# WORKING WITH FAMILIES
# OF THE POOR

# THE GUILFORD FAMILY THERAPY SERIES
## Michael P. Nichols, *Series Editor*

*Recent Volumes*

# WORKING WITH FAMILIES OF THE POOR

Patricia Minuchin
Jorge Colapinto
Salvador Minuchin

THE GUILFORD PRESS
New York   London

© 1998 The Guilford Press
A Division of Guilford Publications, Inc.
72 Spring Street, New York, NY 10012
http://www.guilford.com

Printed in the United States of America

This book is printed on acid-free paper.

Last digit is print number:  9  8  7  6  5  4  3  2  1

**Library of Congress Cataloging-in-Publication Data**
Minuchin, Patricia.
    Working with families of the poor / Patricia Minuchin, Jorge
Colapinto, Salvador Minuchin.
        p.      cm. — (The Guilford family therapy series)
    Includes bibliographical references and index.
    ISBN 1-57230-406-5. — ISBN 1-57230-373-5 (pbk.)
    1. Family social work. 2. Social work with the socially
handicapped. 3. Family psychotherapy.  4.  Problem families—
Services for.  5. Poor—Services for.  I. Colapinto, Jorge.
II. Minuchin, Salvador.  III. Title.  IV. Series.
HV697.M55      1998
362.5—dc21                                                    98-3805
                                                                      CIP

# Acknowledgments

This book represents the effort and experience of many people. We want first to express our deep appreciation to friends and colleagues at Family Studies, Inc., a training and consultation center in New York that sponsored and conducted most of the projects on which the book is based. The group included Evan Bellin, Anne Brooks, Ema Genijovich, David Greenan, Richard Holm, Daniel Minuchin, Wai Yung Lee, and George Simon, in addition to the authors, and was well served by the able secretarial assistance of Loretta Duke.

Although there were no particular fiefdoms during staff meetings or hallway discussions, members of the group were involved in different projects, and their work has contributed especially to certain chapters: David Greenan, as well as Ema Genijovich and Daniel Minuchin, to the chapter on substance dependence (Chapter 6); Daniel Minuchin to the chapters on psychiatric services for children and home-based services (Chapters 7 and 9); Anne Brooks, Evan Bellin, and Ema Genijovich to the chapter on foster care (Chapter 5). Richard Holm and George Simon were involved in projects that do not constitute separate chapters, but they have informed our thinking, provided examples, and generally enriched our understanding of the field. Together with the authors, this group of people ran the gamut of experiences and emotions that accompany the effort to introduce change into the helping systems. We are grateful to them all. In the very best sense, they are responsible for the book, although we absolve them of all blame.

We are grateful as well to the people who invited us into their agencies to work with them; the administrators and staff interested in our approach, who tolerated our activites when we stepped over boundaries, and who certainly taught us as much as we taught them. Throughout the book we have tried to protect their privacy by leaving institutions and locations unidentified, and we must follow that policy here. What follows is a list, inevitably incomplete, of people from a variety of settings who facilitated our work and advanced our thinking: Anstiss Agnew, Machelle Allan, Gretchen Buchenholz, Vince Caccamo, Demo Carros, Susan Egelko, Gloria Faretra, Hope Fontaine, Peter Forsythe, Marc Galanter, Fatima Goldman, Irma Gordon, Phyllis Hersch, Betty Jones, Jay Lappin, Pat Mahoney, Patrick McCarthy, Jim McGuirk, Bob McMahon, Mary Odom, Theodora Ooms, Connie Prescott, Ann Sullivan, Tom Ring, Steve Rutter, David Tobis, Giovanna Todini, William Tucker, and Barbara White. In addition, literally hundreds of workers were involved in the training at different agencies. Although it's impossible to name them all, we take this opportunity to thank them, apologize for the bad moments that seem to accompany any teaching–learning enterprise, and express our hope that this book will meet with their approval.

We thank our editors, Kitty Moore and Michael Nichols, for sage comments and specific suggestions concerning the manuscript. They've made it a better book than it might have been.

Finally, we want to thank all the families—the families who came to the agencies for help, as well as our own families—for making the book possible and for shaping its tone. Working with families who are poor and faced with multiple crises is a constant reminder of both their difficulties and their strengths; they deserve compassion and respect in equal measure. Our own families provided insights, inspiration, and support. They have our love and gratitude.

PATRICIA MINUCHIN
JORGE COLAPINTO
SALVADOR MINUCHIN

# Contents

# PART ONE

# Fundamentals of Thought and Practice

Services for poor families are widely available and almost always well intentioned, but they are frequently flawed as well. Because services are often fragmented and uncoordinated, they're less effective than they might be; and because interventions are focused on individual people and problems, they do not tap the healing possibilities that reside within families and communities.

In this book, we will present a way of thinking and working that is aimed at providing more effective and integrated human services. The approach is based on two fundamental principles: a focus on families and a systems approach to intervention.

In Part I, we will describe our concept of systems and our perspective concerning families, followed by a discussion of the skills and procedures necessary for working within this framework. In Part II, we will concretize the approach by specifically exploring foster care, chemical dependency, residential and psychiatric services for children, and family-centered, home-based services.

But before embarking on the presentation of principles, skills, and applications, we must bring the problems of poor families to life. We will start, therefore, with a prologue, describing the people involved in a particular situation, the issues they face, and the interventions by social agencies. The case of Angie and her family is, of course, unique, as any story must be, but it is also typical. It conveys the complex reality of life among the multicrisis poor, the mixture of helpful and confusing services that are offered or man-dated, and the reactions of those involved. Her story will begin our journey through this book, highlighting the way we think about Angie, her children and family, and the many interventions that address their needs.

# CHAPTER ONE

# Prologue

## ANGIE, HER FAMILY, AND
## THE COMMUNITY OF HELPERS

### ANGIE AND HER FAMILY

Angie is at the center of this case, but she is not alone. Her world includes her companion, the father of the two younger children; three children, each living in a different home; the foster families with whom the children reside; and Angie's parents, siblings, and assorted aunts and uncles. A simple description of Angie's network communicates some of the complexity, but not the harsh reality of life amid poverty, drugs, difficult living conditions, and poor health. That reality is more clearly conveyed by the roster of relevant settings and the list of professional helpers involved in her case. Angie and her family have passed through courts, hospitals, shelters, housing programs, drug centers, rehab clinics, day care centers, and foster care agencies; and they have been attended by lawyers, investigators, parole officers, doctors, social workers, drug counselors, foster care staff, and therapists. The helpers are serious about their roles and want a happy ending for some, or all, of the principals. Inevitably, however, they have jostled each other and the family, and often it has been unclear how everyone's work fits together.

Angie, a troubled woman in her early 20s, has experienced the kind of chaotic childhood and family history that is so familiar among the multicrisis poor that we could reconstruct her past without knowing the details. As a foster child, she was abused intermittently and raped more than once. As a member of a large, disorganized family, she was sometimes ignored and sometimes a caretaker for other people. Over the years, she has lived in shelters, been addicted to drugs, grappled with drug programs, and maintained an on-and-off relationship with her male companion. She has seen her children placed in other families and has tried to comply with the conditions for their return. She has told her story in multiple agencies and therapeutic groups, and has found counselors she trusts and others she doesn't. Depending on one's focus, Angie is uncertain, depressed, and irresponsible—or assertive, realistic, and resilient. Actually, she is all of the above. So how can we understand her life and her context, and what can we do, optimally, to help?

There is an old story about the horrifying spectacle of people hurtling headlong downstream and the response of two observers to their plight. One tries to pull them out as they go by, while the other, after a moment's thought, goes upstream to find out how they got into the river in the first place. The moral is clear: Prevention is more effective in the long run than repair. That is certainly true, but if we move past the obvious, the tale provides a useful way to think further about Angie and others like her. In such cases, the situation upstream is complex and raises some questions: Do people like Angie jump into the water (via drug addiction, irresponsibility, psychological distress) or are they pushed (by poverty, poor education, multiple trauma)? Probably both, so any helpful interventions at the source would require an acknowledgement of all the factors and a sophisticated understanding of how they interact.

For helpers at the water's edge who pull the people out as they go rushing downstream, there is another important question. Is each person struggling in the water an isolated individual, or are some connected with others? Who else is moving downstream with Angie, for instance, and how must the rescuers handle the connections among the separate people and problems? The reality of those connections, and the need to see and work with them, are central themes of this book.

Consider the people whose lives are connected with Angie's.

Although the adults are not married and the family isn't living together, there's a nuclear family at the center. It consists of two parents and two children: Angie; Harlan, her companion; Jocelyn, who is 3½ years old; and Gail, who is 2 years old. Harlan is the father of both children, and he and Angie clearly consider themselves a couple, although their relationship is volatile.

Harlan suffers from a chronic disease, but is surprisingly competent in managing his severe handicap. He appears to have no permanent housing, and he supplements his income by panhandling. He's often vague and unrealistic when he talks, yet has a strong sense that they are a family. He wants the children to live with Angie, and has a special, intense interest in Jocelyn, who has inherited his illness. He feels he can help her cope with her condition.

Jocelyn has been in foster care for 2 years. She is unable to walk, her growth is restricted, and she appears much younger than her age in speech and intellectual development. But she plays, does some things for herself, and is affable and responsive. Jocelyn regularly receives treatment for physical rehabilitation and attends a day care center for handicapped children. Vera, the foster mother, has received special training to deal with her needs. Jocelyn and the foster family have adapted well to each other, but, because Jocelyn lived with Angie until the second little girl was born 2 years ago, Angie feels that she and Jocelyn have a continuing bond.

Gail has been luckier than Jocelyn, since she has not inherited her father's disease, but her life has not been smooth. Angie was drug dependent when this daughter was born and Gail was immediately placed in foster care. The bonding in this foster home is strong. Angie knows she never had a chance to connect with Gail, but she and Harlan both want her returned to live with Angie. Gail is a beautiful little girl, wide-eyed, quiet, rather somber and watchful—at least in the company of Angie, Harlan, and Jocelyn.

Although fragmented and living apart, these four people are interconnected. They are also connected with the two foster families and with Angie's parents, who have been caring for her first-born child, a 5-year-old son, since his infancy. There are no obvious answers to how things should proceed, what arrangements should be maintained or changed, and under what conditions. In pulling Angie out of the torrent, however, it should be understood that other people are traveling downstream along with her, that they are and feel connected—whatever their uncertainties—and that their relationship deserves to be considered.

## THE COMMUNITY OF HELPERS

Social organizations have made multiple efforts to provide services for Angie and members of her family in order to protect them and to prevent further difficulties. Certainly, the worst disasters have been averted. The city has provided shelter, Jocelyn and Harlan have received medical attention, the children are cared for, substance abuse programs have helped Angie with her drug dependence, and counseling has been offered at different stages and in a variety of settings.

But these interventions have had complex by-products. The system has shaped Angie's responses, sometimes in the direction of lesser competence, and the family has been fragmented by procedures that solidify the separation and make a viable reunion difficult. If we are to be helpful in such situations, it's necessary to understand not only the good intentions and positive effects but also the systemic problems that accompany traditional forms of intervention.

We can consider four areas where services have been provided and questions must be raised: professional assistance, housing, foster care, and drug rehabilitation. The issues in these and other areas appear throughout the book and are dealt with elsewhere in more detail, but it's useful at the beginning to see how the interventions are experienced and play themselves out in relation to this one family. The four areas, only briefly reviewed, do not cover the whole spectrum, but they serve to point out the weaknesses as well as the strengths of the helping systems.

### Professional Assistance

The number of social service workers involved in Angie's life over the last few years is overwhelming. It may seem good that so many people have tried to help, or wasteful that so much time and money has been poured into one case, but the important point is that this degree of involvement is inevitably uncoordinated. In talking with

Angie, the workers have gone over the same ground and have duplicated each other's efforts. Angie has memorized the number on the file that makes her anonymous, and, as the file is handed from one worker to another, feels impatient with the repetitious quality of the questions they ask and the answers she gives back ("I'm sick and tired of telling my story to all these people"). She says that, as a result of the turnover at one agency, she had to deal with six different people over a short period of time.

Inevitably, perhaps, Angie has learned to work the system, and has been something of an advocate for "us" (the recipients) versus "them" (the system and the staff). Workers have found her difficult at times—"a woman with an attitude." She describes how, although workers at a women's shelter used to hold meetings to ask the women's opinions, "you had to do what they want anyway, so why ask?" There's little recognition on Angie's part that the staff must work within certain rules, or that they may genuinely want to incorporate group opinion when they can. At the same time, one can understand her sense of frustration and her impression that the system is inefficient and chaotic. She claims that she doesn't trust any of the workers, except for Mona, her current counselor, whom she considers an exception. Mona is an experienced and talented social worker, whose way of functioning must generate both respect and concern in a thoughtful observer; respect because she is an empathic and skillful coordinator, concern because she seems to have taken over much of the executive part of Angie's life. Angie's dependence on the system and its workers is ingrained and grows deeper with time, even while she feels hemmed in and resentful.

## Housing

The urban population of the homeless and/or drug-addicted includes a high percentage of women like Angie whose children have been removed and placed in care. According to both Mona and Angie, they all know the Catch-22 policy established by the housing, legal, and foster care systems: "You can't have housing unless you have your children . . . and you can't have your children until you get housing."

Angie has been relatively fortunate. While living in a single-occupancy female shelter, where she could not have her children with her, she was contacted by a women's advocacy group and moved into their housing facility. Women at this facility share living quarters with each other while they wait for official action, and their children can visit them there. Once the children are returned, a family apartment is provided, along with day care for the children and ongoing counseling for the mothers.

The new housing facility has solved some of Angie's problems but has also  created others. For example, the policy does not provide for male companions or fathers, who are generally viewed as absent or unwelcome. For Angie, that has meant that neither a reunion with Harlan nor an apartment for their nuclear family could be arranged at this facility.

## Foster Care

It would be a distortion to discuss the foster care system as if it had completely failed this family. The children are cared for and Jocelyn receives the special services required by her physical condition. Nonetheless, the separate services have pulled family members away from each other so that, in the ordinary course of events, they will grow increasingly distant. Jocelyn and Gail are in the care of different foster agencies and do not live with the same foster family. The agencies are geographically distant from each other, have no contact, and it is a logistical problem to arrange family visits. Angie describes the setting for visits organized by protective services as "like a warehouse . . . junk, stuff, cluttering up the spaces . . . it's dirty . . . the toys are old . . . I can't let the girls play on the floor." Nobody's fault, perhaps, but an indication that family contacts have low priority. It's difficult for parents to maintain the visiting sched-ules, which are usually evaluated as a sign of interest in later court hearings concerning custody.

Even if visiting is maintained and plans for family reunification go forward, there's little understanding of how complex such a transition would be after so many years of separation coupled with a growing attachment in the foster families, or of what might be required to make the transition successful. Angie is clear about the limitations of the mandatory parenting classes she has attended: How can she answer questions about the way that she disciplines her children or what games they play when they don't even live with her? Observing her during an arranged visit, it's clear that she's loving, wants contact, and has some good ideas, but she has few parenting skills for issues that arise in the course of a day with one child, let alone two—one of whom is severely handicapped and requires special care. Angie expresses both a strong wish to have her children with her and a deep anxiety about whether she is ready and can handle it. Her ambivalence is understandable.

Other matters have never been addressed, including Harlan's role as a father, the difficult process through which Angie and Harlan could forge a viable pattern for coparenting, and the relationship between this family and the foster families important to the children. In Part II of the book, we will discuss a systemic and family-oriented approach to foster care in which different structures and procedures would be available for working on such issues.

## Drug Rehabilitation

Chemical dependency, especially in women with young children, is also the subject of a chapter in Part II of the book. We refer to it here because it was a major factor in Angie's story, and because the problem of addiction demonstrates how different interventions may push and pull in different directions, externalizing the ambivalence that Angie feels about her choices.

Angie spent time in a residential drug center as part of the required activity for getting her children back, and as part of her own effort to become free of drugs. She comments that the program helped her to face herself, understand her life, and control her habit. But, despite the benefits, she left long before the allotted time. She says, "If I stayed up there, I would learn that I could live without Harlan and without the children and be my own person, and take care of *me* . . . but my concern is toward him and the children, and there it was head-on dealing with me."

From Angie's point of view, the program jeopardized her relationship with her family while it explored her personal problems, which presented her with a dilemma. However, the confusion was not only internal: It was a function, as well, of the different and simultaneous interventions current in her life. In a meeting that brought together drug counselors and foster care workers, it became clear that each of the two services had its own priorities and was delivering a different message. The foster care agency was concerned with family relationships and the workers were attempting to coordinate Angie's contacts with Jocelyn and Gail. The drug program focused on Angie as an individual, maintaining that she needed to understand herself and her past, be honest about what she wanted, and become strong as an individual before she could deal with other issues.

When a visit with the children—arranged by the foster care agency—upset Angie, the staff of the drug program placed a moratorium on such visits. At that point, Angie faced the contradiction and made a choice, opting for continuing contact with the children. Drawing on her own strength, and choosing from among the contradictory supports that had become ever-present features in her life, Angie left the residential program, hoping to remain drug free with the help of counseling—and understandably uneasy about an uncertain future.

In offering the story of Angie and her family, we stop at a point of uncertainty. We have wanted only to create an image of the people served by the helping systems, and to highlight issues that often arise in the course of providing services. It's our task in the remainder of the book to discuss alternatives, and to consider how things might go differently for people like Angie and her family when they're pulled out of the rushing waters and offered help.

# CHAPTER TWO

# The Framework

## A SYSTEMS ORIENTATION AND A FAMILY-CENTERED APPROACH

This book is about working with the multicrisis poor and with agencies that serve their needs. We've started by looking at a particular case, in which the services for Angie and her family have been specifically targeted and funneled through a variety of independent systems. The fact that Angie, Harlan, Jocelyn, and Gail are part of one family has had little influence on the way services are framed or delivered.

Fragmentation of this kind is the norm, rather than the exception, and is both inefficient and hard on families. In presenting a different way of working, we are emphasizing an approach that is more integrated, systemic, and supportive of families. The practical implications appear in succeeding chapters, but we begin by providing a general framework, first presenting the basic elements of systems theory and then describing our concept of families—particularly in relation to the multicrisis poor.

## THE SYSTEMIC ORIENTATION

What does it mean to be a systems thinker in general? In relation to social agencies? In relation to families?

We all know about systems. It's a term we use in conversation and that carries a certain weight. We talk about social systems, nervous systems, the solar system. The term is so familiar we don't need to think about its meaning. Clearly, it has to do with connectedness, with the poetic idea that when you take a flower in your hand you discover that it is connected to the universe.

Yes, a systems perspective has to do with connections, but in a special way. It highlights the particular ways that parts are related, and therefore has a predictive component. Because the universe is a system, scientists can predict the moment in which the moon will be positioned between the sun and the earth to produce a lunar eclipse, and they can describe the consequences for the earth and its inhabitants. It is our understanding that parts of a system affect each other, and that these effects repeat themselves, which makes systems interesting to study and prediction possible.

Systems of different kinds have specific features, but any system is organized and characterized by repetitive patterns. Neither the solar system, the welfare system, nor a family is haphazard in the way it functions. The sun will rise tomorrow and the welfare system will follow particular procedures for supporting dependent children, just as a family will follow organized and predictable patterns of its own.

Here we need to pause in order to consider a contradiction. The connections among living organisms seem to be understood as a universal truth. When ecologists tell us that wolves and deer are interconnected in an ecological balance, we accept it; we understand that if too many deer die, the wolves will go hungry until the ratio reestablishes itself. Despite an almost organic understanding of how systems work, we celebrate our national figures as if they acted and triumphed alone; heroes and victims remain disconnected from their environment and other people. A kind of tunnel vision overrides the understanding of connections, which has major implications for service delivery. It means, for instance, that Angie's drug counselors insist that she concentrate on healing herself first, without recognizing that her "personal problems" include a concern for the important people in her family.

If we are to understand how systems ideas apply to people, we must always keep in mind the idea of connections and repetitive patterns. We need, as well, to pay attention to other features of any system: the presence of subsystems, the way in which their parts influence each other, and the fact that every system inevitably goes through periods of stability and change. These ideas are crucial for understanding how families function, but they apply as well to the larger social systems that affect family life; for example, hospitals and social service agencies.

It's clear that the surgical, outpatient, and social work departments of a hospital are subsystems of the larger institution: Each has a particular function, is related to other departments, and is regulated in its functioning by hospital policies and procedures. Perhaps less obvious is the complex and circular way that parts interact. Maybe the approach of the social workers has broadened the surgeons' way of thinking that "Patient X is a kidney problem." Maybe the surgeons have taught the social workers something about the urgency of emergencies. We're aware that policies tend to travel from the top down, but we pay less attention to the fact that the departments affect hospital policy through the ideas they funnel to administrators, and the way they implement or resist directives.

Of course, mutuality doesn't necessarily mean equality. The influence of hospital subsystems on overall policy depends on the flexibility of the system, and within any structure the power of the different parts is apt to be uneven. In most settings, for instance, the social work department has less overall influence than the surgical division. The point arises again in a family context, particularly if we think about families who are poor and dependent on help from organized institutions. Those families are seldom able to influence patterns of the systems that serve them, and constructive intervention is often a matter of trying to redress that imbalance.

However it's organized, no system remains static. It inevitably must go through cycles of stability and change. During periods of stability, a system functions through familiar patterns and, for the most part, repetition is adaptive. Hospitals don't need to reinvent the admission procedure with each new patient, and families don't need to establish new rules for bedtime every day. But all systems that involve living creatures are open-ended. New events occur at intervals, and as a result stable patterns are perturbed. For instance, the hospital might merge with another, and be run thereafter by an HMO. The current procedures would then be challenged. Even if the hospital had been functioning smoothly under the previous circumstances, it would need to reorganize structures and procedures. The staff would go through a transitional period of confusion, in the process searching for patterns that preserve what is valued from the past while adapting appropriately to the new reality.

Like hospitals, social service agencies are organized systems, and their reality is almost always complex. They're generally embedded within larger social and political structures, subdivided into internal subsystems, and coexistent with other agencies that serve many of the same families. An adoption agency, for instance, is embedded in a social–political context that determines legal requirements, the official or unspoken policy on interracial adoptions, the attitude toward gay couples who want to become parents, and the speed with which parental rights are terminated in cases of alleged neglect. These combined factors increase or decrease the number of children eligible for adoption.

Within the agency, work is divided into sections. Particular departments are responsible for different functions, such as locating and evaluating potential adoptive parents, handling legal aspects, or monitoring placement through follow-up visits. Each department has procedures of its own, and the different departments must coordinate their relations with each other and with agencies that work with the same families. Logically, the communication between the department that selects families and the department that monitors placement should be extensive, allowing each to adapt to the realities faced by workers in the other section. An adoption agency should also be in constant communication with services relevant to particular cases, such as the residential center where a child has been living for 2 years before coming up for placement, or the program for children with special needs in the local area where a child is about to be adopted. The connection should be more than a matter of paperwork, especially when a difficult transition—such as adoption—is planned or underway.

Integrating the work of different subsystems and agencies is apt to be time-consuming, but perhaps no more so than handling the negative effects of poor coordination. "Turf" problems between subsystems of an agency have a corrosive effect, as do communication failures between different agencies. Training is a useful and necessary way to introduce change, but the positive effects are limited if training touches only one corner of a complex system. We've learned, for example, that the ability of line workers to sustain new ideas and procedures depends on the support of their supervisors, as well as the possibility of influencing agency policies so they can move in the same direction.

A systems orientation is not an academic luxury; it's a necessary tool. Understanding that different agencies are interactive forces within the network encompassing a family is a cornerstone of collaborative work, and is essential for handling interventions at cross-purposes. If professionals can accept their connections and find alternative ways of handling their differences, they will increase the efficiency of the system and improve the quality of help offered to their clients.

We move now from this brief description of systems that provide services to a more detailed look at the families who are the recipients.

## FAMILIES

A family is a special kind of system, with structure, patterns, and properties that organize stability and change. It's also a small human society, whose members have face-to-face contact, emotional ties, and a shared history. We need especially to understand the families served by social agencies. We can approach that understanding best by means of a more general discussion, considering families first as systems and then as small societies.

## FAMILIES AS SYSTEMS

### Patterns

When we describe families as having a structure, we mean more than a map of who's in the family. We're referring to patterns of interaction that are recurrent and predictable. These patterns reflect the affiliations, tensions, and hierarchies important in human societies, and carry meaning for behavior and relationships.

In most families there are multiple patterns of alliance, involving people who are emotionally close and mutually supportive. Jerry and Clarissa Brown have been married more than 20 years. The way they enjoy leisure time together, deal with their family, and handle problems clearly illustrates a stable alliance. But there are other kinds of alliances, less obvious than theirs. For instance, Grandma and Jenny have a special bond. They spend time together; Grandma is Jenny's confidante and both enjoy the fact that people think they look alike.

Sometimes alliances take a different form. They involve people who are drawn together by an opposition to other family members—and their alliance is more accurately described as a coalition. These coalitions are frequently transient and may be relatively benign. In one family, for instance, the adolescents gang up against their mother whenever she proposes a weekend visit to an unpopular aunt and uncle. In another family, however, the coalition is more stable and less good-humored. The daughters are in alliance against their stepfather, finding a host of ways to oppose him, although they're not close to each other in most other matters.

Patterns that organize the hierarchy of power appear in every family. They define the family pathways for making decisions and controlling the behavior of its members. Patterns of authority are particularly important aspects of family organization. These patterns carry the potential for both harmony and conflict and are subject to challenge as family members grow and change.

Authority patterns that are clear and flexible tend to work well. Clarissa and Jerry Brown have developed a viable process over the years. They defer to each other's authority in particular areas, consider the input of the children when important family decisions are to be made, and have yielded increasing power and autonomy to their children as each one has entered adolescence. Other families, however, have less functional patterns for arriving at decisions and few skills for resolving their differences. Families often come for therapy because their discussions are rigidly organized around winning and losing, and they can't manage to change the patterns that increase family conflict. Authority problems aren't always a matter of rigidity, however. Control may be erratic rather than inflexible, with unfortunate by-products that aren't recognized. In three-generational, single-parent families with young children, for instance, authority sometimes may rest with the mother, at other times with the grandmother, and at still other times with uncles or older sisters—depending on who happens to be around. Messages that are unclear and contradictory confuse the children and interfere with their understanding of acceptable behavior.

Some patterns are ethnic in origin. By and large, families in the Latino community have different patterns for expressing affection, voicing disagreements, and cuddling their young than do their Northern European neighbors. But most family patterns are particular, worked out over time in the family's own setting. One mother, for instance, always steps in to protect the baby from his older sister, and she always gets angry with her 12-year-old son when he's in conflict with her male friend. Her behavior is predictable even when the specific content looks different. The mother will protect the baby whether his sister is hitting him or simply including him in a dangerous game, regardless of whether the roughhouse comes from his sister or a playmate in the park. And, for her own reasons, she will get angry at her 12-year-old any time he fights with her male companion—even if she has moved on to a new relationship, and even if she suspects that the adult has triggered the trouble.

Organized patterns are the concrete expression of implicit rules. Because they define expectations and limits, family members know what's permissible and what isn't. Nina, the oldest daughter of a single parent, knows that she's in charge and can boss the younger children when her mother is out—but everybody understands that she's not allowed to hit them or frighten them. What is useful can also become confining, however. Because patterns are habitual, they don't invite change, and they don't mobilize the wider repertoire of family members. If Nina is drafted too often as the resident baby-sitter, which limits her social life and creates a reservoir of unspoken resentment, it's time for the family to break a pattern that's no longer useful. Perhaps they can tap the potential of her 13-year-old brother, or modify her mother's working hours, or even negotiate a reciprocal arrangement with a neighboring family.

## Subsystems

There are many subsystems within families, as in any complex system. Age and gender create family subsystems, as do other factors. Adults have functions and relationships that separate them from their children. Adolescents form a group with special interests. Males are one unit and females are another. And within a "blended" family there are subgroups of "his," "hers," and "theirs." Spoken and unspoken rules govern relationships between the units: The younger children may not disturb the adolescent when the bedroom door is closed; the children will tattle to adults only when beset by injustice; the mother's children will not expect to go on a Saturday outing with their stepfather and his son unless specifically invited; and Grandpa can stand up for a child in trouble with his or her siblings, but not when the parents are enforcing discipline.

The concept of *boundaries* is important in relation to sub systems, as it is in relation to the family as a whole. Boundaries are invisible but, like the wind, we know they exist because of the way things move. All of the examples in the previous paragraph refer to boundaries, marking thresholds that should not be crossed, as well as the conditions under which they're more permeable. The permeability of boundaries expresses the realities of access and privacy.

The firmness of subsystem boundaries varies with a family's particular style. Thanksgiving dinner at the Smiths brings together three generations, with lots of crowding and a high noise level. That arrangement would make no sense to the Barrys, who put the children at a separate table and call for quiet when the kids act up. In both families, however, there will be developmentally appropriate changes over the family life cycle. The boundaries between adults and children will inevitably grow firmer as the children move toward adolescence. Parents usually intervene if the 5-year-old's teasing brings her little brother to the brink of a tantrum, but when the children become adolescents they're usually expected to fight their own battles, and are likely to draw boundaries that provide them with more privacy. As the parent's generation becomes older, the boundaries may change again, reflecting the needs of the elders and the increasing involvement of their offspring in their health and well-being.

When family patterns are not working well, it's useful to look separately at the different subsystems. Meeting with just the group of children, for instance, provides a view of family hierarchy and family crosscurrents from the bottom up, rather than from the top down. It may also shed light on the repertoire of family members, some of whom may function very differently in different subgroups. Twelve-year-old Mario, for instance, may be a creative and fair-minded leader with his siblings, even though he clams up or is surly when his father is around. That observation provides a useful lead for helping a family explore their own functioning and develop patterns that encompass the needs of particular members.

## The Individual

The individual is the smallest unit in the family system—a separate entity but a piece of the whole. In the framework of a systems approach, it's understood that each person contributes to the formation of family patterns, but it's also evident that personality and behavior are shaped by what the family expects and permits.

This view is more revolutionary than it may sound. It challenges both prevailing theory and the usual organization of social services, which focus on the individual as the natural and sufficient unit. We emphasize this point throughout the book, maintaining that a focus on individual history, dynamics, and treatment is insufficient, and that it's necessary to work with people within the context of their families and their extended network.

If we think of individuals as part of a system, we must have a different view of how self-image is formed and how behavior is governed. Families define their members partly in relation to the qualities and roles of other members. In so doing, they create something of a self-fulfilling prophecy, affecting the self-image and behavior of each individual. Joe is described as shyer than the other children, and he thinks of himself that way. Annie, the oldest girl, is expected to help with the cooking and the little ones, and she absorbs the role of "parental child" without question—at least until adolescence. Mother is the one who handles contact with the schools and other institutions. The shaping of behavior by the family often involves the recognition of individual qualities, but it may also lock behavior in place, restricting exploration and limiting elements in the concept of self.

From a systems point of view, behavior is explained as a shared responsibility, arising from patterns that trigger and maintain the actions of each individual. It's customary to think that "my child defies me" or that "my partner nags," but these are one-way, linear descriptions. In fact, the child's defiance or the partner's nagging is only half of the equation. The process is *circular* and the behavior is *complementary*, meaning that the behavior is sustained by all the participants. All of them initiate behavior and all of them react; it's not really possible to spot the beginning or establish cause and effect. We can say with equal validity that, when Tamika is defiant, her mother yells, Tamika cries, and her mother hits her—or, that mother yells at her daughter, Tamika cries, her mother hits her, and

Tamika becomes defiant. Their interaction is patterned, and we cannot explain the behavior of one without including the other.

The concept of complementarity has offered a useful, if somewhat startling, way of looking at diagnosis, as well as cause and effect, but it has also raised some cautionary flags. Behavior may reflect a circular pattern, but some behavior is dangerous or morally wrong, exploiting the weakness of some family members and endangering their safety. Feminists have made this point in relation to male violence toward women, and all of society condemns the abuse of children. In such situations, the primary task is to protect victimized individuals and to take an ethical stand, while working with the family to change recurrent patterns that are dangerous or morally unacceptable.

## Transitions

All families go through transitional periods. Members grow and change, and events intervene to modify the family's reality. In any change of circumstances, the family, like other systems, faces a period of disorganization. Familiar patterns are no longer appropriate, but new ways of being are not yet available. The family must go through a process of trial and error, searching for some balance between the comfortable patterns that served them in the past and the realistic demands of their new situation. The process, often painful, is marked for a period by uncertainty and tension.

Some transitions are triggered by the normal cycle of development. When a child is born, the helplessness of the infant calls for a new caretaking behavior that changes the relationships among adults within the household. As children grow, there are increasing demands for privacy, autonomy, and responsibility that upset the system and require new patterns. As the middle generation become seniors, problems of aging and frailty require a shift in some functions from the older generation to their adult children. Some transitions, of course, are not developmental at all. They reflect the vicissitudes of modern life and the unexpected events that may happen to any family: divorce, remarriage, unexpected illness, sudden unemployment, floods or earthquakes.

Whatever the stimulus, it's important to realize that behavioral difficulties during periods of transition are not necessarily pathological or permanent. They often represent the family's attempts to explore and adapt. Anxiety, depression, and irritability are the affective components of a crisis. Although the behavior may seem disturbed or dysfunctional, it's not helpful to crystallize the reaction by focusing on pathology.

This is an important point in relation to multicrisis families, a fact that we will highlight in later sections. These families often face recurrent and dramatic transitions, many of which are created by the intervention of powerful social systems. The quality of shock and disorganization in the reactions of family members is not usually understood as part of the process that accompanies transitions. The behavior is often judged as if permanent, with consequences that compound the difficulties.

## FAMILIES AS SMALL SOCIETIES

There's something impersonal about discussing the family as a system, probably because it bypasses the feelings and complexities of human interaction. If we come closer, we can pay attention to the emotional forces that tie people together and pull them apart.

People in a family have a special sense of connection with each other: an attachment, a family bond. That's both a perception and a feeling. They know that "we are us" and they care about each other. When we work with families, we know that its members are concerned to protect, defend, and support each other—and we draw on this bond to help them change. We know also that tension, conflict, and anger are inevitable, partly because of the ties that bind. As some earlier examples have suggested, a family limits and challenges its members even while it supports them.

The sense of family is expressed by feelings and perceptions, and by the way members describe their history, their attitudes, their style—what some refer to as "the family story": "We're a family that keeps to ourselves; we don't want trouble in this neighborhood"; or "We had a hard time moving from the islands, but we're doing OK now"; or "We can't ever seem to resolve anything without getting into a battle"; or "All the women in our family suffer from depression." There are alternative stories, of course, told by different members, but families usually share some version of who they are and how they function.

The counterpart of family affection is family conflict. All families have disagreements, must negotiate their differences, and must develop ways of handling conflict. It is a question of how effective their methods are: how relevant for resolving issues, how satisfactory for the participants, how well they stay within acceptable boundaries for the expression of anger.

Families sometimes fall apart because they can't find their way through disagreements, even though they care for each other. Most families have a signal system, a threshold above which an alarm bell sounds that registers the need for family members to cool down and avoid danger. It matters how early that warning comes, and whether the family has mechanisms for disengagement and crisis control or typically escalates to the point of violence.

Conflict and violence are major concerns in working with multicrisis families. We will discuss these concerns further in the next section, which looks specifically at the multicrisis poor in relation to our general concepts about families.

## "AGENCY" FAMILIES: THE MULTICRISIS POOR

Principles of family structure and function are generic, but have special features when applied to families served and controlled by the courts, the welfare system, and protective services. For one thing, the affection and bonding in these families is often overlooked. We hear that people are so spaced-out on drugs that they can't form attachments, that mothers neglect their children and fathers abuse them, and that families are violent and people are isolated. All truths for some families, but only partial truths that highlight the most visible aspects of individual and family misery while ignoring the loyalty and affection that people feel for each other. For example, Harlan wants the children to go back to Angie because he feels that they're a family, no matter how they look to others or how fragmented they have become as a result of interventions that have both helped them and split them apart. Observant foster parents tell us that foster children love their biological mothers and want to be with them, even if they have been hit or neglected. An illogical state of affairs, but an instance of the deep feeling and emotional ambivalence that accompanies family attachments.

One recurrent and disturbing fact about such families is that they do not write their own stories. Once they enter the institutional network and a case history is opened, society does the editing. Angie's folder goes from place to place, transmitting the official version of who she is and which members of her family are considered relevant to her case. A friendlier approach to families elicits their own perspective on who they are, who they care about, and how they see their problems.

Just as connections and affection are not usually recognized, neither are the family structures: the actual membership of the family and the patterns that describe their functioning. Families served by the welfare system often look chaotic; people come and go and individuals seem cut off. That instability is partly a life-style, amid poverty, drugs, and violence, but it's also a by-product of social interventions. Children are taken for placement, members are jailed or hospitalized, services are fragmented. The point is not whether such interventions are sometimes necessary but that they always break up family structures. The interventions are carried out without recognizing the positive emotional ties and effective resources that may have been disrupted as well. When all the children in a family where the infant fails to thrive are taken for placement, the mother's adolescent protector against an abusive boyfriend also disappears, and the mutually supportive group of siblings is disbanded.

Boundaries are fluid in these families, and workers enter with ease. Often, the family's authority structure, erratic to begin with, disappears. The decisions come from without, and the children learn early on that adults in the family have no power. The worker may unwittingly become part of dysfunctional subsystems, influencing the patterns in a way that is ultimately unhelpful. If the worker supports the adolescent daughter, for instance, allowing her to invoke the power of protective services in battles against her mother, the possibility for the family to manage its own affairs is diminished rather than enhanced.

Violence is a major fact of life for these families, and it takes two forms: the violence that occurs within the families themselves and the violence brought about by social interventions. The former comes to mind first because it is the more conventional association. Poverty, impotence, and despair are both existential and embedded in the family cycles of this population, often leading to shortcut solutions: drugs, delinquency, impulsive sex, and violence.

When we look inside violent families, we see a derailment of order. The usual fail-safe mechanisms that protect family members and ensure the survival of society don't hold. Any worker who deals with inner-city welfare families faces moments of ugly reality: brutal punishment, incest, abandoned children. As consultants and trainers, we have always been invested in the concept of family preservation and we support interventions that keep children in their own homes, but we pay serious attention to the problem of family violence and to the question of how to assess and ensure the safety of family members. The official pendulum that swings through extremes, from removing children to maintaining the family unit to removing the children again, fails to provide a sophisticated solution to this basic issue. The mandates are procedural and global. They are well intentioned but not helpful enough in specific situations. A worker must be able to explore family conflict and to assess the family's potential for positive change before making a decision of this nature. We will discuss this important matter further in succeeding chapters.

The second form of violence is external. It comes from intrusion, and from the absolute power of society in exerting control. The rhetoric, and sometimes the reality, is that of protection for the weak, but the intrusion into the family is often disrespectful, damaging ties and dismembering established structures without recognizing that the procedures do violence to the family. Because there is so little recognition that individuals and families are profoundly interconnected, legal structures and social policy set up an adversary situation, with an associated imbalance between the rights of the family and those of the individual.

An article illustrating this pattern appeared on the front page of *The New York Times* in 1996. Titled "As Courts Remove Children, Lawyers for Parents Stumble" (June 10, 1996), the article detailed the discrepancy between the legal resources available to parents, when children are removed, and those available to the city system and the children. The court-appointed lawyers who serve the parents are described as "overburdened and ill equipped." Their pay is poor and they are compensated at a better rate for appearing in court than for preparatory work, so they frequently do not conduct interviews and research that would strengthen the parents' case. In recent years, the article noted, legal experts "have come to regard much of this work as seriously flawed." The outcome in most cases is preordained: The parents do not win their case. Hardly anybody notices, as a front-page article in a prestigious newspaper is an exceptional and ultimately noninfluential event, but the net effect is to render the family impotent. They are, in a sense, the victims of unintentional social violence.

Social interventions are often necessary, although less often than they occur—and not in the form in which they are generally carried out. Recognizing that the family has structures, attachments, recurrent patterns, and boundaries that have meaning—even if they do not work well or avert danger—changes everything. The approach to the family shifts emphasis. We begin to look for relevant people in the family network and accept unconventional family shapes. We notice subsystems and the rules that govern family interactions, both those that lead to crises and those that indicate strength. We realize that social interventions create transitions, and that families will go through temporary periods of confusion, anger, and anxiety that should not be treated as typical or permanent. We also become aware that when they are actively intervening, workers are part of the family system. Their role in working with poor families is far more powerful than the role carried by teachers, physicians, or ministers in relation to more stable and privileged families. Recognizing these realities, and managing the interventions so that the worker assists the family to help themselves, is the driving force of a family-oriented approach.

What is the current reality? How close do the helping systems come to this view of families and of service delivery? Working for many years as trainers and consultants, we know that it's difficult for most agencies to adopt and implement a family systems approach, and we have grappled with the question of why that should be so. We know that changing from one way of working to another is always difficult, but we need to look deeper, to examine the combination of factors that dominate current practice and make it particularly difficult to move toward a family-oriented approach. The most likely explanations lie in three areas: the nature of bureaucracy, the training of professionals, and the attitudes of society toward the poor. We will now look at those factors in the next section of this chapter.

# OBSTACLES TO A FAMILY
# SYSTEMS APPROACH

## The Nature of Bureaucracy

Bureaucracies become top-heavy by accident. They begin by identifying necessary tasks and developing the structures to carry them out. Certainly, the social institutions that serve the poor were created to be helpful: to cure suffering, to protect the weak, and to provide a safety net for society and its members. But the increase in poverty, homelessness, drugs, violence, and the endangerment of children has imposed new demands on protective systems. Ideally, increasing demand would be met by a creative and efficient comprehensive plan to govern the integration of services and the allocation of funds. But in fact, the situation has typically given rise to a patchwork of distinct and disconnected elements: shelters, temporary housing, and police action to deal with homelessness; a variety of programs to treat substance abuse; a spectrum of agencies that offer foster care, adoption, residential placement, or clinical therapies, for children at risk; and so forth.

The elements of the social service bureaucracy have become specialized turfs, rather than interactive subsystems of an organized structure, and they compete for funds. Although the level of funding is always inadequate to meet the needs, an increase in the flow of money would not, in itself, correct the situation. The fundamental problem is that services are not integrated and money is earmarked for specific categories: babies born with positive toxicity or pregnant teenagers or workfare initiatives. Categorical funding labels the territory, points toward certain procedures, and supplies an ideology for preserving artificial boundaries. There's little leeway or encouragement for thinking through an optimal, innovative approach. As a result, agencies and departments vying for financial support shape their language, procedures, and training in accordance with available funding opportunies.

Over the years, the social service bureaucracy has grown complicated, impersonal, and rigid, and that reality is a major obstacle to the adoption of a family-oriented approach. When a complex system is organized along fixed lines, it becomes a Herculean task to introduce a change in focus.

Social services tend to be organized around the individual.

Every case centers on an identified client who has been referred to a particular agency for help with a specific problem. The by-products of this emphasis have been described in earlier sections, especially in relation to Angie and her family. The problem is not that Jocelyn's physical development is in the hands of medical experts, or that Angie is counseled by people with knowledge and experience of drug addiction. That kind of specialization reflects the competent functioning of the system. The problem is that the drug counselors erect a barrier around Angie-the-person, following their customary procedures for handling addiction, without any official input to remind them that she has connections to her family. Similarly, nothing in the organization of services or directives to the staff at Jocelyn's rehab center suggests that they should be training Angie to exercise the special skills necessary to parent a child with special needs.

It's difficult to challenge this individual orientation because the procedures are tied to well-entrenched bureaucratic structures. Budget allotments, caseloads, and insurance reimbursements are based on individual appraisal and treatment. Arrangements of this kind are both elaborate and cumbersome and don't yield easily. In addition, the emphasis on the individual is taken for granted, not only by the officials who manage the system but by most of the professionals who work within it.

## The Training of Professionals

When professional workers ask themselves "What are we here for?", the answer is usually simple: "To help the patient" (or the abused child, the pregnant teenager, the heroin addict). The focus on the individual is a legacy of professional training that usually emphasizes individually oriented theory, case material, and therapeutic techniques. Social workers, psychologists, and psychiatrists approach their professional work with a framework of ideas about personality, pathology, and treatment—along with particular skills for dealing with the individual. Perhaps it's natural to respond to individual qualities and actions, especially if people are in pain. It requires a complex kind of training to respond to the person in context, and to apply healing procedures that go beyond individual distress in order to mobilize the system.

We have yet to reach that point. In the current climate, the individual focus begins with intake. Workers are expected to follow prescribed procedures, to gather the required information about the person who is referred, and to work toward a definite decision that will move the case to the next step. Although they may enter the system with innovative ideas, workers generally survive by learning how things are done, who's in charge, and what it takes just to keep track of the case load. It's often assumed that the established procedures are inflexible laws or official mandates: You must do intake and fill in the forms in this way. . . . You have to arrange visits by following these procedures. . . . This is how and when you do discharge planning. . . . The professional staff are generally overworked and are apt to view a family orientation as an addition to their jobs rather than a useful approach that's central to the work. They must survive in a system that holds them responsible, and that expects the equivalent of "billable hours" in the form of diligent effort along prescribed lines.

Workers know they're vulnerable if they don't follow established procedures. The media aren't understanding when something goes wrong, and the bureaucracy doesn't protect an employee who has not worked according to the rules. The reality of the job doesn't lend itself readily to time spent searching for families, exploring their strengths, and handling the complexities that multicrisis families present. A worker must be very determined to adopt such an approach when faced with colleagues and supervisors implementing the more typical, individually oriented practices characteristic of their preparation for professional work.

## Social Attitudes toward the Poor

Within social agencies, the effects of the bureaucratic structure and the traditional concentration on individuals are compounded by a view of poor families that is essentially pragmatic and often moralistic. In many settings, the definition of family is narrow. The social work staff must arrive at solutions, and they tend to define family in relation to information that must be funneled to courts or child welfare departments. Who can supply information about this child's early physical and social history? Who might be able to take this neglected child in a kinship foster care arrangement? Where can this pregnant adolescent go with her baby when the infant is born? The staff looks for who might be available to help, and who must be ruled out because the record suggests they have been destructive in their relationship with the client.

Although definitions are often narrow, judgmental attitudes tend to be broad. Moralistic attitudes toward poor families are submerged but pervasive in the culture. The families are blamed for their substance abuse, homelessness, and economic dependency, and viewed as a burden on society. Separating or ignoring families is partly a reflection of disapproval—accompanied by a missionary spirit when children are seen as the victims. There's a countertrend, of course, which is certainly just as valid. From this different perspective, poor families are viewed as the victims of bad economic times and reactionary policies, reacting to the hopelessness of their condition with self-destructive and socially unacceptable behavior. In practice, however, criticism and social impatience tend to outweigh compassion, especially when the political pendulum swings in a conservative direction.

Even when families aren't blamed for their poverty or their social behavior, they're often blamed for the plight of the client. They're seen as part of the problem rather than part of the solution. Marina drinks because her boyfriend is abusive, her parents always made her feel a failure, and other family members are also drug dependent. Jamal has been neglected by his mother, the grandmother doesn't seem interested, and the uncle said he would come in but he never showed up. The home environment is so bad that Jane took up with this boy and got pregnant. And so forth.

There's some truth in these judgments, but such a one-sided analysis doesn't acknowledge what the system has squelched, who might be available as a source of strength, or how the family's resources could be tapped to create a more protective and effective context for its individual members.

## WORKING TOWARD CHANGE

A social service staff that can see the family as a resource is a giant step ahead, but the staff may be unable to work productively because they don't think systemically. They often have little understanding of how a family functions: how the behavior of the client reflects his or her position in an interactive system, how the actions of courts and agencies reverberate through a family, and how positive changes depend on working with the network within which their particular client is embedded.

There's an interesting paradox here. Unlike the practitioner in private practice, professionals who work in social agencies are experiential experts on the meaning of an interactive system. In their own working environment, they're aware of hierarchies, rules, coalitions, alliances, subsystems, and conflict. They're also aware of their particular place in the system. They know that their roles and possibilities are formed and constrained by the way the system works, and that, when they modify or challenge the rules, it has repercussions elsewhere and for other people. It's interesting—and a bit puzzling—that the idea of the family as an interactive system doesn't resonate for staff members, although many features of their own working environment apply to this other, smaller system as well. In particular, it should be obvious that the individual doesn't function independently, and that the effects of individual effort are unlikely to be sustained if the relevant system doesn't change.

Traditional training, social attitudes, and the bureaucracy of large systems work against the implementation of new ideas, but other factors exist as well. Agencies responsible for service delivery have constraints of their own. They have all the features of any complex system, including a strong resistance to change. In bringing new ideas and procedures into discussion, we realize that the process of change will probably not be easy, especially if well-trained professionals are asked to modify their familiar ways of thinking, the policies that guide their work, and the organization of their services. No matter how sincere the effort, a journey toward change is always uphill.

In the remainder of the book, we will focus on the details of interaction between professional workers and family members. That interaction is the bottom line of service delivery, more fundamental in efforts to change the system than laws, social policies, or available money. Even when the system is reorganized through changes in these broader factors, the daily activities of service providers may not reflect the difference. In our experience, a staff encouraged to work with families often is uncertain how to proceed. Workers who aren't accustomed to thinking about family systems lack the skills for effective interventions, and therapists who have worked with system concepts may not know how to apply their skills to agency families. The material of this book is aimed at advancing practical knowledge. We try to provide concrete illustrations of a systems framework, and specific examples of interventions that can be helpful in the delivery of service to this population.

In the following two chapters, we will present the material that is most important for training a staff in a family-oriented approach: the skills necessary for working with families as well as the details of effective procedures. However, it may be useful to note first that we've had a particular role in these agencies, and that the professional role of the reader may be either analogous or different. As consultants or trainers, we're outsiders, which gives us certain advantages: some freshness of perspective when we look at the agency's structure and way of working, and some freedom from the alliances and tensions that subdivide the insiders. It also brings disadvantages: We must take time to learn how the agency functions, and we miss important subtexts obvious to any member of the staff. Some readers probably share the role we have carried and can read the material for its direct application to what they do. Others may be responsible for training within their own agency and will have a different context for processing the material. The basic points, however, and much of the detail, should make instant sense to any reader who has worked with the complex problems of the multicrisis poor, and should provide some guidelines for people who are planning to move into this field of work.

CHAPTER THREE

# Working in the System

FAMILY-SUPPORTIVE SKILLS

Social service workers bring two sets of skills to their work: a way of thinking about their clients and a way of functioning to encourage change. If workers are to increase their mastery of interventions that support families, they must develop both a systemic, family-oriented framework and an expanded set of techniques for implementing new ideas. Practical skills are the most direct, involving interaction with clients, but they're not optimally useful or self-sustaining unless accompanied by a mind-set in which the importance of the family and a knowledge of how systems shape behavior are firmly established ideas.

In this chapter, we will discuss *conceptual skills* (elements of a mind-set for understanding a family and organizing the information) and *practical skills* (procedures that help families to mobilize and develop their resources). For the purpose of discussion, we will treat them separately but they're actually linked, and in the following sections it will become clear that they overlap. We will concretize the ideas with examples that involve some intervention and describe interventions against the background of our thinking. That is, of course, how skills are implemented in actual practice.

In practice, services are necessarily specific, molded to the particular tasks of the setting. In a drug-rehabilitation clinic, for example, the staff must learn to protect or repair the client's connections with his or her family, providing necessary supports so that a person like Angie doesn't have to choose between taking care of herself and remaining in contact with her family. In an agency concerned with pregnant women, the staff must be aware that the baby has a father who may feel involved in the pregnancy, that it's important to explore connections with family members from whom the mother may be cut off, and that it's vital to fortify her bonding with the infant. Families whose children are in care must be supported during the period of placement, and workers must be skillful in promoting a process of reunification that will be successful for both the child and each family. These are specific issues, but they reflect a general orientation. In that sense, the examples in this chapter apply by analogy to a variety of social services.

## CONCEPTUAL SKILLS: THINKING ABOUT FAMILIES

In the previous chapter, families were described as systems and small societies. Now we will make those ideas concrete, documenting how we might train or supervise a worker to think about the individual as embedded within a context, and to focus on patterns, connections, subsystems, boundaries, and transitions in order to understand and describe a family.

For simplicity's sake, we can say that the conceptual task of a family-oriented approach is twofold: to "think big" and to recognize the organization of the family. Thinking big means going beyond the individual in order to understand important features of a case. It also means a willingness to pause and look around—to push the definition of the relevant system beyond the people who come most readily to mind. Recognizing the organization of the system means an alertness to matters such as the quality of connections among people, the typical patterns of family functioning, the implicit rules that govern interactions, the nature of boundaries, and so forth. This can be illustrated by describing Tracy and her family.

### Thinking about People, Patterns, Rules, and Boundaries

Tracy, a mother of three, gets into fights with her 12-year-old son, Abel, screaming at him and hitting him when he refuses to go to school. A neighbor files a complaint and an agency takes on the case, with mother and son as the identified clients. The staff perspective at this agency is that people are free-standing individuals whose behavior is determined by their psychological makeup. They place the mother in a therapy group so that she can explore her own childhood experiences of abuse, and they send Abel for individual counseling. Later, when Tracy reveals the existence of a live-in boyfriend who is verbally abusive to her, the worker recommends that he also should be seen individually for some sessions. In effect, the staff is treating Tracy's punishment of her son, Abel's school phobia, and the boyfriend's abusive language as separate, unconnected problems.

If the staff perceived behavior in terms of interactions and wanted to understand the prevailing patterns, they would need to proceed differently, starting with a larger cast of characters. Tracy and Abel are at the center, but also included are Tracy's boyfriend, John, and Abel's two sisters, who live in the same household. With some exploring, it would become clear that they must include Tracy's mother, who has considerable influence on Tracy and the children, and Tracy's siblings—as well as her godmother, her uncle, and a close friend. Also relevant are those who are neither family nor friends, but who form part of the network that regulates the life of poor families: a worker from Child Protective Services who has been monitoring the home for two years and school personnel, including the truant officer with whom Tracy maintains an antagonistic relationship.

Initially, many of these people will be invisible to the worker, or, at least, their relevance and their interconnections may not be apparent. Family and friends may not come forth as resources because they are unaccustomed to such a role, or because they're in conflict with the client or each other. And the fact that other professionals shape the family's reality may never occur to the staff. Whether and how these people are included in the work is a separate decision, but knowledge of their existence is important. A large canvas is required for creating a map of the human context. The staff should proceed on the assumption that every family's reality requires a mural rather than a closeup, and that the larger picture must be reconstructed if problems are to be understood and resources mobilized.

To explore relevant patterns, it's useful to begin by spotting

central subsystems. The crucial patterns of alliance and antagonism may lie within a particular relationship, in the interaction
between subsystems, or both. In Tracy's case, we would know
where to look from the nature of the presenting complaint and
from the information emerging about John's presence in the
household. We know that Tracy and Abel form a problematic
subsystem, Tracy and John another. With an educated guess, we
also can assume that the triad of Tracy, John, and Abel occupies
a central position in the organization of the family. Alliances and
coalitions involving Abel's sisters and Tracy's mother are certainly
part of the equation, but probably not the point of entry. Experienced workers know they must focus, once they understand the
family map, concentrating on the parts of the system that are
clearly dysfunctional, or that they know from experience have
difficult issues to work out.

In this case, the staff might explore subsystems in which
interactions become abusive, noting ways in which Tracy and her
son trigger each other, as well as events that bring Tracy and John
into conflict. However, they also would pay particular attention to
the triad of Tracy, John, and Abel, knowing that boundaries and
authority often are unclear when an outsider joins an established
unit of parent and children. In this family, the rules of authority
were certainly unclear to its members. Tracy and John disagreed
about discipline. Abel did not get along with John and felt protective toward his mother, explaining, in part, why he stayed home
from school. And Tracy's efforts to control her son escalated to a
screaming frenzy, but only when John was present and her mother
was not—or when threats from the truant officer became more
pressing, Abel more recalcitrant, and John more critical. The
members of this network were part of a web of interaction; their
individual reactions served as stimuli and responses to the behavior
of others.

The particular patterns that emerged in this case are unimpor-
tant at the moment, as is the fact that the situation could not be
resolved without bringing in other members of the family and
school personnel. The point here is that the difficulties of Tracy
and her son could only be fully understood in the context of this
family's organization. The options for intervention were increased
by looking at how different subsystems functioned, and by coming
to understand the confusing rules governing family interactions.

## Thinking about Transitions

The discussion about Tracy's family provides a useful example of
how diagnosis and treatment possibilities change when one thinks
systemically. However, an understanding of the family's patterns
isn't always sufficient, although it provides an essential base. Individuals and families travel along a time line, and sometimes are in
transition. The factor of change may be one of the most powerful
forces in their lives. Families who have just moved into a shelter,
or whose children have been taken for placement, or whose teenage
daughter has become pregnant, are all in transition. Their behavior
can best be explained if the staff pays attention to the meaning and
impact of changing events.

Megan and her family are in this situation. She is 15 years old
and 2 months pregnant. Her mother filed a petition for "children in
need of services" (CHINS), and Megan was referred to a residential
center for pregnant teenagers, where she will live until she goes into
labor. There are multiple services available: medical care, schooling,
and classes focusing on the special issues of pregnancy, birth, and
child development. The staff monitors relationships in the living
quarters, encouraging friendships and mediating quarrels, and there
are group sessions for the girls. Individual counseling focuses on fears
and problems and explores decisions about the future. What's missing
is an interest in the family. The staff receives information about why
the girl was referred, usually including some commentary about
family problems, but lacks the mind-set for exploring family relationships while the girl is at the residence.

Megan is a mildly rebellious adolescent whose excellent grades
in school have dropped, and whose close friendship with 16-year-
old Jamal has resulted in a pregnancy that frightens her. Although
the center of the situation, she is by no means the only one
involved. She comes from an intact African-American family that
is actively involved in a strict religious sect. The parents have
brought up their five children with firm rules and a tight rein. If
the staff were family oriented, they would think it important to
explore the prevailing patterns, authority structures, alliances, and
tensions that have brought this girl to a residential center. It would
soon become clear that the father is a strict disciplinarian; that,
although the mother and aunt are close to Megan, they never
challenge the father; and that the four younger children obey the

family rules. The fundamental point for our discussion, however, is that the pregnancy is experienced as an unexpected and shocking event, catapulting the family from a coherent, well-organized entity, in which all the members know the rules, to a system in a state of confusion.

Megan's family is in transition, attempting to cope with a disruptive event through familiar patterns that have usually gone unquestioned. The father is in charge, and has handled the situation by ejecting the culprit. The remaining family members go on as before, superficially, but the change is profound and the situation unresolved. There will be a baby, a new member of the family, and Megan will become a parent—ready or not.

The staff needs to consider some basic questions concerning the period of pregnancy and future developments. Will Megan and her baby be permanently banished? Is that what she and the family really want? What are the younger children thinking and how will this affect their adolescence? What about Jamal and his family: Are they interested in the baby? Megan's pregnancy is a transitional period, with fluid properties that will settle eventually into new patterns. Without help, the members of this extended family may settle into their reactions, with boundaries that are too rigid, emotional bonds that aren't honored, and distress that remains unexpressed.

Helping this family will involve practical skills: The worker will have to meet with the family, acknowledging their anger and pain while exploring alternative means for helping Megan and her baby. The first step, however, is conceptual. The staff must understand the traumatic implications of the situation for this family, including the fact that they are in the midst of a profound transition.

Transitions are open-ended. They bring confusion, but also provide opportunities. A worker who thinks creatively is likely to approach a situation like Megan's with the intention of preparing the groundwork for change, and with a long view of the possibilities for reuniting the family. We have worked with families who are angry or distant during the pregnancy but whose availability changes dramatically when the baby is born. The birth of the child is, after all, another major transition, with the appeal of an infant at its center.

If the staff thinks in these terms, they will bring both patience and thoughtful preparation to their work during the pregnancy. In some cases, they may need to reach beyond the immediate family, exploring with the adolescent the resources of her informal network. That network may well include people, such as godmothers, church members, older siblings, or friends, who care about her and will be concerned for the baby. But unless the worker has this mind-set, the development of a support system is likely to be haphazard rather than planful.

The transition that has disrupted a family may be less obvious than an unexpected pregnancy. In some situations, professional workers proceed with diagnosis and treatment without ever realizing that a family transition has occurred, and that it is relevant for the case at hand. Liliana's arrival at a local hospital is an example. Sixteen-year-old Liliana was admitted after telling her parents that she wanted to die and then taking a large dose of pills. The first reactions of the staff invoked familiar theories for understanding individual pathology. They saw her as a depressed, suicidal adolescent. In this case, however, the adolescent came from a family of recent immigrants. The staff was encouraged to broaden the scope of their thinking, and in particular to consider how the daughter's problems might be related to the family's sense of displacement after migrating from South America.

The family was invited to come in for an exploratory discussion. In the course of the meeting, the staff became aware of the importance and complexity of the transition. The family was faced with a new language, a loss of friends, the challenge of supporting itself, the frightening reality of living in a neighborhood run by armed gangs, and the daughter's involvement with an adolescent group whose life-style was unfamiliar. Both staff and family developed a different understanding of Liliana's problem. They came to see her symptoms in relation to the context, and to understand that Liliana was caught between two worlds, unable to resolve the contradictions and live by the rules of both, while the controlling behavior of her parents expressed their fear and lack of power in an alien culture and dangerous neighborhood.

## Preparing for Change

Recognizing family patterns, context, and the impact of transitions allows the staff to approach problems and solutions with a fresh outlook that includes some optimism about mobilizing family strengths. A family always has a broader potential repertoire than appears in its repetitive patterns. Tracy's abusive behavior only partially represents her. Given a different set of circumstances, one might see her sense of responsibility, her tenderness, and her easy humor, as well as her boyfriend's sense of commitment to Tracy's family that lies behind his domineering behavior. Megan's family has strong bonds of loyalty underlying their strictly regulated routine. And, like other immigrant families, Liliana's has some experience with tackling the unfamiliar, even if they have suffered in the process. These aspects, although temporarily invisible, are part of the latent strength of a family. With help from an agency staff that recognizes this potential, family members may be able to use different parts of themselves in ways that contribute positively to their collective life and individual development.

Recognizing that workers and clients shape each other's behavior is another way of preparing for constructive change. The patterns established in the helping situation may or may not be useful, and even a responsible, well-meaning worker may become part of the problem. For instance, in one situation the mother of an adolescent daughter came to an agency serving parents of difficult teenagers. She was "at her wit's end." Trying to describe how difficult things were between her daughter, Gina, and herself, she mentioned an incident in which she had lost her temper. The worker's antennae went up, almost automatically, and she reacted with concern. She switched from her role as advisor and resource for the mother to a position of advocacy for the girl, forming an alliance that increased tension within the family. The mother was bewildered. She became more defensive with the worker and more helpless in relating to her daughter, while Gina was split between loyalty to her mother and the feeling of power she had acquired through the intervention of the authorities.

In a different situation, however, the staff of a residential center recognized the agency's role in a repetitive (negative) pattern, and were able to work constructively with the family. In this case, violent confrontations between a 12-year-old and his stepfather routinely landed the boy at the institution. The staff understood that the child's placement provided temporary relief from the chronic tension between the stepfather and the boy's mother and that the situation would continue unless the cycle was broken.

They helped the parents negotiate internal differences without involving external sources of control, and they normalized the family's perception of the transitional difficulties that occurred whenever the boy returned home after a period of inpatient therapy.

Preparing to change systems that aren't working well involves ever-expanding circles, including relationships among agencies that serve the same family. Interagency problems, discussed in the previous chapters, crop up surprisingly often in individual cases. When workers make contradictory diagnoses of the family's needs and spend time arguing diverse views, their behavior may mirror the conflicts and unsuccessful coping patterns of family life.

A review of case coordination must always be part of a systems approach. If the agencies are many and their participation is intense, it may be necessary to recognize that "we have met the enemy and they are us." Changing the pattern of agency involvement may require something basically simple, such as reducing the number of agencies in the loop so that coordination is more effective. As a positive by-product, such a move may mean that the family will spend less time traveling to meetings, telling their story over and over, and falling into a pattern of manipulating agency differences to obtain what they want. Whatever the remedies, nothing can change unless a staff is alert to the realities of how things are working, both in the families themselves and in the larger systems that serve them.

## PRACTICAL SKILLS: HELPING FAMILIES CHANGE

A broad view of the relevant parties and an understanding of patterns, boundaries, and transitions does not translate automatically into effective service, especially when the primary goal is to engage and empower the family. Many poor families are unaccustomed to taking such an active role. They expect social service agencies to do something *for* them (finding housing or keeping an adolescent off the streets) or *to* them (taking the children away or making surprise home visits). The mother of a boy admitted to a residential center may be glad of the respite, the sibling of a recovering addict may prefer to stay out of her sister's rehabilitation experience, the parents of a child placed in foster care may be angry at workers in general. Changing those expectations so that the family becomes an active agent in solving its problems requires subtle skills with a paradoxical feature: The staff must learn how to work hard at taking a backseat.

While training agency workers to establish an interactive relationship with families, we emphasize new skills in four areas: gathering information, reframing family assumptions, exploring alternative patterns of interaction, and handling conflict.

## Gathering Information

The process of gathering information begins with the first contact. The initial meeting provides an opportunity to convey a respectful interest in how the family sees their situation, even while the worker is learning how the family functions. The basic aim is to make the family feel welcome and involve them immediately in a joint effort. There's a relatively low-key mode for gathering information that consists of listening, observing, and reflecting back an understanding of the family's viewpoint. In the family therapy literature, this is referred to as "joining," and is the first step toward forming a cooperative unit. A more active mode includes mapping the family structure and encouraging the enactment of typical interactions that can help the worker understand how the family handles issues and relationships.

### Joining, Listening, and Observing

Families may come to the first session under duress because they have been told by the court or protective services that they must attend meetings at the agency. Or they may come voluntarily, hoping that the agency can somehow fix their troubles. In either case, the worker first must listen to the family's concerns—their own story of what has been happening and why, what they hope for, and what they're afraid of. Their version is valid in its own terms, just as valid as the official case presentation—sometimes even more so. A busy caseworker may feel impatient with the family's report. It may conflict with the material in the official file and thus may seem self-serving or evasive. For the family, however, it is the reality. To listen to their presentation with respectful attention is a skill, and to reflect back an understanding of the difficulties is part of joining:

> A young mother whose children were taken away on charges of neglect says: "I don't know what I'm doing here. You people have me running in circles. I don't get any answers."
> The worker says: "You're fighting many battles."
> The mother continues: "I'm fighting her, him, her . . . (*points at family members and another worker in the room*). I'm only one person."
> The worker nods: "You're right. It's too much for one person. How do they fight you?"

The worker acknowledges the mother's point of view and encourages her to continue. Before they have talked much longer, she has gathered information about bureaucratic tangles that aren't part of the official record but are relevant for handling the situation constructively.

When a family begins to describe their reality, the worker must listen with what has sometimes been called the "third ear," picking up on what is said indirectly and registering information obscured in the telling. It's especially important to listen for accomplishments and areas of strength that never may have been openly valued. We know that poor families often present themselves as weaker than they are, especially when they interact with representatives of the system, and that they describe their problems and realities without giving themselves credit for competence. The young mother who has been complaining to the worker says: "They kicked me from the apartment and we ended up in this rat hole without any heat or hot water." The worker asks when that happened and the woman tells her it was a year ago. The worker says, with some force: "You spent one year in that place, with the children!! How did you manage?" She has responded to the part of the story that suggests strength rather than dysfunction, slowing down the narrative to acknowledge the terrible circumstances in the environment—and to highlight the skill that enabled the family to survive.

Listening and observing proceed together. The heritage of psychoanalysis has labeled therapy as the "talking cure," but skillful therapists have always noticed the nonverbal cues of posture, facial expression, and movement. Family therapists have also understood that the family drama takes place, to an extent, right before their eyes.

Observing begins as soon as the family enters the room. The worker must take in patterns and interactions as well as individual behavior. Of course it matters that the girl looks as if she has been crying, but the worker must scan the group, noticing that her sister looks protective and her mother impatient. How family members seat themselves around the room will also tell a lot about family organization and relationships. Who sits next to whom? Who talks first? Who talks most, and who seems silent, deferential, or uninterested? Which family members support each other and which ones keep their distance? Who relates to the protective service worker who accompanies the family, and who does not?

What about disagreements? As the family describes their situation, its members often tell different stories. It's less important to arrive at "the truth," which is, in any event, always partial, than to discover the family pattern for handling contradictions. Do they interrupt to correct each other, and what happens when they do? Do they argue or insult each other? Does the grandfather ally himself with the children? Do family members compete for the attention and good opinion of the worker? And what of behavior that doesn't fit the family's description? The family may agree, for instance, that all the children ignore the mother's boyfriend, and the worker may accept that as a fact. A look at the videotape, however, reveals what she failed to notice at the time: The youngest boy gravitates repeatedly toward the boyfriend, leaning against his knees while the family and the worker are talking.

By listening to the family and observing them closely, the staff can pick up leads for the aspects they want to reinforce. In the following vignette, the social worker has captured and woven together information that suggests caring, connectedness, and interdependence among family members—even though that behavior is played down in the family's own version:

PAULA: Nobody cared. They knew I was using drugs. They knew I was a prostitute. I don't blame them.

WORKER: But Lisa said she used to go out and look for you.

PAULA:  Yeah, that's true. She knew where to find me. But that's it. She's the only one.

WORKER (*to Lisa*):  What made you go out for her?

LISA:  We would get worried. We heard things.

WORKER:  We? You and who else?

LISA:  My mom. She would hear something . . . the neighbors talking . . . and she'd tell me, "Go get your sister."

Here the worker has not only underlined the positive concerns of family members, she has moved from an amorphous "they" to particular people, clarifying the details of who belongs in a map of Paula's family.

## Mapping

A worker who thinks systemically gathers information that provides a picture of the family. Mapping is a concrete way of recording and sharing that information. Family scope, connections, functions, and relationships become more apparent to both workers and clients when represented graphically.

It's helpful to draw a tentative map of the family, even before the initial meeting, as a way of carrying a visual image of "family" into that first encounter. The map shows the members in the primary client's network, as the worker understands it from the referral: their genders and ages, how they are related to the person who has been referred, and their living arrangements.

The caseworker may know, for instance, that the grandmother has lodged a complaint stating that the two grandchildren have been beaten, and that the mother, who denies it, is coming in to see him with the children. The caseworker is unsure about some facts, however. Does the grandmother live with the family? Is there a father or boyfriend who hits the children, even if the mother doesn't, and, if so, does he live with them? Does the mother have siblings, and are they close? He draws a preliminary map (also called a genogram), which reflects his tentative knowledge and, perhaps, his questions (see Figure 3.1).

When the caseworker and family meet, it's useful to involve the family in drawing up their own map. Enlisting their participation can be matter-of-fact: "Could you just show me here who's in

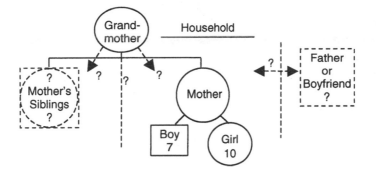

**FIGURE 3.1.**

your family? You can draw a circle for the women and a square for the men. Ask the other people in the family to help you." Inviting family members to place the people and write their names inside a circle promotes a recognition of their mutual belonging, an awareness that "these are us." It invites them to think about which members are stable, which are transient, and who should be drawn closer together because of their connection.

The family's construction of their map provides useful information and usually is a pleasurable activity. However, an experienced worker surveys the product with an understanding that the picture may be partial. The first version often fails to include some people—an aunt, or the oldest daughter's godmother—although they participate actively in the life of the family. Interested questions contribute to expanding the map: Who else is concerned with Carla's drug problem? (Her godmother? If so, draw her in.). Who might be relieved when she finally joins a program? (Her godmother and aunt? Then add the aunt as well.) Are there people in the extended family who think she shouldn't keep her new baby? (Her brother and the mother of Carla's boyfriend? Then add them.) While those procedures are useful, it remains important to be sensitive to reservations on the part of the family. It's early and, as yet, they don't trust the worker. The larger picture may fill in over time, as the worker and family become a cooperative unit and new people emerge as a result of their joint efforts.

Sometimes family members disagree about who should be included or where they should be placed on the map. Such disagreements are, of course, meaningful. Crystal says, "Daddy needs to be there, too." The worker asks why she thinks he should be there. "Because he's my dad," she says. Her aunt says, "OK. Put him there," but as Crystal writes her father's name inside the circle, her aunt says, "No, he shouldn't be in the circle, because he doesn't live with us, right?"

In some situations, the worker might use mapping to represent more complex aspects of the family's organization. The closeness and distance of family members can be indicated by their placement on the map. Involvement can be indicated by a double line ($=$) and overinvolvement by a triple line ($\equiv$). Conflict can be indicated by wavy lines ($\approx$) and a break in the relationship by broken lines (–\ \–). Where useful, symbols can also indicate the difference between clear boundaries (_ _ _) rigid boundaries (——), and diffuse boundaries ($\cdots$).

The Jones family, for instance, consists of mother, stepfather, 16-year-old Lewis, 13-year-old Sheba, and the maternal grandmother. The grandmother doesn't live with them but is interested and available. The father of the children has moved out of the area and has no contact with his former wife or his children. As in many stepfamilies, the mother and her two children form a close subsystem. Lewis is in constant conflict with his stepfather, and the mother is protective of her son, coming into conflict with her husband over issues of control. Sheba and her mother have always been especially close.

Figure 3.2 illustrates this situation. There's a clear boundary separating the grandmother from the rest of the family. A rigid boundary, as well as interrupted lines, separates the father from the family, indicating a lack of contact. The placement of mother and children on the map, as well as the boundary around them, marks this group as a subsystem, and the triple lines between the mother and Sheba suggest overinvolvement. The wavy lines between Lewis and his stepfather, and also between the mother and stepfather, indicate a conflict in these relationships.

Every staff, of course, can develop its own set of symbols, choosing indicators best suited for the families with which they work. A map of this kind helps the staff to think about interactions among family members. Even in its simplest form, mapping gives the staff and the family a shared understanding of the family's scope and membership. It's also a way of normalizing the first contacts

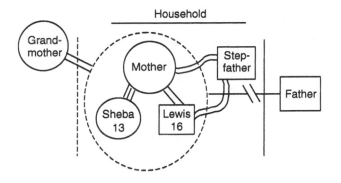

Household

**FIGURE 3.2.**

between them, moving the meeting away from a persistent focus on problems. As more information emerges, it can be a useful way to record the stability and fluidity of membership, the nature of subsystems, and the family's view of who matters in their lives.

### Encouraging Enactments

A map provides a picture of how family members are situated and connected to each other, but family behavior is what offers a handle for useful interventions. An alertness to spontaneous events is an important source of information and a skill in itself. However, the role of the worker is not purely that of an observer. To understand family patterns, the worker must encourage the enactment of typical family patterns, which requires a more complex skill.

When family members are interviewed together, they tend to behave typically. Even if they're cautious or suspicious, they handle relationships and events in ways that come naturally, provided they're given space and opportunity to do so. That is a big proviso. Professional workers occupy the central position in an interview and have been trained to take charge—directing questions at particular people, handling tensions and interruptions. It's difficult for people in the helping professions to step out of the action, letting it evolve and spotting the useful moment to intervene. If the family members short-circuit their usual patterns by turning to the staff, the most useful procedure in many situations is to channel the interaction back to the family. In the following excerpt, the worker encourages a fuller enactment of family behavior, as it probably would occur in their own home setting. The caseworker is listening to Miryam's account of the difficulties she is experiencing with her two children, 9-year-old Anthony and 7-year-old Michelle, while they play in the background. Suddenly Anthony pushes Michelle, who begins to cry.

MIRYAM (*angrily*): Now what was that?

Both children start to respond at the same time. Miryam ignores them and resumes talking with the worker. The worker, however, sits back in her chair and looks alternately at Miryam and the children. Miryam hesitates, then turns toward Anthony.

MIRYAM: You come here.

ANTHONY (*to the worker*): She hit me first!

WORKER: I don't know. Tell that to your mother.

Miryam and the children initiate a three-way conversation.

Here the worker is skillfully nonresponsive. She indicates, by posture and by discontinuing her conversation with Miryam, that she will wait for Miryam to handle the situation. Her response to Anthony is direct, indicating that she's unavailable as an ally or judge, and that she regards his mother as the appropriate person to mediate. With these simple but skillful moves, the worker has picked up information about the family pattern: for instance, that Miryam may ignore the children's efforts to appeal to her authority, allowing the turmoil to escalate, and that Anthony is quick to enlist other people. As she watches the interaction that she has encouraged, the worker will also see how Miryam handles conflict between the children, and will gather clues about aspects of Miryam's parenting that she can reinforce or help Miryam change.

Although the worker's behavior may seem simple enough once it has been pointed out, it is, in fact, not easy for professional workers to hold back. Even experienced therapists are apt to enter too soon and talk too much. Effective enactments empower the family, allowing them to express their usual ways of functioning and to explore new pathways on their own. The worker must be strong enough to take an active leadership role while resisting the tendency to take over.

## Reframing Family Assumptions

Constructive intervention is a matter of punctuation, selecting from the emerging information and zeroing in on transactions that are relevant for the worker's task. Part of that task is to help the family members reframe their assumptions about themselves. When a family tells its own story, it's almost always too narrow, and, with multicrisis families in particular, the stories frequently are too negative. Reframing often involves an emphasis on positives, a search for indications of affiliation and affection among family members, and an alertness to suggestions of strength in the way the family copes.

At other times (or simultaneously), the task is a matter of challenging negatives. Challenging the family's rendition of a story should not appear as an aggressive act. Rather it should offer new options. It may involve helping a child experience how he can make himself understood, although he has learned to give up before he starts; or helping a boyfriend understand that his opinion counts with his girlfriend, even if he expects to be ignored by her family; or helping a mother realize she has a better grasp of her child than she thinks.

In one situation, for instance, Jamie's mother tells the worker, "I don't try to get him to listen anymore. . . . The only reason he listened before was [that] I used to hit him, but that's child abuse." The worker tracks the comment: "Are you saying that you don't try to discipline him because the only way you know would be abusive?" The mother says: "Right. I used to, but I don't anymore." The worker has been preparing for this moment, and is able to say, "But 5 minutes ago you told him very firmly that he had to put that toy back, and he put it back."

The staff will often need to "catch" a family when they're describing their connections and strengths without realizing what they're doing, or acting in ways that belie their summary of how poorly they function. At that moment, the worker reframes the discussion or the action so that a different aspect comes alive for the family. In talking with Paula about her drug addiction and sexual behavior, the worker caught the moment when Paula described the activities of her sister and mother, and was able to underline the caring and connection in the family. In meeting with Miryam, the worker listened as she talked with her children and was able to comment later on her competence: "That really calmed things—the way you explained to Anthony how he's supposed to behave here. That was very effective." Through this comment, Miryam's assumption that she can't handle her children comes up for review, introducing a different perspective and planting the seeds for change.

There are many instances when behavior will seem less than acceptable. Parents may seem too sharp with their children, or abdicate their role as authorities or guides. The family's own narrative, which casts the mother as critical, helpless, or out-of-it, may seem fairly accurate. Nonetheless, the staff must become adept at reframing that behavior in more positive terms—not because it is more true but because it is *equally* true, and because it helps people who feel defeated and self-critical mobilize some other, stronger, part of themselves. When Miryam criticizes Anthony sharply, the worker can say, "You know, I can see you're a very concerned mother, and you have a strong sense of justice." When a mother with three young children watches them banging on the chairs and says in despair that she doesn't know how to stop them, the worker can say, "Yes, it's a problem for you, but you're also very patient with them." That broadens the story of how the family functions, and is a prelude to exploring more effective ways of controlling the children.

It may not seem easy to inject comments of this kind, but it's probably helpful to remember that certain positive features characterize most people forced to endure very difficult circumstances. The multicrisis poor often develop an ability to tolerate frustrating situations that would try any of us, along with useful skills for seeking and using help, a generous and empathic attitude toward other people in similar circumstances, and so forth. With this reality in mind, a worker may find it increasingly easy to recognize commendable elements, and to reframe the meaning of behavior in positive terms.

The effort is important. By shaking up the family's automatic assumptions, the worker creates space to entertain new perspectives and possibilities. Reframing, however, is part of the process rather than its ultimate goal. An alternative view of family strengths and possibilities lays the groundwork for different behavior but usually is an insufficient stimulus for change. It's important to reinforce words and ideas by providing an actual opportunity to explore new patterns of interaction.

## Exploring Alternative Patterns of Interaction

Dysfunctional families are partially paralyzed. They're stuck in repetitive patterns that don't work well but that carry some sense of security because they're habitual. The dysfunctional family is often afraid to change, nor do they know how. They need skilled help, which is the job of the staff. Once family patterns are understood and perhaps reframed, the staff must actively intervene to help the family explore new pathways, enabling them to build muscles where there have been none before.

In the systems terms we have used to describe family functioning, one might say that the family needs help to create new boundaries around subsystems and to change the usual rules for communicating. In more down-to-earth language, one might say that family members need different ways of connecting with each other, better ways of expressing their feelings, and a larger, more effective set of skills for resolving conflict.

To overcome the inertia that accompanies habitual behavior, the staff needs to structure interactions atypical for the family, asking them to handle the situation and supporting their hesitant new steps. The staff must keep the effort going, highlighting behavior moving in a more functional direction and redirecting behavior sinking back into old patterns. By encouraging explorations, the staff enlists the family as primary actors. The eventual goal is for family members to implement new behavior themselves.

For example, the staff person working with Tracy, John, and Abel asks them to talk with each other about the increasing pressure from the truant officer. How can they work out a way for Abel to get up in the morning and go to school? The grouping itself is new, at least as a problem-solving unit. When John suggests that he could be in charge of waking Abel, Tracy objects, fearing a blowup. The worker then asks John and Abel to discuss the idea while Tracy looks on, creating a new pattern with atypical boundaries. As John and Abel begin to talk, the worker beckons Tracy over to sit near him, physically underlining the invisible boundary around the two males and lending the support of his proximity to Tracy, who is anxious.

John says he can wake Abel at 7, and Abel says not until 7:30—if he isn't already awake by then. Holding Tracy quiet with a gentle gesture, and before John can say that is clearly too late, the worker compliments them on their negotiation, says it's a good compromise, and why not try it. He's basically supporting a new pattern, punctuating the discussion when it shows some progress, and before it runs into trouble and escalates into an argument. These few minutes are only a beginning, but they represent an opening up of new possibilities.

Or, consider the situation of 15-year-old Megan, who is living in the residential center, cut off from her family while awaiting her baby's birth. The staff invites her family to the center to plan for the infant. As Megan breaks down in tears, it is her 14-year-old sister, Saral, who puts an arm around her and offers a tissue. The worker says this is a hard time for all the family, but that she realizes they are respectful of life and probably concerned for the baby. She asks Saral to help Megan talk about how she feels, what she wants, and how she might talk with her parents. The worker goes slowly, knowing that this family doesn't discuss their feelings openly, and that the children don't usually talk together about important matters without parental intervention—especially from the father. When Megan tells her father she would like to come home on weekends and he doesn't answer, the worker asks Megan to "say it a different way so your father can hear what you're trying to tell him." The worker needs to enlist family members to help each other in a difficult situation, reinforcing all efforts to communicate and normalizing the expression of anger, pain, and dependence. Although the exact procedures evolve with the situation, staff intervention to help families explore their own possibilities and solutions is important.

Finally, there is the example of the Silva family, which we can briefly track through the gathering of information, the reframing of the family's assumptions, and the exploration of new patterns.

The worker has received a report of child abuse, stating that Ms. Silva has allegedly hit her 14-year-old daughter, Tina, with a stick. The worker has little other information about the family and his preliminary map includes only these two people. He asks Ms. Silva to come in with Tina. Early in the meeting, they are exploring the reported incident and the following interchange takes place:

WORKER (to Tina): Do you remember what the stick looked like?

TINA: It was from the broomstick.

WORKER: Where did she hit you?

TINA: Well, she started beating on my leg. My grandmother was telling me, "Run." She said, "Run." My mother was swinging at my face. Then I run to the room, and . . .

WORKER: Wait a minute. Where did your grandmother come from?

TINA: This was in my grandmother's house.

MS. SILVA: That time that I hit her, right. That weekend I went to my mother's house. My mother sent her to the store and she left, and was away for hours, and I hit her.

WORKER: Let me ask you a question. How often did you do that, hitting her with a broomstick?

MS. SILVA: Only that time. Other times I hit her, but not with a broomstick.

WORKER: Well, do you think if that had happened in your home, just with the two of you, you'd still have hit her with a broomstick? Let's say that you are in your home and she takes off without permission.

MS. SILVA: She did do that here.

WORKER: But you didn't hit her with a broomstick.

TINA: She wasn't allowed to. It would be child abuse.

MS. SILVA: No, it's not that I wasn't allowed to. I try to control myself

WORKER: When you are at home. Do you have broomsticks in your home?

TINA: Of course, she does. She can't sweep without a broom.

WORKER: But she never hit you with a broomstick at home.

MS. SILVA: See, but with my mother she knew how to get her way, when my mother sent her to the store.

WORKER: She tricked your mother.

MS. SILVA: Right. Here she could do the same thing. She's done it. But I don't let her get away with it.

WORKER: So maybe the one you wanted to beat with a broom was your mom, for letting your daughter get her way.

TINA: She told my grandmother that if my grandmother didn't

walk away she would hit my grandmother. And my grandmother said, "What? That you are going to hit who? I will beat
you!"

MS. SILVA: No, it wasn't like that. I told her to move out of the
way, because if she didn't she was going to get hit with the
stick, not that I was going to hit her with it. My mother didn't
want me to hit my daughter.

WORKER (to Tina): I think you got hit with a broomstick because
your mom was trying to teach a lesson to your grandmother.

TINA: And my grandmother would beat her butt.

In this brief interchange, the worker has gathered information
and begun to reframe the situation. He has picked up on a passing
mention of the grandmother, realizing that the central cast of
characters must be expanded. In the subsequent discussion, he
reframes the abusive behavior, highlighting the interaction of the
mother and grandmother as an important factor.

In planning to explore new patterns, the worker utilizes information he has gathered and considers how the family could most
usefully explore new possibilities. The worker has noticed, for
instance, that Tina has learned to ally herself with one adult against
another. She has been strengthened in challenging her mother's
authority, not only by her alliance with her grandmother but by
invoking the power of the authorities in monitoring child abuse.
The protection of children from physical harm is an important
responsibility of the state, but is not helpful when used as a weapon
in the conflict between an adolescent and a parent—especially if
the parent's behavior is neither habitual nor severe. In this case the
worker decides to focus on the family triangle, and to draw a firm
boundary between family members and the authorities. He will
encourage an open discussion between mother and grandmother,
challenging the coalition between grandmother and Tina in opposition to Ms. Silva, and removing Tina from the inappropriate
position of power that increases tension between mother and
daughter and leads to physical action.

The worker meets with Ms. Silva, her mother, and Tina. He
asks the two adults to discuss their views of how to control Tina.
When Tina intrudes to make a comment, the worker stops her: "No,
this is something they have to discuss without you." As the discus-

sion develops—or at another meeting, if things go slowly—there will be time to help the mother and/or the grandmother to take over the role of preventing Tina from entering their discussions. That is a new pattern, which must be integrated by the family into their daily life and become self-propelled and automatic. At the same time, the worker and the family need to recognize that Tina is a young adolescent looking for more autonomy. Mother and daughter will need to negotiate some new rules that take into account her changing needs.

In all of these situations, the examples are partial, only suggesting what skills are required. As the work evolves, the staff needs to follow developments, helping the family rehearse new patterns, accept setbacks, and take responsibility for creating its own new and more functional reality.

## Handling Conflict

Some of the examples in this chapter involve family conflict, but the question of how to handle conflict is so important that it bears further discussion.

To begin with, there is a theoretical issue about working directly on negative family patterns. Especially for a population that has experienced so much misery and has internalized so much social criticism, it's important to highlight family strengths, reframe negatives, focus on solutions, and empower family members through respect for their viewpoint and support for their efforts. In this chapter, we have focused principally on ways to implement that approach. However, accentuating the positive may be insufficient if a family has not learned to handle their disagreements and their anger. People need mechanisms for managing the tension that is buried, that arises and erupts, or that jeopardizes affection and breaks important connections.

Family disagreements are a part of life. They can be bitter and unyielding in any family, sustained by the unresolved issue of who's "right," by hurt feelings, and by the frustration of efforts that seem to go nowhere: "I've told him over and over and nothing works"; "She doesn't listen; she doesn't understand"; "Nothing gets through unless I hit him." People get stuck in repetitive patterns, hurting each other and unable to see alternatives. The anger may go underground, erupt and escalate, or find its solution in drink or drugs.

What does a worker do? Certainly the staff must assess the degree of danger. They must be concerned to protect the weaker family members and short-circuit incipient tragedy. But there are many stages of family conflict before truly dangerous levels are reached. One definition of empowerment or resilience is that the family has learned to tolerate their differences, and has developed a repertoire for resolving conflict.

Every professional worker knows how useful it is to vent anger. Allowing a client to rail at the system or even at another family member often clears the air, if only because there is a tolerant ear as well as a release of pressure. But conflict goes beyond internal pressure; it is an interactive matter, a failure of communication and resolution between people. The staff cannot tiptoe around that reality if they want to help the family.

Being willing and able to relate to conflict requires a variety of skills. The worker needs to be prepared to stir up disagreement when the family is sidestepping their differences, tolerate conflict when it arises spontaneously, and mediate what is getting out of hand. A tall order, perhaps, but the staff doesn't work alone. Members of the family are often effective allies, helping to explore the issues and develop new pathways. The worker initiates and orchestrates the action but may select certain family members to coach, help break silences, or get past the shouting.

For instance, Megan's sister, Saral, is her ally, who also manages her father better than Megan does. The worker asks Saral to coach Megan on how she can tell their parents what she wants for the baby and herself. When the silence is broken, the father erupts in anger and the family sits frozen in their chairs. The worker then enters to stir up further discussion: "I understand your pain and your disappointment—and so does Megan—but she's afraid now, and she needs to plan for her baby. Can you and your wife and Megan talk now about what to do?"

The worker is sometimes a traffic cop, keeping some people out, putting others together, providing some with the possibility of venting their anger, and others with the experience of resolving an issue before anger takes over. Tina's mother and grandmother need to talk together as adults, expressing their mutual disapproval of the other's way of disciplining Tina, and Tina must be kept out of the discussion. Abel and John need to negotiate the rules for getting up in the morning, while Tracy sits on the sidelines and the worker waits to punctuate the discussion at the earliest point of semiagreement. In this case, the worker decided that these family members needed to resolve something before their discussion escalated to a conflict—whether or not the plan was optimal.

Tracy and John would need to have their own discussion about how he treats her and what triggers his abusive behavior. When they talk, they will probably shout at each other—an event the worker will need to tolerate—and talk over each other so that neither hears the other—a situation in which the worker will have a role to play. There are various possibilities, and he may use all of them: He may introduce some version of "Hold it! He doesn't hear you. It's too noisy and he's heard that before. Say it in a different way." Tracy would then say something and the worker might say, "Good. Find out if John understood. . . . Ask him." She asks. John shrugs, then says he doesn't mean to talk her down but he can't stand the way she gets on his case. Tracy is silent. The worker says, "Find out what he means."

The worker is a coach, sometimes part of the discussion and sometimes deliberately on the sidelines. He stirs the pot, sometimes illustrating how a dialogue proceeds when everyone has a say, meaning is explored, and discussion has a longer duration than is usual for family members. It's a new pattern, and it begins to create a new pathway for resolving conflict: fragile, not yet self-sustaining, requiring practice, but potentially significant for the survival of this couple.

The worker has other possibilities that are not always verbal. One worker handled situations in which everybody talked at once by calling a halt and holding up a pencil: "This is the talking stick (or 'the magic wand'). Whoever has it can talk; the others listen." Or, in order to make subsystem boundaries concrete, the worker asks the family to change or move their chairs, indicating that certain people will talk about their conflict while other people, who usually intervene when anger rises, will sit at a distance and remain out of the battle. The worker stays out of the discussion but is alert. She may enter to jump start the discussion again, if it comes to an angry halt, or intervene to say to the mother, "This is when your daughter gets frightened and is afraid you'll hit her, so she shouts or runs away. Can you take a minute to listen to her, then you can respond." Or she may bring in a helper from the family to work on different ways of communicating.

The repertoire of skills is broad and the worker uses them flexibly as the contact with the family evolves. At some point, with any family, it will probably be useful to use most of the skills we have described: to ask people to discuss their disagreements, to keep other family members from smoothing the situation or taking sides, to introduce other family members in helpful but atypical roles, to mediate—when that seems indicated—by stirring up or slowing down the action, to offer talking sticks or metaphors or even humor as a way of facilitating alternative ways of interacting, and to explore new, more constructive patterns for the resolution of conflict.

Lurking behind this discussion is the specter of violence, the knowledge that disagreement can escalate to rage, and that rage can express itself in physical aggression. It's the responsibility of the staff to assess the level of violence, and if the decision is made to work with the family, to make the starting point clear: "It's not permissible to hurt the children. There are other ways to do things and we'll explore them, but that's the ground rule. That has to change."

It's not easy to work with family conflict. The staff is often personally uncomfortable, as well as worried. It's a relief to emphasize strength, respect, and support, but agency families—like any others—need ways of moving off their battlegrounds without leaving carnage behind. Or, to soften the image, they need to learn how to avoid severing family connections that are sources of potential support in a difficult world. Megan and her baby need an extended family. Tracy, John, Abel, and Abel's sisters should be able to live together as a family, negotiating their disagreements and their anger. Tina's mother should be able to control her daughter without a broomstick, and Tina should be able to speak up for her rights without pulling in a social worker and calling on the power of the state. In all those situations, conflict can be resolved without harming family members, and without invoking the social interventions that dismember the family.

To work effectively with family conflict, the staff needs to factor in a realistic evaluation of their level of skill at any particular time. They can move on to more difficult situations as they acquire more experience, being sure to maintain the essential staff structures that offer supervision and support during the process. If the workers are to empower families, however, the effort and the risk are necessary.

## FAMILIES AND LARGER SYSTEMS: HELPING AT THE JUNCTURE

Many of the problems that beset a family lie at its juncture with larger systems. The multicrisis poor don't manage their contacts with agencies, workers, and institutions very well. The issues at hand are similar to those already existing within the family: confusing pathways of communication, unclear boundaries, weak skills for conflict resolution. In this particular situation, the problems are compounded by the fact that the system is skewed, with families in a less powerful position than people in authority. Rebalancing the system often requires procedural changes within agencies, as well as systemic changes in how different services coordinate their efforts.

It's possible, however, for staff to help the family relate to service systems more effectively. They can do this by actions that empower the family: withholding professional competence, shedding power, strengthening the boundaries between agency and family. Although such actions seem mostly a matter of stepping back, they involve some skill. They require a letting go on the part of professionals who are trained to take charge, and a stepping forward on the part of people who have grown accustomed to a more passive role. Knowing when and how to cede power to the family is a significant skill.

Some opportunities to strengthen family participation occur during ordinary moments of contact with its members. If the worker isn't alert, they will slip by unnoticed. During an initial interview, for instance, a teenager recalled being molested by a neighbor as a young child, and the worker and mother concurred that "she needs to talk with somebody about that." There was no suggestion that this was not purely a professional matter, that the mother might be up to the task, or that other family members might be useful participants in the discussion of her feelings. In a different situation, when a young mother was holding her infant during a scheduled visit and the baby began to cry, the foster mother automatically extended her arms and the mother promptly returned the baby to her. Everybody took it for granted. The worker never suggested that the mother try to soothe him herself, or that the foster mother advise her about the ways that seem to work best.

In these situations, competence, power, and expertise remained with the representatives of the system. To empower the family instead, would require the motivation to break the usual patterns, as well as a development of practical skills. The staff would need some trust that family members will find their way, tolerance of their fumbling, patience in the face of their efforts to turn again to the expert, and some simple coaching skills when that seems useful and unintrusive. Suggestions by the foster mother about soothing the baby, along with a comment that it doesn't always work, would give the young mother some guidance, without interrupting her relationship to her child or short-circuiting the growth of competence. She can only develop confidence and an ability to parent through contact with her infant.

One way of shedding power is to search assiduously for resources within the family before automatically making a referral. To do this, the worker must accept that there is a trade-off. The family is apt to be less knowledgeable and efficient than professional helpers, but they can probably use the mechanisms they work out themselves in a more sustained way. Maybe a young boy's uncle, rather than a worker, can coach him on how to stay away from fights in school. Maybe the grandparents who have their grandson in kinship care can negotiate directly with their daughter about the conditions for visitation, rather than following the set rules of the agency and registering their complaints through the worker.

It may be particularly difficult to let go when there's conflict in the family, or when child-rearing practices seem faulty. The staff needs to monitor the safety of individuals in the family, but workers often claim control over "gray areas" when it's questionable that they should do so.

Here are two simple examples:

Emma Jones is the kinship foster parent of her grandson, Paul. She and Paul's mother, Gwen, engage in loud arguments whenever Gwen comes to pick him up for the weekend. The worker intervenes to prevent them from arguing in Paul's presence, announcing that from now on she will pick the boy up at Emma's home, transport him to Gwen's house, then bring him back.

The child protective worker has successfully engaged Margo, who is pregnant, in a drug rehabilitation clinic so that her baby will not be placed at birth. Both are pleased with this. On one of the worker's visits, however, she observes that Margo is unjustly reprimanding her 5-year-old daughter, and she tells her that she will have to learn to be fair to her daughter before her case can be closed.

In these situations, the workers are using their positions of power as leverage to promote specific ways of relating—or not relating—among family members. In the first example, the worker is preventing the two women from arguing, at least in front of the child; in the second example, the worker is demanding fairness in the mother–daughter relationship as a condition for closing the case. The intentions are good and the prescriptions for family life are intrinsically positive, but the effect of these injunctions is a loss of autonomy for the family. The relationship between Margo and her 5-year-old daughter is now shaped more by the worker's rules than by their interactions with each other. And Emma and Gwen will not learn to negotiate their conflicts; their contact has been broken and their disagreements suspended—unresolved.

To help families regain control over their lives, the staff must rein in their own controlling behavior, in each instance questioning whether the intervention is necessary. Is it really imperative that Emma and Gwen refrain from arguing? Are there alternative, less controlling ways of responding? Might it be more helpful to suggest that conflict is normal under their circumstances, and that a three-way meeting to discuss their differences could be useful? And is it sometimes worth considering whether the staff is being pulled into a controlling stance by the clients themselves, for instance, by the "unfair" mother who may be challenging the worker as well as reprimanding her daughter? Whatever the answer, there should be a pause between impulse and action on the part of the worker, such that control becomes a function of necessity rather than of role.

Sometimes, of course, a controlling stance is unavoidable.

When that happens, the worker must find a way to keep the issue from dominating the relationship. When Jane missed her appointment for a urine test at the clinic, the worker was required by law to notify the agency. At the next session with Jane and Jerry, her boyfriend, Jane was angry.

JANE:: I don't feel like having a session today.

WORKER: How come?

JANE: I'm pissed. I miss one f_____ test and you report me.

WORKER: Well, the rules are that if you miss a test I have to report it and I did, but I wrote down your explanation as well. I'm glad you came in, though. I know you're angry at the agency these days and I think you might try to find out from Jerry how he thinks you should handle that.

In general, the worker wants to strengthen the boundary between family and agencies, stepping out of the action, withholding expertise, and asking family members to talk together about their issues— even those concerning problems in dealing with agencies. In the following interchange, involving parents whose children have been taken into care, the worker wants the parents to develop a sense that they're a team, that they probably have useful ideas, and that together they may have some power. The couple begins with the assumption that all the decisions lie outside of them.

WORKER: Have you talked with your husband about what you need to do to get your children back?

MOTHER: He's not the one who took them away. It's the people who took them away who's got to give me some answers. We can't do anything until we get some answers.

WORKER: Who have you been talking to?

MOTHER: This woman, McSomething, at protective services.

WORKER (to father): And you?

FATHER: Nobody. I don't talk to those people. I tell her it's no use.

WORKER: I think you need to work as a team. Why don't you talk together now about how to deal with this.

Many poor families have difficulty focusing on their own internal processes, precisely because the intervention of external agencies is a chronic fixture of their lives. A family may be involved simultaneously with multiple agencies, each with its own agenda, and all of them regularly penetrating the family's boundaries. Contradictory agendas sometimes reflect the conflicting attitudes of various family members. The relationship between these members and their respective champions may become just as relevant as the relationships among family members themselves.

In helping families strengthen the boundary that differentiates them from regulatory agencies, some workers use themselves as border guards. They invoke their expertise to keep the regulators "off the family's back," or they vouch for the family's competence whenever others express concern. That's useful, up to a point. However, there are some pitfalls that workers must be aware of: They must handle the increase of concern in the agency about what is occurring in a family that the worker seems to be protecting, and they must understand that, if they play this role consistently, the family's ability to protect its own boundaries will fail to develop. As an alternative to *becoming* the family's boundary, the staff may work to *nurture* it, signaling in the various ways we have suggested—as well as some of their own invention—that they respect the integrity of the family as a unit with internal resources.

As indicated earlier, the problems that lie at the juncture between families and larger systems cannot be fully handled by agency workers, even those who are skillful and well intentioned. Progress often depends on procedural changes in how the agency functions and on the coordination of services among the various agencies that serve the family. We will discuss procedural matters in the next chapter, and consider communication among professionals at various points throughout the book.

## A SUMMARY OF SKILLS

Because skills described in this chapter are so basic to working effectively with families, we will close the chapter by summarizing and rephrasing its main points.

Workers must first *think* about families (Points 1–5), then must exercise *practical skills* to help families change (Points 6–10):

1. Families are social systems. They organize their members toward certain ways of thinking about themselves and interacting with each other. The behavior of family members becomes constrained, over time, by family rules, boundaries, and expectations. What the staff sees when they meet a family is predictable behavior that defines "the way things are" in the family.

2. The typical behavior of family members may be preferred, but alternative patterns are available—even if seldom used. This fact encourages a hopeful view of possibilities, providing incentive for exploring the family's repertoire. Assessment of a family should always include the invisible roster of strengths and resources.

3. Individuals are separate entities, but are also part of a web of family relationships. The staff is often presented with an identified client whose symptoms or behavior are defined as the problem. They can accept the presenting complaint, but must be aware that control of the symptom lies in the interaction between family members and the client.

4. Families move through transitional periods in which the demands of new circumstances require a change in family patterns. The family may respond by adapting and evolving, but families sometimes get stuck, maintaining patterns that are habitual but unadaptive. Symptoms or disruptive behavior in one family member may reflect the family's distress. The problems are potentially transitory, and the function of the staff is to help the family through a period of disorganization.

5. When they intervene, workers become part of the family system, and are likely to be pulled toward accepting the family's view of who they are and how they should be helped. The staff should understand that the pull of the system narrows their view of the family. It's important, even if difficult, to think about the family in a different way and to highlight their capacity for expansion.

6. The staff's first efforts to help families change should explore how they define their problems, questioning and expanding what the family has taken for granted. The skills for gathering information and exploring possibilities include listening, observing, mapping, reframing, and helping families explore agreements and disagreements through spontaneous and guided enactments.

7. Workers are the catalysts of change. They help the family recognize dysfunctional patterns and explore the possibility of relating in different ways. Family members are encouraged to connect, whenever alienated, and to explore constructive approaches to conflict.

8. The staff empowers families by focusing on family strengths, but they must also work with conflict. If conflicts aren't resolved, they may alienate family members from each other or erupt into violence. The staff should explore this area, listening for disagreements, helping the family to handle conflict safely, and exploring new ways of relating under stress.

9. Intervention is most effective if the staff can restrain their expertise, using their skills to encourage family members to see each other as a resource, and to mobilize help from within their own network. That may involve a new role for workers, requiring a less central position than is customary, and a less active effort to solve the family's problems for them.

10. The staff should consider the extended family as its own primary resource, expanding their initial view of who might be available to help. A request for additional professional services may not be necessary and should be considered carefully. When many agencies are providing a family with multiple services, it's important to evaluate the balance between help and confusion. One of the most useful interventions on the behalf of a family may be to induce organizational changes, so that services become more collaborative, family-friendly, and effective.

CHAPTER FOUR

# Changing the System

FAMILY-SUPPORTIVE PROCEDURES

T he implementation of a family approach depends on the skills of professional workers, and the success of their efforts in turn depends on the support of their agencies: in effect, a circle of mutual dependence. Agency support is partly a matter of attitude, but it's also a matter of structure, in which the details of policy and procedure allow the staff to exercise a repertoire of family-oriented skills. That situation is not easily come by. It's often necessary to review established procedures, looking for details that obstruct or facilitate a family approach, and modifying procedures so they provide a supportive context.

From our perspective, procedures such as intake, assessment, planning, and service are part of one continuing process. If they aren't consistently organized to include the family from the beginning, it becomes increasingly difficult to do so at a later stage. Consider the following situations:

Sandra vanishes from a drug rehabilitation clinic after a period of attendance. The worker contacts Sandra's boyfriend, Colin, thought to be supportive of Sandra's involvement in the program. Colin says there's nothing he can do.

Angela, a depressed mother of four who lives with her children in a temporary shelter for homeless families, gets into trouble for curfew violations. The shelter workers invite her husband, who is staying with his mother, to a meeting. He gently scolds Angela for her misbehavior while also praising the progress she has made in battling her drinking problem. Angela responds like a contrite child, and that same night she violates curfew once again.

James, an 11-year-old, is living at a residential center because of violent behavior at school and at home. He has just completed 3 months of residential treatment and, according to the staff, is ready to participate in family therapy sessions to prepare for his discharge. During the first session, James and his mother engage in a heated argument and the stepfather storms out of the room, swearing that either James will have to leave the family or he will.

Laura's newborn, Wanda, is placed in foster care so that her mother can attend a residential drug-treatment program. After 6 months, during which Laura sees her daughter once every other week, the child welfare and foster care agencies decide that mother and daughter are ready to be reunited. The foster care staff increases the frequency of visits and complements them with weekly family sessions for Laura, Wanda, and Laura's new boyfriend. However, the couple seems uninterested, misses appointments, and hints that Wanda might need to stay longer in foster care to give her mother time to adjust.

In all of these situations, the workers were trying to apply their newly acquired family intervention skills. When Sandra precipitated a crisis by leaving the drug program and Angela broke curfew, the workers reached out to family members. And when James and Laura were deemed ready, the staff began to reconnect parents and children. In every case it was too late. None of the services had created an involvement with the family before this moment. James and Laura had been purposely separated from their families so that their individual problems could be treated without interference from the issues of daily life. The men who were important to Sandra and Angela had already been cast as peripheral by the time they were asked to participate. Sandra's boyfriend had escorted her to the program the first day and Angela's husband came to the shelter for sporadic visits, but neither had been contacted by service staff along the way.

If agency procedures had been different from the start, subsequent events might have taken a different course. What if Angela's husband had been encouraged from the beginning to remain involved with his family? Angela might not have violated curfew. Or, if his impulse to leave the family had been openly discussed, he might not have been considered the best resource for Angela, and other avenues of support might have been explored. What if Sandra's boyfriend had participated in the admission interview and attended joint sessions with her? Perhaps Sandra would not have dropped out. Or, if she had, he might have been in a better position to encourage her return to the program. What about James and Laura? When it was time to consider discharge for James, he and his family may have been at a further point had their sessions together started earlier. Similarly, the relationship between Laura and her baby might have been more solid if they had had frequent contact during those first 6 months after Wanda's birth.

But the families were excluded from involvement. In each situation, the workers were following an established mode of interaction with clients, codified into the procedures for intake, assessment, and service. Angela's application for a place in the shelter was treated as if she had been a single parent; her husband was not part of the planning. Sandra was interviewed alone for the drug program while her boyfriend waited outside. James' family also waited outside—both literally and symbolically—while their child was treated at the residential center. And Wanda was placed in some kind of layaway while her mother was sent to recover from drugs. The procedures began with the individual as the focus of concern, leaving little room for the practice of family-oriented skills, and making it unlikely that family members could respond helpfully at a point of crisis or transition.

The first contact with the agency establishes the tone of everything that follows, and consequently is crucial. Therefore, we will begin our consideration of family-supportive procedures with a discussion of intake.

## INTAKE: FORMING A PARTNERSHIP WITH THE FAMILY

When a new case comes to an agency, there's a flurry of urgent work to be done. Intake is a period for gathering information, filling out forms, and making decisions that will connect the client both to a new setting and to the professionals who will provide services. Not necessarily a crisis, but not a time for dallying either. Agency workers feel the pressure: They're aware that the relay race started farther back and higher up, that they must carry it forward, and that they're responsible to the larger systems that made the referral and expect accountability in return. The pressure and official forms often dictate the intake process, leading to a focus on the diagnosis of individual dysfunction ("drug addiction," "depression," "acting out," "poor parenting skills") and on the familiar categories of information that usually fill the official record (individual history, cognitive and emotional status, diagnosis, motivation, prognosis).

Within these parameters, the inclusion of the client's family at the point of intake may seem complicated, troublesome, and perhaps unnecessary. Even if the agency expects to work with the family, it's often the policy or assumption that such work will come later, when the client is deemed ready. First it's necessary to deal with the presenting problem of the identified client. Procedures and planning must move along established pathways.

If an agency wishes to create an active partnership with families, it must usually arrange a radical revision of the customary procedures, beginning with the inclusion of the family in the intake process and a concerted effort to maximize their involvement. The family should emerge from the first contact with a sense that the staff is respectful, supportive, and concerned that they understand the family's perspective. The staff should make it clear that the agency will regard them as partners in the development of solutions, and that their continuing involvement in treatment is essential. Given the critical importance of this initial phase, we will look at the procedures in detail.

What follows is a discussion of who to invite, what to cover at intake, and how to assess and relate to the family. We take these procedures step-by-step, indicating what to consider, what decisions must be made, and the sequence of events. This process is basically in the hands of the workers who receive the family. In order to follow the procedures, however, the staff must have agency support at several levels, ranging from flexibility in timing to new intake forms that guide the interview toward family matters.

## Whom to Invite

The question of whom to invite harks back to a family-oriented mind-set and to the mandate "think big." Here are the identified clients: Sandra, Angela, James, Laura. Who are the important people in the life space of each? In the previous chapter, we traced that through for Tracy and Abel, knowing we must include John, Tracy's mother, and Abel's sisters, at the very least. Likewise, we have also populated the personal world of the four people introduced in this chapter by noting the central role of husbands, boyfriends, parents, and children. How does the staff arrive at an understanding of the relevant people, and how do they decide who to invite to the very first meeting?

As suggested earlier, it's useful to make a map from the known facts on the referral sheet, but it's also important to consider the probabilities. Teenagers usually have a parent somewhere out there, even if they come in alone, and they may have concerned aunts, grandparents, siblings, or close friends. Children often have more than one involved adult in their lives, even if the mother fills a lot of that space and is a reliable source for all the usual questions. Workers would do well to have an automatic checklist in their heads of who might be involved, including not only immediate kin and members of the household but stable or transitory companions, siblings who don't live at home, foster family members, church and school personnel, and a variety of workers who may provide continuity from the past and facilitate an assessment of current realities and resources.

If all were included at the outset, the stage would be crowded and the process possibly unproductive. It's important, however, to consider who might be relevant and then make choices from a broad array of people. The fragmentation created by the system, or by the erratic life history of the client, should not limit the caseworker who sets up the initial meetings.

What actually happens is controlled by the worker's judgment and by practical realities. Sometimes the very first contact is created by happenstance. Angela and her children may have been brought to the shelter on a bitter winter evening by the police: No husband in sight, and no grandmother, church member, or worker from the housing unit. James may have been brought to the residential center by his mother after a violent tantrum at school and an emergency referral by the school counselor: No stepfather, no siblings, no representative of the school. Of course the process must begin at that point, with admission and a few essential papers. But conversation is crucial, and should include the assurance that staff and family will explore this situation together as soon as possible. It's at this first encounter that the worker establishes the necessity of family participation, mapping out with Angela or James and his mother who is important in the larger picture, and who should be present at the next meeting.

Through this first contact, or even from the official records, it may be clear who should participate in the intake, but they don't necessarily gather together with ease. Some family members are reluctant to attend because they're at odds with each other, or because they fear being blamed. Parents whose children have been forcibly removed may be resentful or depressed, and don't see any point in making contact with the foster care agency. James's stepfather may blame his wife for the boy's behavior and decide it's best if he keeps his distance. Sandra may be reluctant to involve her family out of anger or fear or pride. And professional workers from other agencies may not want to attend a meeting after moving a client off their case load; they have too much to do and are unfamiliar with this procedure.

The staff must meet these situations with a clear message about the necessity of participation that can be heard by the clients and that fits the possibilities of the setting. For example, a residential center in Sweden brings the family in to live for a week with the child, and a hospital director in the United States has redesigned space on the children's ward so that the family can spend the first day and night together. Those are bold measures and not always possible, but there are many other ways to convey the message and accommodate the participants. A foster care agency may need to make an extra effort to contact and involve the child's biological family at the point of placement. The invitation to this family should carry the message: "We need you. Without your help we will have more difficulty making this placement work for your child."

Sometimes a matter-of-fact approach is useful. In a drug rehabilitation clinic, for instance, it's possible to make family participation a condition for admission. As the director of one clinic put it, "We can take the position, as we do with urine samples, that the

family intake is not negotiable." Similarly, when a child comes in
to a ward or residential center, the staff can convey the idea that
of course the father will be involved—even if the mother is the
parent who usually deals with outside institutions. As fathers,
working mothers, siblings, and other professionals may find it
difficult to leave work or school to attend the intake, the agency
will need to accommodate, offering flexible scheduling that includes evening or weekend hours.

The ideal of broad participation must be tempered by the
judgment of the staff as well as by practical considerations. When
family therapists first meet with a family, they usually want to see
all the relevant people, but subsequent meetings are arranged with
subsets and combinations, depending on what they deem useful.
The same kind of appraisal is required in the agency setting,
although the context and complexity of the families sets up a
different challenge. The main purpose is to establish connections
and not overwhelm the primary client or the family. For that
reason, it may be unproductive to start the intake with everybody
who appears relevant, although it's always important to expand the
cast beyond traditional expectations.

The very first contact provides some idea of who the client sees
as allies or adversaries, and what the sore spots are. It would have
been clear from the first conversation with James and his mother
that the mother and stepfather disagree about how to handle him,
and that the godmother, who lives nearby, supports the mother and
is an important force. It would also have been evident from talking
with Sandra that she has complex relations with her mother and
sister, that her father has abused her, and that none of the family
approves of Colin, her boyfriend.

Armed with that information, in each case the worker decides
whether or not to invite people whose presence will increase the
tension, and may plan to build further contacts in a series of intake
meetings. In James's case, a worker might invite the two parents
first, because their conflicting viewpoints are a central part of the
situation and usually are expressed indirectly, adding the godmother, 14-year-old sister, and school counselor in subsequent
meetings. Angela's husband would be included immediately, to
acknowledge his role and assess their relationship, while later
sessions might include his mother, the housing worker, Angela's
sister, and a friend from Angela's church. The intake for Sandra

would include Colin, who accompanied her to the center, and then Colin and her mother and sister—but might hold off contact with Sandra's abusive father.

These decisions involve clinical judgments, and must include multiple factors. For newly trained workers, decisions must take account of their fledgling skills and their level of comfort in handling conflict. Any intake worker must expand the cast of characters beyond the individual, but workers finding their way in the face of family resistance may need to gauge the balance of conflict and support in the family system so that those invited to the meeting will not bring an unmanageable level of family tension. In this evaluation, the preference of the primary client can be useful. In one clinic, the staff offers reluctant clients the option of inviting two family members of their choice to the session. They assume that people chosen in this way will offer a broader perspective and will also support the client through the early stages of admission and participation.

Intake may actually take place over several meetings, during which relevant people are invited sequentially and central information is gathered over time. Even officially required data can be gathered in this way. However, in order to exercise judgment in each case, the worker needs the support of the agency, as well as a clear understanding of the extent to which the system can be flexible. Whatever the pacing, relevant members of the network should be included early enough so that they understand their important role in the work at hand, and so the staff can proceed on the basis of an enlarged set of possibilities.

## What to Cover

There are three primary goals for intake interviews. First, the staff must convey the agency's family-oriented point of view and conduct the meetings so that the family understands its central role. Second, they must impart information that the clients will need and in turn obtain the information that's officially required. And, finally, they must assess the family, looking for problems and conflicts, repetitive patterns, strengths and resources, as well as preparing the way for continuing family involvement. These goals overlap, and the staff is usually conveying an attitude, imparting or gathering essential information, and assessing family patterns all at once. Everything we have discussed in earlier sections is relevant to the question of how to do this: a broad concept of family, an interest in the family's perspective, a respectful attitude, an orientation toward strength, and the development of skills for observing, listening, and encouraging family interactions. It's useful, however, to discuss the details, and we do so in the following sections.

## Communicating the Need for Family Involvement

Inviting the family to intake meetings is the first communication about the agency's point of view. It's a powerful message, establishing the priorities in very concrete terms. While one might expect families to be gratified, they're sometimes startled or confused. If they've been through the system before, they're already veterans, trained to travel the same pathways to which most workers are accustomed. They don't expect to be involved in the planning and delivery of services and need more explanation. The approach of the agency must make sense, particularly since it will involve time and effort. There are many reasons why family members may not respond when invited to participate, and the staff must have a repertoire of mechanisms for communicating the rationale and importance of this policy.

The staff is a step ahead when the identified client is a child. Most families feel responsible for their child, even if they also feel angry or defeated, or relieved to be turning the child over to professionals. When James and his mother appear at the residential center, the first discussion should convey very clearly that the center cannot change the behavior of a young boy by itself. The family is the most powerful force in the child's life, and the staff can only help by working closely with family members. Rather than calm the family with reassurances that the child is now in good hands, it's important to preserve the sense of urgency and to convey the need for the family's continuous involvement.

Different situations and ages require other details. When a pregnant teenager comes into a residence, the intake worker may face an angry family. The family may feel that they have lost control over this adolescent, that she got what she deserved, and that they're giving up on her. But she's young and vulnerable and people in her world may be concerned for her. It's often not difficult to corral a family around the reality that there will be a new baby in the family, and that involvement of the extended family in planning and support is essential.

Intake at a foster care agency is another matter. Everything in the process of removal, court action, and placement has already suggested that the biological family is out of the loop. It's the task of the foster care worker to underline the continuing rights and responsibilities of the child's family, conveying the message that an infant like Wanda must bond with her mother while she remains in care, or that the secure development of an older child depends on continuing contact with his family during the period of placement.

With adult clients, the family may be estranged or critical, or may assume that each adult must handle housing, treatment, or detox programs on his or her own. In justifying the request for family involvement, the worker has two main arguments: Family support is an important component of treatment and changes in the client will impact family life. The intake worker may know, for instance, that a mother's investment in her children will provide the most powerful incentive for abstinence from drugs, and he discusses this immediately with the grandmother, who has custody of the children. He helps her understand that family participation will be an important part of the drug treatment, increasing her daughter's chances of improvement. The worker also discusses the implications of change: Her daughter's improvement will bring about a reorganization of relationships and living arrangements that will affect everybody, and the family needs to work on this together. Hope and logic are communicated at the same time.

In all these situations, the worker is hooking the family into the beginning of the process and laying the groundwork for their continuing participation. To do this effectively requires some of the skills discussed earlier. The worker must convey the conviction that family involvement is crucial for progress and that it's an agency ground rule, but the message is only effective if combined with an emphasis on family strengths. If the worker can convey respect for the family's concern and knowledge, as well as a clear position that the experts cannot do it alone, the family will usually accept the rationale for their participation.

## Exchanging Information and Assessing the Family

Even with family members assembled and some understanding established, it's often difficult for workers to change the usual procedures. They may feel obliged to complete the intake forms, a task which may take up the entire first meeting. If that happens, the family assumes the agency has an official understanding of the problem and family members are only present to hear what the program has to offer and comply with bureaucratic requirements. These passive activities reinforce the conception that the agency is taking over.

A family-oriented intake needs to follow a different procedure, one in which the family takes an active role in identifying problems and working toward solutions. The worker does best by remaining privately skeptical about the official background information, suspending opinions, checking facts with the family, and looking for a richer picture of the family's reality. During this kind of intake the worker focuses on information that only the family can provide, such as the opinions of various members about the nature and origin of their problems and their views about possible solutions. What do they expect from their involvement with the agency? What has been their experience with previous interventions? As a family, do they share an agenda or are they pulling in different directions? At times the worker moves out of the center, allowing for enactments of family style and functioning so she can assess family patterns.

If James, his mother, and his stepfather had participated in this kind of intake, the residential center would have been well on its way to working productively with the boy and his family. The worker might have learned how each parent sees the origin and history of his violent behavior, how James sees his place in the family vis-à-vis his sister ("the good one"), what the parents resent and accept about the school's complaints, and what happens when James's restless tapping on the arm of the chair disturbs the conversation. The worker would have had the opportunity to comment on the family's concern for the child, noting in particular their wish to manage disagreements, control James, and stay together.

Because intake forms guide so much of staff thinking and effort, it's advisable for an agency to review the forms they traditionally use and to create guidelines that facilitate a family orientation. In

Appendix 4.1, we offer an example of questions that might be included in such a form at an agency where children are the primary clients. The items direct attention to family concerns, opinions, expectations, and characteristics—for example, who's in the extended family, how the family is affected by the child's problems, what the family considers the most important focus for help, what solutions they have already tried, how they expect to be involved, and how they describe family stressors and strengths.

Naturally, each agency has its own needs and constraints, and must create or adapt its own forms. However, if the family is seen as a source of information and a resource for further work, intake forms will embody that orientation.

At some point, of course, the worker must gather the historical information that satisfies agency, system, and insurance guidelines on record keeping, and must impart practical information to the clients. Official data often can be gathered late in the session, after a collaborative system of family and agency has been established, or even at subsequent meetings, but the first session cannot finish before the family learns some important facts about the agency. How do things work? What's special about this program as compared to programs they have known in the past? What rules and regulations determine the freedom of interaction between staff and families, such as the mandatory reporting of suspected child abuse? If intake workers can postpone delivering this information until they've learned something about the family and established a relationship, they're in a better position to pinpoint areas where the agency may be relevant to this family's needs. Rather than presenting a litany of available services, the worker can make focused observations and recommendations: "In your situation . . . "; or "Do you think this kind of service would be important for you?"; or "I think you should look into this. We can help, if you're interested"; and so forth.

Workers from referring or associated agencies may be especially useful for imparting information during intake, or for reviewing past and present services. The counselor from James's school, for instance, might describe conditions for his readmission and services available at that time. However, the intake worker has the responsibility for maintaining the tone of the session, directing the discussion of issues, and keeping the constructive involvement of the family in the foreground.

*Laying the Groundwork for Continuous Family Involvement*

Intake almost always terminates in a plan for continuing service, no matter what the staff orientation. If the agency is family oriented, intake should move toward a preliminary "contract," an understanding with the family concerning its future relationship with the agency. In a residential center, the contract might include an agreement about the frequency of family sessions, the availability of family members when crises arise that involve the child, and the responsibility of the staff to keep the family informed about treatment procedures and details of the child's life within the center. In a foster care agency, the focus might be on the frequency and location of the biological family's visits with the child, the ways in which the two families will maintain ongoing contact, and the means for ensuring that the family will participate in important matters such as medical appointments, birthdays, and school functions. In a drug rehabilitation clinic, the family might be asked to provide support for the recovery efforts of the client, and to participate in multifamily groups designed to facilitate the reentry of the ostracized member.

## NURTURING THE PARTNERSHIP AND MOVING THE FAMILY ON

If the process of intake has been successfully managed, the client and family emerge energized and connected to the agency, but the ensuing weeks and months are a time of potential drift. The danger is that agency and family will settle into parallel routines that don't require very much interaction. It's up to the staff to keep things vital; the initiative must come from the agency, which needs to find ways to reach out to families and keep them involved.

### Outreach

Nurturing the relationship with families may require some simple institutional changes, such as modifying the setting to provide pleasant and inviting public spaces, or expanding center-based activities to include family members. However, continuing contact also requires direct outreach, as well as specific efforts to handle developments that suggest family resistance rather than drift.

Direct outreach should be case-specific. The worker knows that James's parents are busy people and have other children. As time goes by, one or the other misses occasional meetings, and neither thinks to inquire about James's behavior in the unit or his educational progress. It's up to the worker to phone them at intervals, conveying the staff's conviction that of course the parents would be interested and that they have the right to know the details of how James is doing.

Or consider Laura, a new mother living without her child and aware of the judgment that she's not yet a fit parent. She doesn't expect to be included in matters that affect her baby, and it probably wouldn't occur to the foster parents to invite her along when they take Wanda to the doctor for a checkup. Nor would they feel they have the right to do so without agency permission. The worker, however, can make that suggestion to both families, planting a new idea and nuturing the connection between them. An invitation to go along on visits to the doctor slows down the mother's drift away from an infant she hardly knows. It enables her to keep up with her child's development, to have her questions answered, and to prepare for when the baby will be released to her care. Expeditions of this kind build shared experience among the network of adults concerned with the infant.

Some forms of outreach can become general policy. In one center for pregnant adolescents, the staff instituted a practice of calling the family twice a week, not to discuss problems or administrative issues but just to touch base. In most situations, parents become used to the idea that they're contacted only when their child is in trouble. A phone call just to talk and exchange information at first comes as a surprise, but then serves to keep open the lines of communication.

If an agency staff thinks together about the practical ways of maintaining contact with families, they will probably come up with a variety of ideas that can be implemented and codified. Consider the following examples, taken from clinics, foster care agencies, residential centers, and day treatment programs. They are actually applicable across the board:

An agency may modify its space. In one foster care agency, a cluster of cubicles was transformed into a room large enough to accommodate several children and the members of both their biological and foster families. In another agency, the boardroom was taken over during certain periods for that purpose. In a day treatment program for drug dependent mothers, space on the unit was allotted for cribs and toys so the children could be close to their parents while they participated in the program. In a residential center, the furniture in the meeting room was rearranged so that families could mingle informally with the staff. The details vary, but the common theme is the flexibility to experiment with an environment in order to create a family-friendly setting.

Other examples concern program organization. Many facilities offer parenting classes to the identified clients, but several have expanded their boundaries, encouraging companions, spouses, and grandparents to attend as well. In some settings, it has become customary to hold family meetings before and after a weekend at home in order to process the events that have occurred during that time. Some residential centers have invited family members to come by to discuss incidents that have occurred on the unit, and in some cases they have even been welcomed to sit in on a staff review of the case. Of course, new procedures require more than energy and creative ideas on the part of the staff. They also require active participation by the administration, especially if there are to be physical changes in the setting, or a reorganization of staff time and activities.

Outreach to the family may be insufficient as a means of increasing contact. Sometimes the primary clients resist the involvement of their families, either anticipating that family members will cause them grief or because they feel defensive and ashamed. The worker can move slowly but need not give up. It's often possible to bring family issues into the discussion, finding ways to underscore their relevance, detoxify the idea of family involvement, and prepare the groundwork for an actual meeting.

The work with Barbara is such an example. She refused to invite her mother and sister to joint meetings at the drug rehabilitation clinic, arguing that she needed to stand on her own two feet and that her relatives' critical attitude would complicate matters. The counselor was certain from the initial meeting, however, that these people were central in Barbara's life and would be important participants in the coming struggle to become free of drugs. She

devoted some individual sessions to an exploration of Barbara's
family relationships. Whenever Barbara brought up the usual topics
that had been occupying previous counseling sessions—her tendency to get involved with violent men, her vulnerability to
temptations of the drug, her feelings of being mistreated by the
foster care agency that had custody of her children—the counselor
would methodically interweave her mother and sister into the
discussion. What did they think about Barbara's boyfriends? How
did they relate to men? Did they also miss Barbara's children who
now were in foster care?

This approach led to the unsurprising revelation that Barbara
felt rejected by her mother, was jealous of her sister, and yearned
to repair her relationship with both of them but didn't know how.
Once this emotional connection became evident, Barbara herself
concluded that it might be a good idea to attempt a rapprochement.
The family was invited in for a series of sessions in which some
tensions were resolved and Barbara developed a stronger sense of
family support. After that, the counselor found a variety of ways to
keep the family connected, encouraging Barbara to call her sister
when there were things to chat about, suggesting that Barbara
invite her family to events at the clinic, and helping to set up an
arrangement allowing Barbara's children to visit at their grandmother's house so that she could see them and the family could be
together.

When family members begin to miss scheduled visits with their
children, as in the case of James's parents, the staff is faced with a
dilemma. If they patiently accommodate to a pattern of no-shows
and keep scheduling appointments for "same time next week," they
convey a sense that such behavior is expected and doesn't matter
all that much. But if they focus on the parents' lack of responsibility,
they end up in the position of prosecutors, leaving the family in the
complementary position of defendants.

In such situations, the procedures chosen must strike a delicate
balance. The worker pursues the family with enough persistence to
emphasize the importance of their presence, but without creating
antagonism. Most of all, the message must stress one basic fact: The
child and staff need their help in order to make satisfactory progress.
It's a litany but it's also the truth, and that fact should lend
conviction to the worker's efforts.

In some situations, it's helpful to use the phone or to communicate by letter so that contact is maintained. In such cases, the worker mentions the issues being discussed with the child, while reinforcing the importance of family participation in the resolution of these problems. She might suggest to James's parents, for instance, that they really need to hear his view of how he's picked on, as compared to his sister, and how only they can straighten out his mistaken ideas about their opinions. It also is useful to reschedule missed appointments for the next day, or as soon as possible, rather than waiting for the usual time to roll around.

When foster care workers reach out to the child's biological family, they face a particularly complex dilemma stemming from the requirement to monitor parental behavior. That's part of their job description, and cannot be waived by the leadership of the agency because it originates at higher levels of power—such as protective services and the courts. Workers feel they must demand explanations for acts of noncompliance, such as missing scheduled visits, because, as we have often been told, "The judge will want to know." Under such circumstances, the partnership between agency and family may fall victim to a power struggle, with little energy or disposition to collaborate on behalf of the child.

When the agency is expected to monitor parent behavior, the protection of the partnership may require both an acknowledgment of the staff role as agents of control and some way of distinguishing between that role and the partnership function. In some agencies it has been possible to organize the staff in teams of two people; one works on compliance with the official mandates while the other is free to focus on enhancing the relationship between agency and family. Because many agencies are constrained in their staffing possibilities, one worker may have to wear both hats. In a particular agency, the worker took to actually wearing hats of different colors, switching them in the middle of the meetings. Although we've said little about the use of humor, metaphor, or playfulness in these chapters, they often carry the day, reducing tension for both staff and family and providing images that help form a bond between them.


## Visiting the Family at Home

Outreach usually involves bringing a family into the agency, but it's sometimes useful to maintain contact through a visit. Home visits require sensitivity to the wishes and reactions of the family. It's important for the family to understand that the staff really wants to know the family better, meet other family members, and understand the nature and environment of daily life. Families are often empowered by meeting in their own setting, but are also sensitive to intrusion and to criticism of their life-style. It hardly needs mentioning that the worker must enter with respect, and that the purpose of the visit should be contact and communication.

The kind of interchange that takes place depends on the relationship already established. A skilled worker may deal with conflict as it arises, or choose to bypass a discussion in favor of handling the matter at another time. It's almost always preferable to work on family tensions when the primary client is also at home, but there may be times when that's not essential. If a child is caught in the middle of repetitive marital conflicts, for instance, the worker may want to handle that issue during a home visit when the child is absent. Again, that's an informed call by the worker making the visit, and the decision depends both on the situation and the worker's skill.

In residential centers, the question of home visits for the client is an important matter. Visits are essential: They keep the family connected and provide realistic current material for ongoing work, whether the problem concerns tension between parents and child or the relapse of an adult into substance abuse. Visits also provide a "dry run" for the later reunion of the family. Agency policy, however, is not always benign. Sometimes it's determined by a reward-and-punishment philosophy rather than a concept that visits are part of the problem-solving process.

The curtailment of home visits should be rare, invoked only when a visit to the family home poses a safety risk. Granting or withholding a weekend pass should never be used as reward or punishment for behavior on the ward, and home visits for a foster child should not be contingent on parental compliance with other aspects of the treatment plan. There's little evidence that these controlling procedures modify behavior, but they do convey the message that complying with institutional rules is more important than maintaining family connections.

If incidents occur during home visits and are tense but not dangerous, the worker can place the incident within the context of the evolving relationship among client, agency, and family. Conflicts can be accepted as normal phenomena, to be expected among people who are trying to adjust to each other while living apart. In effect, every visit involves a series of transitions for client and family. The family must expand their patterns of behavior to include the client, then reorganize again when the visit is over. The client must adapt to family realities after adjusting to expectations on the ward, then readapt to the routines of the institution. That's not easy, and should be discussed as a normal but difficult phenomenon when the family meets with the worker.

## Moving On: Discharge and/or Reunification

Finally, there is the matter of "moving on." Discharge from the services of a particular agency creates a period of transition, with all the uncertainty and discomfort accompanying any change, even if the move is positive. Paradoxically, supports often dwindle and disappear exactly at this point of increased vulnerability. The case is removed from the worker's roster, which is immediately filled with new clients.

In order to reduce the number of situations where discharge doesn't work, an agency would do well to modify discharge procedures so that attention is intensified. Successful transitions depend on preparatory, carefully processed encounters involving the people and situations that the client will be facing, whether family members, a new foster home, a halfway house, or a different agency. People need to experience the next setting, knowing that this is where they will be living; and the people in that setting must prepare for the entry or reentry of the client. Adaptation is a process, evolving through the period before, during, and after the actual transition.

The organization of agency procedures should provide staff time for preparing the transition and for helping clients and families afterward. When Wanda returns to her mother's care, Laura and her boyfriend need the help of a familiar worker to tide them over the first adjustments. When Angela finds housing and her husband joins the family at home, workers at the shelter need to help with the move, or put them in contact with people who can be available. When Sandra leaves the rehab center to live with her boyfriend, it's important to focus some sessions on this transition, and on the changing relations with her family. And when James returns home, the family needs both preparatory visits and follow-up sessions in order to deal with their apprehension, and with the viability of patterns they have been developing for living together.

Such efforts must be a matter of agency policy. The extra sessions in preparation for change require approval. The continuing involvement of a worker in the lives of a family after official discharge requires an understanding that this is part of the worker's caseload for a period of time. The implementation of such a policy may be facilitated if the agency understands that this is probably the most economical way to service a family, reducing the likelihood that they will fail to adapt and will return through the revolving door. Some percentage of an agency's clientele moves on as a result of improvement, and because the staff believes they can make a go of their lives when they leave the agency. It's tragic to undermine that potential by an abrupt and unsupported transition during the last stage of the process.

## APPENDIX 4.1. SUGGESTED QUESTIONS FOR A FAMILY INTAKE*

### Identifying Information

Who is in the family?

(If not volunteered, ask about family members beyond the child and parents: grandparents, siblings, aunts, and uncles. Ask also about people who may be important although they are not kin, such as godparents. If possible, ask the informants to make a family map.)

### The Child's Problems

Why is the child here? What does the family think the reason is, and are there some family members who have different opinions?

When did the problems first appear? What else was happening in the child's life and in the family at that time?

Who else has been affected by the child's problems? How?

What solutions have been tried?

---

*The questions are adapted from a form developed by Ema Genijovich. They are intended as a supplement to questions required by the agency or necessary for official purposes.

What has been the involvement of child welfare, or of the medical, court, or school systems, in working with the child and family? Has that been helpful?

(If the child has not been described as having problems but has been placed in the care of the agency because of family difficulties, focus the questions on child characteristics, development, and relationships, as viewed by the family.)

## The Family: Strengths and Stresses

What are the family's strengths?

(Spend time on this area. If not volunteered, ask about support systems, coping mechanisms, qualities the family is proud of, such as family loyalty, resilience, mutual respect, protection and education of the children, and so forth.)

What are the stresses?

(Consider social and economic factors, such as unemployment, racial prejudice, homelessness, limited education, migration, and language difficulties, as well as personal and family factors, such as illness, drug or alcohol dependence, a death in the family, divorce, and marital tension.)

## Family Expectations and Role

What do members of the family want from the agency? What do they hope will be accomplished? What do they think is the most important concern to focus on first?

Since family members are an important part of the agency's work with the child, which family members should be attending all the meetings?

How might the agency contact family members who don't usually become involved but might be a valuable resource?

# PART TWO

# Interventions in Different Settings

We move now to specific areas of service delivery. In the following chapters, we will discuss foster care, the treatment of drug-dependent pregnant women, residential and psychiatric settings for children, and home-based services for families. The framework presented in the first section covers all of these areas. In each case, we will take a systems-oriented, family-centered approach to the description of the territory, applying skills and procedures already discussed to the particulars of the service.

In all of these chapters, the content is about expansion and collaboration. That may not be obvious because the individual chapters are seemingly quite different from each other. Every chapter includes case material, interviews, and examples, but the experiences on which they're based are distinct, and the chapters do not follow a general outline. In relation to foster care, we present a comprehensive model and a format for training. The chapter on addiction is essentially a case history, demonstrating the problems of bringing a new approach into an established system, as well as the possibilities for evolution and expansion. The chapters on residential centers and psychiatric wards for children are set in a broader framework. They indicate how the nature and organization of these services have been influenced by social and professional forces. The chapter on family-centered, home-based services deals with "trouble in Paradise." We look at both the promising aspects of this approach and the problems of effective implementation. Despite the variations in form from one area to another, the underlying concern with expansion and collaboration is consistent, creating an emphasis on the need to think more broadly, move beyond the individual client, and connect the fragmented parts of the relevant systems.

We are under no illusion that difficult problems have quick solutions. In preparing these chapters, we have concentrated on offering alternatives to customary practice, a kind of map for exploring pathways that are probably bumpier than the well-worn tracks but may prove more serviceable for approaching the destination. The models of intervention would require adaptation to fit specific settings, and the many short examples are guidelines rather than formulae, geared to holding open what is shutting down, and expanding the focus of the work.

In reading the chapters, it will be useful to keep two other points in mind.

First of all, children are at the center of this book. Every chapter is concerned with services that affect their well-being. With regard to foster care and residential or psychiatric centers for children, that focus is obvious, but it's also the case in other areas. The chapter on substance abuse describes a program for perinatal women and their infants, and the chapter on home-based interventions concerns a service targeted for families whose children are at risk for placement outside the home.

Although the young are central, we have not dealt directly with the serious problems of development and adjustment that appear among the children of this population. That's partly because such problems already receive considerable professional attention, but also because we believe that the problems of the children cannot fully be understood or alleviated in isolation. In order to help the children, it's necessary to work within the relevant context: the families of the children, and the systems that take responsibility for their care.

Finally, it seems likely that the discussions and examples in these chapters will seem closer to the working life of the reader than the material in the first section—more related to the daily tasks that face a foster care worker, a drug counselor, or a staff psychologist in a psychiatric hospital. Nonetheless, it's important to remember that the separation into specific areas may not represent reality from the perspective of the clients. In order to go deeper, we have had to fragment the field, dealing with one issue at a time. However, we know that the same multicrisis families appear and reappear in all these settings. Substance abuse, homelessness, and foster care may be related facts of life for the members of a particular family, even when the problems are defined separately and handled by different agencies.

Nobody can take on the world. Professional staff must work within the framework of their organization and the definition of their task. Nonetheless, workers who understand that family issues often cross boundaries are better able to understand the concerns and behavior of their clients, and may be more prepared to facilitate the contacts essential for the well-being of children and families in their charge.

CHAPTER FIVE

# Foster Care

AN ECOLOGICAL MODEL

M any people would be startled by the sheer number of children in foster care: close to half a million nationwide by the last years of the 1990s, and apparently climbing. Coontz (1992) reminds us that our image of the nuclear family, with Mom and Dad shepherding the children through adolescence and into their adult working lives, is more sentimental than historically accurate. In earlier times, the death of parents and economic hardships meant that many children grew up in single-parent households or were farmed out to work. Nonetheless, the current reality is disturbing. We now know more about the psychological trauma of separating children from all that is familiar, and have reason to be concerned that the mood and legislation of the late 1990s leans toward increasing placements, the earlier termination of parental rights, the facilitation of adoptions, and the growth of orphanages run for profit.

The current trend is influenced by a mix of factors, including financial considerations, efficiency, and the legitimate concerns of society for protecting children. Clearly, some reports of abuse and neglect are warranted. It's important to identify the serious cases and remove children from potential danger. But many situations are not best handled by taking children from their homes and, when such measures are deemed advisable, the process that follows may not serve either the optimal development of the children or the potential of their families to function differently. The challenge is

91

to develop a foster care system that's effective and compassionate, protecting the children while preserving family rights, and increasing the family's ability to care safely for their children.

The stated aims of foster care have usually reflected this philosophy, noting that the goal is to alleviate stress in an overburdened family, to care for the children during an interim period, and to facilitate family reunification as soon as it is safe and feasible (see the report of the Foster Care Committee of the Mayor's Commission for the Foster Care of Children, 1993). In practice, however, the process of evaluation, placement, and continuing service has often defeated the basic aims, suggesting a necessary change in framework and procedures. Our work has focused on bringing foster care practice closer to the stated aims.

The approach to foster care as described in this chapter, was developed during the early 1980s (S. Minuchin, 1984). Based on general concepts about families and systems, the model was adapted to the specific realities of the foster care situation, and subsequently applied to staff training in foster care agencies.*

In general, the approach is aimed at reducing trauma, building family strength, and increasing the possibility of successful reunification. In order to achieve these goals, the model emphasizes connections among parts of the system, empowerment of the child's family, and the expansion of roles for both professional staff and members of the foster and biological families. The model is unique, but the aims are shared by other family-oriented organizations. The Annie E. Casey Foundation, for example, supported a broad Family to Family Initiative in the 1990s (Sharkey, 1997), and the National Resource Center for Family Centered Practice has distributed material describing foster care efforts with similar goals (see, e.g., The Prevention Report, 1992).

In this chapter, we will consider how the conceptual framework described in previous chapters applies specifically to the foster care system, and we will illustrate the process of training and consultation in foster care agencies. We will begin by describing the organization of foster care in a large metropolitan area; the involve-

---

*Developed by Salvador Minuchin, the model was supported in the initial stages through grants from the Edna McConnell Clark Foundation and the State of New York, and was implemented by the staff of Family Studies, Inc.

ment of municipal departments, courts, and foster care agencies; and the process that goes from the first complaints through place-ment and subsequent procedures. It is the context within which we worked when we first implemented the model, and it illustrates the combination of supportive and corrosive features dictating which aspects of the system we tried to change.

## THE CONTEXT: LARGER SYSTEMS AND THE PROCESS OF PLACEMENT

The process leading to foster placement usually begins with a phone call to protective services reporting a suspicion of child abuse or neglect. An investigator is sent to the home, and may decide that there is no basis for the allegation, or that the situation can be handled by direct services to the family. In other cases, the worker decides that the children must be protected by removing them from the home. Sometimes the decision to take the child for placement is obviously correct. In other cases the decision is questionable, reflecting limited information, the evaluation of a poverty-stricken household as a negative environment for children, or the worker's fear of criticism if the children remain and come to harm. When tragic cases come to public attention, there's a new urgency to the unofficial mandate "When in doubt, remove the children."

After removal, the children are usually sent to a foster care agency that selects foster families from their accredited pool and monitors subsequent care of the children. Court hearings and legal procedures, with separate lawyers and caseworkers for children and family members, set the terms of reunification. The plan may call for drug treatment, parenting classes, acceptable housing, and/or personal counseling. Subsequent action always requires a judicial review in which the court will consider progress as reported by child protective services and by relevant agencies.

During the period of placement, visiting arrangements vary but certain procedures are typical—especially if geographical difficulties exist in bringing people together or if the agency is primarily concerned with protecting the foster families. In many cases, the biological families do not know the address or phone number of the families caring for their children, and visiting is scheduled once every two weeks on agency premises. When home visits are mandated, the child is accompanied by an agency worker. Contact between biological and foster families is minimal or nonexistent.

The intention is protective, but the narrow individual focus, limited understanding of family connections, judgmental attitudes, and bureaucratic fragmentation of services that were discussed earlier create obstacles to an optimal approach. Under these conditions, the situation often drifts. The child's relatives begin to miss visits, and the child and foster family bond while child and biological parents become increasingly detached. The process is not supportive of families, and family reunification, if it occurs, is often unsuccessful. In describing a different approach, we're concerned with both the guiding ideas and practical procedures in this system.

## THE ECOLOGICAL MODEL: SIX BASIC IDEAS

Foster care has some unique features. Unlike most social services, foster placement involves *two* families: the biological family and the foster family. There are also two sets of agency "employees": the professional staff and the foster families. When we enter an agency, we look at the situation from an *ecological* perspective, meaning that we take into account the complexity of this structure and include many elements in how we think, set goals, and plan the training.

The ecological model has six basic ideas, which we elaborate upon in the following sections.

### Foster Placement Creates a New, Triangular System

As soon as a child is separated from home and placed in a foster family, a new three-part system comes into being that consists of the biological family, foster family, and foster care agency. That reality is not often acknowledged within the foster care system. Indeed, the usual procedures tend to create a sharp demarcation between the two families, and the fragmentation of services often means that professional workers miss the connections.

If we observe people within their context and consider the larger picture, we're better able to understand how the two families and agency are inevitably connected through their shared involvement with the child. Within that network, there are important subsystems: the unit of foster and biological families, the team of social worker and foster family, and the child within the context of each family—a participant in the patterns of both. From the perspective of this model, the existence of a superordinate triangle, and of subsystems within it, is a basic fact.

## The Triangular System Should Be Collaborative Rather Than Adversarial, and Should Include Members of Both Extended Families

If the first basic idea is a description of reality, this second one is a statement of goals—perhaps the core of the approach. To the extent that we can help policymakers and professional workers think in these terms and organize procedures accordingly, we can consider our intervention to be effective, and the system well on its way to improving the experience and probable outcome (see P. Minuchin, 1995).

Collaboration implies that people are in contact with each other and that they function as a network on behalf of the child, sharing information and solving problems by mutual effort. It's clear from the description of the typical foster-care process that members of the triangular system are seldom in continuing contact, either as a triad or as a dyad of foster and biological families. Furthermore, professional work is often limited to the one adult in each family who seems primarily responsible for the child—usually the biological or foster mother. The workers are busy; if they don't have a broader framework in mind they seldom search for members of the extended biological family who might be a resource, even if they don't live with mother and child. In the same way, contact with the foster family is often limited to the foster mother, even if the child has moved into a home that includes a foster father and children of various ages, all of whom affect how the child is accepted into the family.

When members of the two families meet, most typically during visits between mother and child at the agency, the contact is usually brief and the tone wary or adversarial. Foster and biological families tend to view each other stereotypically, and their attitudes are often negative. When Roger and Alva Lincoln took Jed into their home as a foster child, they were told only that he had been neglected by his parents, and they wondered aloud how anybody "could do that to a child." Jed's mother and father were bewildered by the speed with which Jed and his sister were removed from the family, and they resented the people "who've got our kids." As with all stereotypes, these attitudes are not easily altered, especially if the families have no contact with each other.

The quality of contact between members of the biological and foster families is at the heart of the matter, and has much to do with the eventual outcome of the situation. Kelsey offers a clear example, since she has participated both in a destructive, disempowering relationship and in a relationship that is sustained and supportive.

Kelsey left home at 13 with a man in his 20s who was drug addicted. She left him after the birth of her second child. She is now 17 and her sons are both in foster care, but they have been placed in separate homes monitored by different agencies. Kelsey has tried to maintain contact with both children, but has had very different experiences with the two foster families.

Kelsey talks first about her contacts with the foster mother of her younger son, now 2 years old, during visits with the boy at the agency:

> "She brings him in when *she* wants to bring him. Like, if I have a visit from 12 to 4, she'll bring him in at 3:30. . . . She tells me, 'Don't pick him up. Don't kiss him. Don't take him outside.' So I say he's my son, and she says, 'Yeah, well he's in *my* care now, so he's *my* son.' And I'll be crying, but nobody does nothing about it. So I just gave up. When I get my son, I'll just take him and go!"

The downward spiral is obvious. The combination of Kelsey's complaints, the critical attitude of the foster mother, and the fact that Kelsey no longer visits with her son will probably lead the agency to consider her a surly, irresponsible mother who's disinterested in her child. Her assumption that she will one day receive her son back and can "just go" is naive, and her expectation that things will be all right when that time comes is doubly so. It's unlikely that she will function well as a parent, if she suddenly were to assume that role with an uprooted, bewildered young child who knows her less well than he knows the foster family.

Kelsey's experience with the foster family of her 3 year old is quite different. This family participated in the training program described in a later section. Kelsey and the foster mother have established a strong relationship. "Julie's cool," says Kelsey.

"When I first came here, I had a nasty attitude. I didn't want to talk to nobody . . . 'cause they had my son! I'd complain about everything: 'I don't like this; I don't like that. Why has he got a scratch on him?'—knowing he's gonna fall . . . knowing when I had him he'd fall. But I'd go on about anything, just to get mad. . . . And Julie, she'd come over to me and say, 'Kelsey, you know boys! Come on now, whyn't you stop that?' And she'd talk to me, and I'd still be . . . like 'grrrrr' . . . and she'd say, 'Well look, let's take Buddy and go get some lunch.' "

Starting with the same anger that she felt when each son was taken away, Kelsey responds to warmth, humor, and the matter-of-fact acceptance of her resentment. She moves on to profit from the small, effective ways the foster mother makes space for Kelsey's relationship with her son, encourages Kelsey's competence, and provides a model for handling the concrete tasks of socializing a young child.

Kelsey says:

"You know, sometimes Buddy'll ask Julie something and she'll say, 'Whyn't you go ask Mommy to take your jacket off . . . or ask Mommy to take you to the bathroom?' Things I didn't know, I wasn't embarrassed to ask her. . . . She potty trained him, and she'd be telling me things . . . so I asked her, 'How did you get Buddy to do that? And how do you get Buddy to go to bed at a certain time?', 'cause with me, if he don't want to go to bed, I won't make him go to bed, right? So, she was saying you have to let him know you're the mother and it's time to go to bed. And sometimes Buddy'll get mad at me, and he'll say, 'I hate you!', and I ask her how am I supposed to deal with that? I ask her things and she tells me how *she* does with him, so when he comes home I can do the same."

The difference in these two experiences is not a matter of foster parent personality, although that is certainly a factor. It's a function of the preparation of the foster family—in terms of understanding, compassion, and skills—and of the agency policies and professional supports that make this kind of contact possible. In training foster care personnel, it's essential to change negative attitudes and to facilitate the structures and skills that make collaboration possible.

## Empowerment of the Biological Family Is Crucial

A collaborative network depends on reasonable equality in the roles of its members. When a child is taken for placement, the biological family is at the low point of the triangle. Society has made a judgment and established a hierarchy of approval: The foster family is competent and the biological family inadequate. The legal decision concerning placement may be justified, but once the decision is made, the process of disqualifying the family must be reversed if they are ever to be reunited. A family is unlikely to manage the period of placement successfully unless the adults can regain the sense that they have rights and responsibilities in relation to their children, and that they have some role in relation to their lives and their fate.

In itself, the removal of a child is depressing for parents who love their children, and confirms the feeling of impotence endemic for many. The process of removal and placement compounds their sense of defeat.

Nelda has four children: a 19-year-old son who has a steady job and lives on his own, and three children who live with her. Tommy is 14 and attends school; Rafie is 4 and mildly mentally handicapped; and Damon is a sickly infant and failing to thrive. When Nelda takes the baby to the hospital, the nurse is alarmed and alerts protective services. A worker sent to inspect the home reports garbage bags standing in the kitchen, little food in the refrigerator, and a general atmosphere of poverty and disarray. She returns the next day with a policeman and they remove the three children, leaving a distraught and bewildered mother with an explanation that it's for the good of the baby and that she will be notified of a court hearing.

The children are placed according to their needs and available venues: the infant in a city hospital, the 4-year-old with a suburban family accredited for the special care of mentally handicapped children, and the 14-year-old in a distant institution for adolescents separated from home. The geography of these placements is daunting. How can the mother keep contact with all the children?

At the hearing the case is discussed, but there's no provision for Nelda to speak for herself. She wants to explain that the garbage bags were waiting for her 19-year-old son, who was coming later to carry them down; that she was going shopping for food that afternoon; that her sister, who lives nearby, is helpful, and sometimes even takes the children while she cleans her house. She wants to explain how she has organized her life and how she copes, and the fact that nobody in power will listen leaves her angry and depressed.

The plan for reunification requires that Nelda attend parenting classes, go for personal counseling, and visit the children regularly. If these are the conditions, she's more than willing and follows the plan. However, when interviewed by a person she trusts, Nelda admits feeling confused and hopeless. The traveling to visit the children is exhausting and the parenting classes seem irrelevant. Most of all, she's bewildered by the counseling. She doesn't understand what's wrong, what she's expected to do, or how she or anybody will know when it's successful. Nobody has explained the reason or the goal. People who trudge through a prescription in this way are disempowered, at the least, and it's unlikely that Nelda will be a more competent and confident person when and if the system returns her children.

The process could be different. The fact that Nelda has raised her two older boys successfully should be part of the equation. It was probably unnecessary to remove the 14-year-old, who was attending school, not delinquent, and not on drugs. The placement of the two younger children, if deemed necessary, could have been handled in a way that made the mother a partner, preparing her to care more effectively for a mentally handicapped child. Nelda needed a more detailed explanation concerning the tasks she was expected to fulfill while the children were in placement, and a more personalized program of activities. She would have profited from continuing contact with the hospital staff and the specialized foster mother, particularly in relation to the care and education of her children. It would have been more useful and seemed more meaningful than generalized parenting classes. Nelda needed to come through the experience with a feeling of more power, and with specific tools for parenting Rafie and Damon, her two younger children.

To be helpful to parents, the foster care system must rethink and reorganize the process of placement and the manner in which it sets the reunification requirements. Once a child is placed, however, empowerment is in the hands of the agency via its procedures for intake and visitation, and through the interaction of social workers and foster parents with the child's family.

As an example of small movements that involve the biological parents and bring their strengths to the foreground, consider the following situation: Two small boys have been placed with a foster family and the parents have not seen them since their placement 3 months earlier. A trainer has been working with the staff, and the foster care worker arranges for the parents to come to the agency and for the foster parents to bring the two boys. Present at the meeting are the social worker, the trainer, the children, and both sets of parents.

When they enter, the foster mother puts the 1-year-old on her lap, unzips his snowsuit, and reaches for a diaper. The social worker suggests that the child's mother can do that. The foster mother is willing—it just never occurred to her—and she hands the child over. The social worker, alert to the importance of communication between these two families, suggests that the foster parents describe their family to the other couple so that they can picture the new setting for their children. The foster parents describe their four children, and the fact that the 6-year-old, their youngest, is a special pal for the two boys. The conversation is friendly, reassuring, and reduces tension. At the same time, it becomes obvious that the foster family has been calling the older boy "Kenny," the name on his official records—although he has been called "Kiko" by his family since birth—and that he has been slow to respond. Furthermore, "We didn't know he could walk till last week, when he got up and ran across the room after the dog!" Even though they did not say so, this family had clearly been treating the 2-year-old as a retarded child, slow to walk, talk, and recognize his name.

The trainer remarked that the child must have been very frightened by the changes in his life, and began to talk with the mother about Kiko's development: When did he sit up? What words can he say? The mother became the recognized expert, and the trainer commented to the foster couple that the parents really know a lot about the children's early life that the foster parents don't know—a point to which all agreed. The families were now on the verge of forming a cooperative system in which all had something to share.

In that situation, the trainer and the social worker were the motors of change, encouraging interaction between the families and bringing them to a new point of equilibrium. When foster families are trained, however, they become the primary agents of empowerment, and are frequently creative and effective.

We asked a group of trained foster parents how they manage to involve biological parents when they have an infant in their care. Since the foster parents are the ones who feed, bathe, and soothe the baby, providing the kind of care that binds adults and children to each other, how do they help the mother to feel connected to the baby when they visit together?

Martha says:

"Right away I give the mother the baby, a bottle, some food, a Pamper. Now it's her baby. I don't tell her that, but . . . I may stay with her a little while and chat, but I move away. I always move away."

Gina nods, and says:

"I do the same thing. Maybe I go to the bathroom . . . and I'll stand outside the door about 10 or 15 minutes, because to me the mother . . . this is strange to her now, when she gets the baby in her hands so I just let her know . . . 'Oh, the baby's hair needs to be combed. Could you comb her hair? I'll be right back. And could you change the Pamper for the baby? I got to go to the bathroom.' Not saying I want her to be able to . . . but she's got to know she's the mother. Not only that, but the baby has to know that's *somebody* in her life."

Empowering biological families is humane; most parents love their children, even if they provide erratic care or poor control, and they generally want to remain a family and raise their children successfully. It's also practical because the restoration of families is a more viable pathway for the system than the constant search for foster homes and the destructive movement of children from one placement to another. Finally, it's psychologically sound. Only a family that feels respected and has some control over their own lives can become a more functional environment for growing children.

## Foster Care Is Marked by Major Transitions, and These Transitional Periods Require Special Attention

Transitions are inevitable in the life of any individual, as well as the life cycle of a family. As suggested in earlier sections, transitions may be normal and expected, like the birth of a baby, or unexpected and traumatic, like the sudden unemployment of a family bread-winner. Whatever their nature, transitions always require a reor-ganization of familiar patterns so that people can function in the new circumstances.

The foster care situation is marked by profound transitions at the point of placement and reunification. Often there are other moves along the way. These transitions are periods of upheaval and vulnerability. How they are handled affects the way in which people adapt and shapes the course of future events.

In working with a foster care agency, we do considerable work around the nature of intake—the first major transition for all participants. Our focus is on the establishment of the cooperative triangle: on involving all relevant parties, developing procedures to support their relationship, and planning together for the future. We also ask the staff to keep the larger picture in mind. Transitions affect not only the child, whose behavior may reflect the trauma of separation and the strangeness of the new situation, but the foster and biological families as well. When a foster child enters a new home, the foster family must expand and reorganize. Time and energy are distributed differently by the adults, and the new 5-year-old disrupts the usual relations between the 4-year-old son of the family and the 7-year-old foster child who already lives there, as well as everybody's place in the family routines.

For the biological family, the change is also dramatic. They must adapt to life without the children, and must fulfill mandates concerning visiting, life-style, parenting classes, and housing that are prerequisites for regaining their children. Hostility or with-drawal are not surprising as first reactions, and, as in the case of the children, may reflect the trauma of the separation rather than a confirmed attitude. Kelsey's comments describe her "attitude" when the children were taken and the process through which it changed for the better.

Visits during placement are also small transitions, and the burden falls mostly on the child. In our training, we describe this with a concrete image (see Figure 5.1), trying to make vivid the child's movement from one family to the other and back again.

In the diagram, the child carries a "knapsack." The knapsack contains the expectations and patterns of the biological family, which the child carries into the foster family, as well as the expectations and patterns of the foster family, which are carried along on visits to the biological family. The child must fit into the patterns of each family, shifting with every move and integrating the mixture, somehow, into an internal map of the family world.

If the family is eventually reunified, the transition is welcome but not simple. It involves some loss for the foster family and a challenge for the biological family, which must create a viable situation although they previously have been judged inadequate. That is anxiety producing and difficult. During the period of placement, these parents and children have not experienced the kind of daily contact through which most of us work out relationships, clarify authority, set family rules, and establish credibility with each other.

A poignant 1995 movie comes to mind. In *Losing Isaiah*, a young black child is moved from the white family he has always

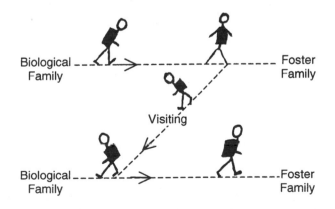

**FIGURE 5.1.** Visiting during foster care placement.

lived with to his biological mother, who is now anxious to raise her son, although they have had no previous contact with each other. There are no clear rights or wrongs in this situation, and the ethnic issues and personal uncertainties are profound. The depression of the child is so deep and disturbing that the two mothers finally come together, beginning to construct a world for Isaiah in which his losses can be tempered and his emotional connections expanded.

We have seen real situations in which, even though ethnicity was not a factor, the transitional difficulties were just as profound. Margo, for example, was now almost 4 and had been in placement for 3 years, since her adolescent mother, Jill, sought help from protective services. Through that period Margo had visited Jill and her extended family in the grandmother's home. Reunification was scheduled for the near future, and the foster care staff arranged to bring the foster and biological families together.

There were visits back and forth, with good will on both sides, but it became clear that reunification would be difficult. The foster family included a boy a little older than Margo, and the two had grown up together as playmates. Separation would be painful. In addition, Jill was pregnant and engaged to be married. Jill and Kevin would be a family-in-formation with an infant to take care of; the absorption of Margo would complicate their task. The staff knew the couple would need help.

Versions of this story are everywhere in the foster care system, varying in detail but not in complexity or the mixture of pleasure and pain. Of importance is the recognition that transitions are critical periods requiring the continuing collaboration of the triangular system. A successful outcome depends on careful planning, an understanding that adaptations take time, and a commitment by staff to continue their work when the children go home until the situation has stabilized.

## A Consideration of Developmental Issues Must Be Integrated into Foster Care Services

The child's stage of development shapes every aspect of the foster care experience: the impact of separation and the adaptation to a new home, as well as the possibility of maintaining a sense of the original family while accepting new people. The reality is very different for infants, toddlers, school-age children, and adolescents—not necessarily easier or harder, at one stage or another, but processed by different levels of cognitive understanding and emotional focus.

Foster care placements are generally arranged with some concern for the fit between the child's age and the foster family. Certain foster families are known to be skillful with very young children; others are considered more appropriate for school-age children or adolescents. Most agencies also prepare the foster families with educational material about the developmental needs of children at different ages.

These are useful first steps, but no matter how conscientiously they're followed, they remain focused on the foster family and the child. Developmental concerns are not considered relevant for the newly formed triad. In our view, issues of growth and development are a shared responsibility of the two families. They should be working together to discuss changes, solve new problems, and create some consistency in the child's two worlds. Collaboration increases the likelihood that parents will be able to handle a child who has grown and changed and is returning home after a period of separation.

The developmental flow brings different tasks to the foreground at different stages. For infants, the basic issue is attachment: the child's sense of security invested in particular people, and the adult sense of emotional investment in this child. When mothers and infants are separated very early, basic attachment is jeopardized. Elena, for instance, has been in and out of hospitals for the past year, and her baby, who was placed at 2 months, has bonded to the foster mother. When Elena picks him up to cuddle during visits, he cries, struggles, and reaches for his foster mother. Both women must work on keeping the biological mother and infant connected, if they are ever to live together, and the social worker must help Elena to deal with her sense of discouragement during the process.

For young children beyond infancy, the developmental challenge is to set realistic limits and work out the balance between autonomy and control. Kelsey had little experience or skill in getting Buddy to go to bed, in potty training, or in knowing when to accept the assertiveness of a 3-year-old and when to draw the line. Her relationship with the foster mother was a frame for learning how to handle issues involved in raising a young child.

With middle-years children, developmental issues arise both in the family and in relation to school. Children of 8 and 9 have legitimate privileges and responsibilities in a household. Families handle these differently, and a foster child carries both models in his or her "knapsack." It's important for the two families to talk about their expectations and differences. Mary's mother, for instance, was religious and wanted her 10-year-old daughter to go to church and Sunday School. The foster family, also religious, found her request acceptable, but the Pentecostal church of one family wasn't comfortable for the other, and both families needed to resolve that dilemma.

Mary had also changed schools, and her experience and progress in the new school setting was an important part of her life. Parents whose children have been removed from home seldom know how to make contact with schools that their children attend. They don't make an issue of being kept abreast, and it doesn't occur either to the agency or the school that parents have the right to be informed and involved. Open communication about Mary's school progress is a task for the triangular network, especially through the contact between families.

The developmental issues of adolescents are familiar and daunting: the mix of independence and responsibility in the family as well as matters of drugs, sex, gangs, school, and violence in the community. Adolescents are often taken from their family because the adults can't control them. Helping a family qualify for reunification is more than a matter of drug programs, individual counseling, or skill training for parents and adolescent. They must develop a viable way of living together. It's neither correct nor productive for the foster family to work on developmental issues without involving the biological family, and it's unrealistic to expect the family to reunite successfully if they have been out of contact.

## Kinship Foster Care Is a Special Case of Foster Placement That Requires Particular Kinds of Services

Most aspects of the ecological model apply to all foster care situations, including collaboration, empowerment, a focus on transitions, a concern for developmental tasks, and the necessary involvement of all members in the extended system. However, kinship foster care is different in one crucial way: When children are placed with relatives, the placement does not create a new system. Rather, it changes the reality of family members who already know each other and have established patterns of relating, carrying authority, and resolving conflict.

Kinship care is generally the preferred form of placement, with clear psychological advantages for the child. It reduces the trauma of separation and doesn't require adaptation to a completely new world of people and places. Placing a child with familiar kin also increases the possibility that the "foster family" will continue to figure in the child's life, and will function as a resource for parents when the child returns home.

But the situation is not always simple. The extended family may be part of the problem as well as part of the solution. Alva's grandmother, for instance, has long disapproved of her daughter's companions and way of life, and when she has the child in care she makes it difficult for mother and child to visit with each other. She argues over the visiting schedule, criticizes her daughter's way of handling Alva, and uses the opportunity to point out again that her daughter's friends are ruining her life. Tensions are relatively common in such situations, even when family members are concerned for each other and want the best for the children. If placement and reunification are to succeed, role confusions, destructive patterns, and boundary issues must be identified and resolved. The creation of a collaborative system is still the primary goal, but the nature of professional intervention may be closer to conventional family therapy than is typical with foster care cases.

The situation with Jill and Margo that was referred to earlier offers an example of role and boundary confusion at the point of reunification. When Margo visited with her family, it was always at her grandmother's house, where Jill would meet her and spend the afternoon. As the foster care worker discussed family reunification, it became clear that Jill and her mother had different expectations. Jill saw them all as "one big family." She expected Margo to return to her grandmother's house, where she and Kevin could visit her often. Jill commented that she had left her mother's home long ago but "not in my heart." The grandmother was startled: "I thought when you left home, you left home!" Although she loved the little girl, she had three other children and serious economic problems. She had not expected to be the permanent caretaker for Margo, functioning as a kinship foster parent, albeit unofficially.

The brief and successful course of therapy centered first on Jill and her mother, and was focused on boundaries and roles. Jill's view that she would be like a big sister for Margo was immature, and placed too heavy a burden on her mother. As that became clear, Kevin joined the sessions, and he and Jill began to plan for their family of four. Together with the social worker, they explored the question of when it would be best to bring Margo home in relation to the birth of their baby, how she might react, and how they might handle this complicated transition. The grandmother was now an interested but peripheral observer, and after some sessions the young couple continued without her. Despite the foster care context, family therapists would recognize this as a familiar situation in which parents and young adult children must clarify functions and boundaries, moving in the process toward a new stage of family equilibrium.

## TRAINING IN FOSTER CARE SETTINGS

How to get from here to there? Concepts and goals provide underpinning for the work, but the training process is a separate matter. It requires a theory about creating change, a sequential plan, and some awareness of the task and structure specific to the agency. Foster care agencies, like other service settings, have line workers and administrators; therefore training must affect both skills for working with clients and procedural policies. The unique feature in these agencies is that the structure also includes foster families who carry out the basic task and must be trained to work cooperatively with the child's family, as well as with the professional staff.

We present here a plan for training and consultation in foster care settings. The plan is based on the ecological model and reflects our experience working with foster care agencies for more than a decade. As a result of that experience, we have also published a *Training Manual for Foster Parents*, intended for use by centers interested in the ecological approach (P. Minuchin et al., 1990). Since its publication in 1990, the *Manual* has been used by agencies and government departments in every U.S. state, suggesting a national need for training of this nature (see Appendix 5.1 for Table of Contents).

Table 5.1 presents an outline of the training plan and sequence. It will be seen that there are five phases, that foster care staff and foster parents are trained both separately and together, and that there are intermittent contacts with administrators. In the discussion that follows, we will describe the sequence of procedures, and some details of our experience during the initial application of this training at three agencies.

TABLE 5.1. Training Plan and Sequence

| | Foster care workers | Foster parents | Administrators |
|---|---|---|---|
| **Phase I** | | | |
| Contact with administrators; arrangements for training | | | Discussions, planning, contract |
| **Phase II** | | | |
| Staff training; four to six meetings | Framework and concepts: activities, tapes, role play, demonstration | | |
| **Phase III** | | | |
| Continue staff training; Begin foster parent training, three to four meetings | Work with agency cases; mapping, planning, interviews, skill building | Framework and concepts: *Training Manual for Foster Parents* | Policy discussions regarding intake, visitation, case coordination, arising from case issues |
| **Phase IV** | | | |
| Training of staff and foster parent teams; skill building | Combined training; work together on issues of intake, visitation, discharge, team collaboration, coordination of roles; meet as teams with agency families | | |
| **Phase V** | | | |
| Training becomes in-house staff development | Foster care staff become leaders; train new staff and foster parents | Foster parents participate in training new foster parents | |

## Contact with Administrators

We entered the agencies as outside trainers, and our first meetings were with agency directors and executive staff. They needed more detail about the project, and we needed to know what they expected the training to accomplish, and how the training would fit into the way the agency functioned. During these first contacts, we also set up the conditions of training: who would participate, where we would meet, what equipment we would need. The discussions were useful, arranging the specifics and establishing a liaison with the administrative staff.

By agreement with the administrators, we began with a general presentation to the staff-at-large, describing our point of view, presenting the training plan, and responding to questions. As the agencies were sizable and the intensive training would be confined to a core group of participants, it was important for the rest of the staff to know what would be going on, and what we hoped would later spread throughout the agency.

During the first meeting with administrators, we specified that we would work with a pilot group of social workers and foster parents, but the process of selection was left with the agencies. They went about it in different ways: One agency sought volunteers among the foster care social workers, while another chose particular people and checked afterward to see if they were willing. In one setting, the selected social workers chose the foster parents who would join them in the training; in another, the foster parents were chosen independently. One agency director was relatively active in the selection process; in the others the process was left to supervisors and training staff.

Phase I will inevitably look different in each situation. An in-house trainer doesn't need initial contacts to meet the administrators and learn about the agency. A staff responsible for statewide training doesn't work directly with administrators. Trainers will get things started through procedures that make sense in their own setting. However, it's important to understand that some issues will require a review of policy and procedures as the training progresses. We returned at intervals to meet with administrators in order to discuss matters such as intake, visitation, and case coordination. Whatever the setting, access to the administrators who shape the procedures is crucial. The training concentrates on case workers and foster parents, but the administrators make policy and are responsible for removing impediments to the new ways of working.

## The Beginning of Staff Training

Intensive training begins with the foster care staff. In the long run, the training is focused on the development of a team approach in which social worker and foster parent share a viewpoint and complement each other, but their roles are not the same. Foster care workers carry the professional responsibility, and in some respects the approach we present is different from the way they have been working. It's important for them to discuss the material and implement the skills in their own group before they're joined by foster parents.

During Phase I we lay the groundwork for changes in attitude and framework. We want the staff to broaden their ideas about who is involved in a foster care situation, to understand that behavior is a function of interaction, and that both biological and foster families establish patterns that are repeated and observable. As most foster care workers are particularly interested in the children, who indeed are the very center of the situation, we also focus on the experience of the child as a member of two families, and as a person who must make the transition from one family to another.

The tools for establishing this groundwork depend on the group in training, as well as the preferences and materials available to the trainer. We used exercises, videotapes, didactic information, handouts, discussion, role play, and demonstration. Many of the exercises and role-play scenarios have been incorporated into the *Training Manual for Foster Parents*, and they are useful not only for the training of foster parents but for any professional group interested in broadening and freshening their own approach.

For instance, we have used an activity described in the first session of the *Manual*, to work with staff on the realities of family life. We ask each participant to map out his or her family, writing down ages and using gender symbols to create a simple picture of family membership and structure. Then, within small groups, individuals are asked to trade maps and to "guess at" one developmental task for another person's family at their current stage of life (e.g., "You've two kids in school; you probably have to keep an eye on homework and how they're doing"; or, "I see you've got your father living with you and he's not so young; maybe you have to take care of him"). We then go on to an exercise in which the family takes in a 5-year-old foster boy and each participant discusses the probable reaction of his or her family: What would the family expect of the child? What rules would he have to follow? How would different members of the family react if he were bossy or aggressive? Who would help him if he were scared?

We might follow that exercise with a role play (from Session 3 of the *Manual*) in which two siblings—10-year-old Tony and 8-year-old Willis—have been newly placed together in a foster family. In the role-play scenario, the foster mother has been talking to Willis, who doesn't look at her or answer, and Gloria, the 11-year-old daughter of the family, begins to make fun of him. The role play begins when Tony speaks up, in whatever fashion the player chooses, and goes on from there. The activity is meant to stimulate discussion about the expectations of a foster family, the roles of the boys in the family they came from, and the relationships of siblings. A reference to the "knapsack" that children carry from one family to another is a useful way to organize the discussion.

In our training we have relied a good deal on videotapes for illustration and discussion. Not all trainers have easy access to videotapes of family meetings, but they are an excellent teaching tool and well worth the trouble to find or create. If a professional staff is expecting to learn how to "do family therapy," they may be especially interested in such tapes, but the therapy is not the point, particularly at introductory stages. The important feature is the interaction of family members. Videotapes offer the possibility of demonstrating how behavior is circular and complementary, and how patterns repeat themselves. The trainer can reinforce a focus on the family by the liberal use of the pause, stop, rewind, and fast forward buttons on the VCR machine, moving back and forth to help a group pick up what they have missed. In this way, the group can rewind to see what's happening (e.g., the daughter changes the subject every time the mother scolds the son and he begins to look explosive), and can then search for the same pattern elsewhere during the session.

Because staff workers often focus automatically on pathology, we have used videotapes to point out indicators of strength and resourcefulness in a family. And because workers are accustomed to listening for content, we have found videotapes useful for drawing attention to nonverbal patterns that illustrate so much about family functioning: who leads the discussion, who comforts other people, who deflects argument, how messages are conveyed through body language, and so forth. Wherever possible, we have taught with videotapes that reflect the same population as the clientele of the agency and contain problems typical of families with children in foster care: families with single parents, problems of teenage pregnancy, drug dependency, physical or sexual abuse, and/or family members afflicted with AIDS.

After the review and exploration of basic ideas, we move on to skills needed for working with families. We emphasize connecting and empowering, and, more specifically, joining, searching for strength, and complementarity. Joining comes relatively easily for trained social workers. The search for strength and complementarity, both forms of family empowerment, are more difficult. Against the background of problems that multicrisis families bring, and accustomed to the professional tradition of emphasizing the pathology that must be dealt with, staff sometimes has trouble focusing on strengths and resources. For people who are helpers by profession and nature, it can also be difficult to step back and leave the control and action to others. However, complementarity means that whenever professionals are active the clients will be more passive, and, conversely, that when staff leaves more room the clients will take a more active role. Both the highlighting of family strength and the effort to withhold competence are important skills for the foster care staff.

A meeting that was described earlier, involving "Kiko," his baby brother, and their foster and biological parents, offers a good example of joining and empowering. The foster care worker suggested that the biological mother take over the care of the baby, and that the foster parents describe their home and family to the boys' parents. The trainer suggested that the mother share the details of her children's early development with the foster parents. The session had many levels that were useful not only for the families but for staff training as well.

What the staff saw was a form of intervention that withheld professional competence, rebalanced the usual pattern of complementarity, and empowered people who were used to being disqualified. Through simple suggestions and behavior, the trainer made space for the social worker, the social worker made space for the foster parents, and the foster parents made space for the biological parents. Additionally, the staff saw that the tension and wariness at the beginning of the session dissipated over time as a result of increasing familiarity and the mutual sharing of information. Finally, they had the opportunity to discuss flaws in the intake process. If the family had been brought in for such a meeting at the start, it would have been clear that Kiko could walk and talk and knew his name, and that his regressive behavior was a reaction to separation and placement.

A trainer doesn't usually determine which families can be utilized for teaching purposes. However, it's important to look for some families who are going through intake and others who are at the point of discharge. That allows the staff to discuss procedures that will be most effective for empowering the family at any particular stage.

## The Beginning of Foster Parent Training

Training of the foster parents begins separately. For one thing, foster parents have their own perspective and should be able to explore the realities of their particular task before they meet with a different group. For another, these first meetings should change the ethos of their position in the structure.

In most agencies, foster parents are actively solicited and their contribution is openly, and even gratefully, acknowledged. Without these families, the children could not be placed in homes, and that fact is understood throughout the system. Nonetheless, the definition of the job, and the process of selection, induction, instruction, and judgment often conveys a message of limited functions (child care) and tight control (obedience to agency rules and mandates). The child-protective motivations for monitoring and control are obvious, but the process of training often misses a valuable opportunity. Training should invigorate the foster parents, even while it conveys necessary information, and should empower them as important, contributing members of the service team.

Almost any agency has both newly recruited and experienced foster parents. Training for the novices must include information about agency procedures and the details of child care, but it's also important to shape their view of foster care at the start, emphasizing the importance of the biological family and the breadth and power of their own role. New foster parents may be particularly open-minded at this stage, but if they're very critical or disrespectful of biological families, it's best to discover this attitude at the beginning.

Experienced foster parents have often taken in and released a number of children over the years, and they know the routines very well. They either may be particularly wise about parenting a foster child or especially resistant to new perspectives—and they're apt to be a little of each. If an agency is to develop a coherent approach, experienced foster parents also must be considered candidates for further training. For this group, training is a matter of exploring attitudes, expanding roles, and honoring the fruits of accumulated experience. At the same time, the training experience should convey the sense that they are moving up the ladder in the hierarchy of the agency.

The *Training Manual for Foster Parents* is applicable to both new and experienced groups, with appropriate modifications. The *Manual* consists of a theoretical section presenting the concepts described in this chapter, followed by instructions for conducting eight training sessions. The central topic and training activities for each session are indicated in Appendix 5.1.

The first four sessions build a framework for understanding families, with particular emphasis on their diversity and strength, and on the experience of the child and the two families when a child is placed. The activities include the range described earlier: mapping, role play, small group work, and discussion of vignettes concerning families and the foster care experience. By the time they have finished these activities, participants generally have a broader understanding of their own family involvement and that of the child's family. They're more oriented toward the potential strength of the biological family and more appreciative of the traumatic features of separation and placement. Most foster parents have some basic understanding of developmental characteristics, since they usually have children of their own. However, a review of child development in the context of foster placement is a reminder that children of a particular age may behave differently than the family's own children; foster children often have had difficult experiences and also have been uprooted.

Once basic attitudes have been loosened and brainstorming has

been encouraged, foster parents often move toward an identification with the plight and perspective of the biological parents. They
frequently produce creative suggestions for establishing connections, and for providing the families with a larger role in caring for
the children and making important decisions.

We have found it fruitful to explore the topic of visitation
thoroughly (see Session 5 in the *Manual*). Visits between family and
child are the lifeline of foster care, and contact between the two
families is essential. An agency's visiting policy should be flexible and
open to negotiation on a case-by-case basis. Foster parents may be
both the most wary members of the triangle, in relation to visiting,
and the most openly creative. If novices, they may hold negative
stereotypes or have heard disturbing anecdotes about intrusive parents. If experienced foster parents, they may have grown comfortable
with agency routines that limit visiting and highlight the protection
of the foster family from the child's relatives. On the other hand, we
have often seen an accepting, matter-of-fact response from foster
parents once the topic is introduced, and alternatives to the routine
visits on agency premises have been suggested: a picnic in the park,
a get-together at McDonald's with children from both families,
shared birthday parties, telephone calls, photograph exchanges, and
written correspondence. For the foster mothers who were part of our
project, the idea of contact between families—and between the
foster child and the biological family—appeared to make sense. As
one foster parent remarked, "The kids handle easier if they know you
like their mother."

In some respects, foster parents are more streetwise than social
workers, and more accepting of the conditions of life in this
population. One exercise in the *Manual* (Session 5) describes a
situation in which a 7-year-old boy is placed in foster care while
his mother serves a 6-month jail term for drug-related charges. A
group of foster parents was asked to discuss whether and how the
child might be taken to visit during this period—an admittedly
complicated situation. Social workers often have particular difficulty with this idea, but the group of newly selected foster parents
reacted with a direct and vigorous discussion. Not all felt easy with
the situation, but this inner-city group of people were well ac-
quainted with the realities of their neighborhoods. They agreed that
the child could not be protected from knowing where his mother
was, that it was important for this depressed little boy to see and

talk with her, and that they would need to prepare him beforehand for the procedures and atmosphere at the prison.

While in their own group, we heard foster parents expressing clear conceptions of their role, as well as their conviction that they had particular information unavailable to the staff.

Myra says:

"What's going on is . . . the agency isn't always able to see what the biological mother is doing. It's *we*. . . . We're the ones who have to observe. . . . Most of the time, the foster mothers have a better understanding of the families and know the parents better than the case workers, so really it's up to us."

Cara looks at the situation from a different angle. She says:

"Some case workers look at the natural mother as a bad influence on the child, and they *feel* this. They're not stupid!"

Janine is less sure. She says:

"Well, if the parent's a drug addict or something like that. . . ."

But Cara feels strongly:

"Whether they're a drug addict, or whatever addict they are, they're still that kid's mother! They're just as human as me and you. No matter how bad the parent is, the child wants to go back to the mother or father. You find the worst parent, the child will still want to be returned to the natural mother."

Marilyn has one more observation to add to this discussion:

"Well, you got some good case workers and some who are not so good. You got some who will work to the bone to unite them with the kids, and you got some who say, 'Oh, she's nothing but a crackhead. . . . She's nothing but a drug user.' "

It may be useful for the workers to realize that foster parents have some unexpressed criticisms of the staff, when the two groups come together for training.

## The Team: Training Staff and Foster Parents Together

When staff and foster parents meet as a team, some attitudes and skills are already in place. Their task now is twofold: to form cooperative teams and to work together with biological families.

Teams are both powerful and complex. When two people work together they often complement each other's strengths, but there are also issues of status, turf, and role. If the status of team members is different from the start, collaboration is often difficult. Some skills that are important for working with biological families are equally useful in this situation: joining, listening to each other, empowerment, and the ability to take complementary roles. Staff members and foster parents need to discuss their understanding of territory, air their confusions, and explore the nature of their autonomy and interdependence.

This phase of the training is basically hands-on. Teams composed of social workers and foster parents will be meeting with biological families connected with the agency. In each case, the team's task is to create a collaborative network in which the child's family can function as a central and respected member of the triangle. As they work together, staff members and foster parents usually come to understand where they fall naturally in the division of labor, where they run into confusion, and what issues they must resolve.

There are many ways to solidify a shared perspective and prepare for meetings with agency families. The comments of Kelsey that were reported earlier were addressed to a combined group of social workers and foster parents in training. Kelsey had been invited to describe her experience as a parent and to offer suggestions about improving the procedures. For the staff and foster parents, this meeting provided a detailed exposure to the needs, frustrations, and sensibilities of the parent. Her description led to a discussion about the impact of foster parent behavior on the child's relatives, the issues that arise in parenting a young child, and the way in which a foster mother—as both model and facilitator of the parent's competence—can increase the possibilities for effective reunification of the family. The discussion also suggested a necessary role for the social worker: to monitor the relationship between the two families, and to enter the situation when the quality of their contact spirals downward.

In order to explore their roles and collaboration, it's important for the teams to meet with a variety of agency families presenting an array of different issues. In one case, the biological mother of three boys was currently estranged from the agency, a situation which presented social workers and foster parents with a complex problem to resolve.

Jana voluntarily brought her three boys into foster care at a point of crisis in her life. They were placed in two different families, and Jana came to the agency regularly for visits. At some point, she found the setting cramped and noisy and asked to take the boys outside. As a matter of policy, the request was refused. Jana was resentful, and, as the situation escalated, she broke contact with the agency and no longer came to visit her children.

As the foster care worker and the two foster mothers were part of a training project, they discussed the situation with the group and the trainer. It was decided that, since they were neighbors and her children were living in their homes, the two foster mothers, rather than agency staff, would be in charge of contacting Jana. Jana agreed to come in for a meeting. In their planning, the team decided that the foster parents would carry the session, but that the social worker would be present and available to help as needed. The goal was to establish contact, to break the stalemate between Jana and the agency, and to begin the formation of a collaborative network.

The meeting began with Jana sitting between Clara and Laura, the foster parents. Maude, the social worker, was present and sat slightly to the side. As everybody settled down, Jana sat with her arms folded across her chest, unsmiling, wary, silent.

Clara spoke first. She had the oldest boy, 12-year-old Bobby, and the youngest, 5-year-old Malcolm, in her care.

"Jana, I just want to tell you . . . you have two beautiful sons."

A gracious beginning. Jana smiles, nods, and relaxes a little.

Laura makes a joke about James being a handful. James is 10, and has been placed separately because he's a more difficult child. Jana comments that everybody petted the oldest and the youngest, but James was the middle one and he had a harder time.

Clara asks now, "Do you like the way I'm taking care of your boys?"

She takes it for granted that Jana has her own standards, and that she has the right to judge how somebody else is caring for her children. Jana says yes, and that she knows Clara is spoiling them. It's a light comment, and they both laugh. Clara continues then in a serious vein. She talks about Malcolm, who had difficulties when he first came to live with her. "He was very emotional. I really needed to give him lots of time . . . he's stronger now."

At this point, Jana becomes an active participant. She talks about the boys, and about the problem of preparing them for leaving her. She comments that she never hid anything from Bobby, who is responsible and very smart, and that although she explained the situation to the two older boys, she knew that Malcolm was too young to understand. As Jana continues talking, it's clear that she's an intelligent, observant parent who is concerned about her children and attuned to their personalities and individual differences.

Laura joins in to talk about the difficulties she's having with James, who gets into fights.

She says, "So, I'm having a little problem with him right now. With you, when he had tantrums, the way he does . . . I mean, how did you deal with it? What did you do?"

This is a respectful vote of confidence. Laura is asking for help in solving a problem of child care and management, acknowledging that Jana has experience in dealing with her son and probably has some useful ideas. It's a first step toward forming a cooperative adult system that can pool resources on behalf of the child. Jana responds in kind. She says that James has behaved the same way with her and that he doesn't like people to tell him what to do. She then describes how she manages him.

Fifteen minutes into their meeting, these three parents were discussing the children and the realities of the situation. Although the behavior of the foster parents was spontaneous, it was based on their understanding that it was important to be connected to the families of their foster children, and reflected the skills they had developed for conveying respect and interest. As a result, they tapped the strength and knowledge of the mother in a very short time and began the process of constructive communication.

The social worker was present but silent through most of the meeting, allowing the new relationship to unfold. If the foster parents had been less skillful or Jana less responsive, she would necessarily have been more active. Since that was not the case, her role was to facilitate by holding back. As events unfold in the future, she will have the central responsibility for evaluating progress, troubleshooting as necessary, and carrying the case forward.

We have learned through experience that professional workers and foster parents are able to learn together and form cooperative teams, working with agency cases as they arise and honing their skills over time. However, such teams are embedded in an agency structure, and the success of their efforts depends in part on an administrative review of policies and procedures.

## Continuing Contact with the Administrators

As training proceeded, we had intermittent but recurring contact with administrators and supervisors. Particular cases often brought policy questions to the foreground. In Jana's case, for example, the policy on family visits required a review. Jana was a responsible mother, and her request to take her boys to the park was reasonable. If the agency insisted on rigidly following the rules, the contact between Jana and the two foster mothers would surely be jeopardized.

We have been impressed by how many procedures are a matter of habit rather than law, and how often they're based on "worst-case" expectations. Many agencies limit family visits to the agency premises, forming policy around the need for control, logistical problems, and the necessary protection of children and foster families. The policy is understandable as a base line, but could it be expanded and made more flexible? Under what conditions? Could procedures be evaluated on a case-by-case basis or proceed sequentially? For instance, could Jana take her boys out, if accompanied by a foster parent, until all participants felt comfortable in giving her free rein?

We explored other situations that require administrative support for new procedures, particularly those involving intake, case coordination, and intensive services at points of transition. It often proves possible to bring the two families together as soon as the child is placed, thereby reducing the trauma of separation. Official wheels turn slowly, and it's only possible to hurry the process of intake and expand the roster of participants if the responsible parties believe it's essential for the children, the families, and the ultimate result. Change requires support at all levels of the agency, with particular encouragement from policymakers.

The same holds true for structural reorganization within the agency. We argued for the coordination of case management within and beyond the agency, using examples of confusion and suffering in particular cases as the spark for policy discussion. We also discussed the possibility of allotting extra staff time during periods of transition. Those moments are both especially difficult and especially malleable. The potential for positive and negative developments is greatest when new systems are under formation, and extra effort at that time is apt to be particularly productive.

Up to this point, the description of training has concerned agency personnel. Although the obstacles to change increase as families, staff, and administrators become involved, the refinement of policies, procedures, and skills within an agency is a goal with reasonable expectations. Beyond these boundaries, at the junctures with other systems, the challenge becomes more daunting.

## BEYOND THE TRIANGLE: WORKING AT THE JUNCTURES WITH OTHER SYSTEMS

In almost every foster care situation, systems beyond the boundaries of the agency affect important decisions and the progress of the case. Consider the network of relevant systems in the following foster care cases:

Mary is eager to have her son back. She has been attending the prescribed parenting and counseling sessions, has been visiting her son regularly, and is in good contact with the foster family. The agency worker thinks she's ready but the worker at child protective services disagrees. She's focused on the court orders and thinks that the primary task for Mary is to complete the mandated sessions. Court hearings have been scheduled, canceled, rescheduled, and postponed. Mary is an articulate woman who feels she can speak for herself, and she complains that whenever there are hearings the judge talks to the lawyers and the protective service workers but never to her. The situation has been unresolved for some time and Mary is deeply discouraged. Involved in this situation are the legal system, protective services, counseling and educational services, the foster care system, and the foster care agency.

Angie's children are in foster care while she participates in a residential drug program. The program focuses on her past experiences, her feelings, and her progress in the therapeutic community. But Angie is concerned for her children and her partner, and leaves the program against the advice of the professional staff. Involved in this situation are the drug rehab community, the welfare system, the foster care system, and the foster care agency.

Alfreda, who is homeless, has three children: two in foster care and one living with her mother. Decent housing is available for her, organized by an energetic and effective group oriented toward women's issues, but it's a single room residence. Most of the women living there have children in foster care. If Alfreda accepts this housing, she cannot be reunited with her family. Involved in this situation are the public housing authority, private housing agencies, the foster care system, and foster care agencies.

Nelda and Angie have children with special needs who are in foster care with specially trained families. Nelda's son is mentally handicapped and Angie's daughter is physically handicapped. Each child receives therapeutic attention through the child welfare system, and the foster parents are supervised in working with their special needs at home. There's no provision for Nelda or Angie to participate in this specialized work, although reunification of these families is a possibility and, at least, they will continue to have contact with their children indefinitely. Involved in this situation are protective services, medical and educational systems, the foster care system, and foster care agencies.

Maureen, 17, and her infant son are in foster care. They're living with a couple who are fond of Maureen and her child and who want to integrate them into their own family. Maureen has continuing ties with her biological family, despite their high level of disorganization, substance abuse, and domestic violence. Contact between the two families is marked by mutual distrust, but the aftercare worker from the adolescent pregnancy center has been attempting to bring them together. Maureen responds to the tension by lying to the foster mother about visiting her father, and she's discovered. The foster family feels betrayed and angry, and the worker from protective services is considering moving mother and child into another placement. Involved in this situation are protective services, the adolescent pregnancy agency, the foster care system, and the foster care agency.

There's a common thread in these cases. Although the central figures are embedded in families, none of the systems or services respond to that fact. The housing authority sees Alfreda as a homeless individual. The drug program works on Angie's ghosts and defenses. The protective and foster care systems consider Maureen and her baby as the only clients. None of them see an extended family as the consumer.

Although there's a problem within every system, it's compounded when several systems are involved. There's blockage at the junctures, a narrowing of perspective when one system overlaps another. Nobody suggests to the rehabilitation experts that they coach the biological parents of handicapped children as well as the foster parents. Nobody thinks Mary should plead for her children in court or describe her family resources. Information is funneled to the judge by the child-protective social worker, who presents the situation from her own perspective. There's no room at this juncture for a consideration of Mary within the context of her family.

Is it possible to influence the communication among systems so that they invest more in the preservation of families? The answer is both no and yes. What can be accomplished within the boundaries of a foster care agency is not easily brought about when larger systems are involved. To create comprehensive changes in the organization of the legal system, the housing authorities, the child welfare system, drug programs, and medical services to the poor, one must work at another level. However, consultants, trainers, and staff workers in a foster care setting are not without resources for influencing established systems. They can function as a force for consciousness-raising, highlighting the results of poor coordination and the expensive, self-defeating effects of policies that don't take families into account. They can enlist the support of policymakers within the agency, and make common cause with people in other systems who share the same goals.

The meeting described in Chapter 1 is an example of such an effort. The meeting brought together Angie and her family, the foster parents of her two children, foster care workers, professional staff from the drug program she had abruptly left, and the training consultant. It was an exploration—an effort to raise awareness concerning the different perspectives and the complex issues important to all parties. How much the adversarial positions were constructively perturbed is unknown. But the discussion was a beginning. It provided for interaction among the representatives of several systems and highlighted the need for integrated services.

Assembling together representatives of the different systems that work with a family is a promising procedure for facilitating change. In the case of foster care, child protective workers are responsible for the execution of legal mandates and hold considerable power. They can veto suggestions for reunification, even when the foster care worker believes that the move is advisable. If the child protective worker is brought into contact with members of the foster care triangle, he may become aware of important new strengths beyond the completion of prescribed court assignments, such as the development of a dependable support system or an increase in child-rearing skills. He may then be able to listen with more confidence to the judgment of professional colleagues within the agency, and is more likely to function as an advocate rather than an obstacle when a parent petitions for the return of the children.

The cases are specific, but they point to flaws in general policies and procedures that should be corrected. The courts should adapt their schedules and routines so that they can listen directly to the plaintiffs, even when justifiably interested in expert opinion. Housing authorities, whether public or private, should respond to the realities of the social context and review the technicalities that keep families separated. The referral systems that organize educational, medical, and therapeutic services for children should take into account the surrounding network, and should work with both biological and foster families. In the long run, such procedures may prove economically sensible, as well as more family-friendly.

At these junctures between foster care and the associated systems that enter family life, it's important to challenge boundaries, connect the participants, and search for integrative procedures. Nationwide movements striving toward wraparound community services and case coordination are moving in this direction. Workers within an enlightened foster care structure may be able to learn from and contribute to their efforts.

## APPENDIX 5.1. TRAINING MANUAL FOR FOSTER PARENTS BASED ON AN ECOLOGICAL PERSPECTIVE ON FOSTER CARE

### Table of Contents

An Open Letter to Agency Administrators and Trainers

PART ONE

The Ecological Viewpoint and Foster Care
    Family Interaction
    Family Patterns
    The Foster Care Situation
    Training Foster Parents

The Themes and Skills of the Training
    The Basic Themes
        Family Preservation
        Outreach to the Extended Family
        Family Empowerment
        Developmental Stage
        Periods of Transition
    The Skills
        Joining
        Mapping
        Working with Complementarity
        Searching for Strength

PART TWO

Session One: What's a Foster Family?

To the Trainer (themes, skills, goals)
Session Activities
    I.   Mapping the Foster Family
    II.  The Foster Family: Developmental Tasks and Family Strengths
    III. Transitions: The Foster Family Receives a Child
    IV. Open Discussion
    Appendix
        Family Map
        Developmental Tasks of the Family

Session Two: The Foster Child: Entering a New Home

To the Trainer (themes, skills, goals)
Session Activities
    I.   Child Development
    II.  Connecting to the New Home
    III. Troubling Behavior: Understanding and Helping
    IV. Open Discussion

Session Three: Roots: The Foster Child's Biological Family

To the Trainer (themes, skills, goals)
Session Activities
    I.   Understanding the Biological Family
    II.  Receiving Siblings into the Foster Family
    III. Open Discussion

Session Four: Different Kinds of Families: Family Shapes
and Ethnicity

To the Trainer (themes, skills, goals)
Session Activities
    I.   Family Shapes
    II.  Ethnicity
    III. Open Discussion

Session Five: Visitation and Continuing Contact

To the Trainer (themes, skills, goals)
Session Activities
    I.   The Meaning of Visits and Family Contacts
    II.  Encouraging Family Visits
    III. Visiting Time: Before, During, and After
    IV. Open Discussion

Session Six: Coordination with Case Workers:
Exploring Functions and New Roles

To the Trainer (themes, skills, goals)
Session Activities
    I.   Foster Care Activities in the Agency: Organized Services and
        New Roles
    II.  Case Worker and Foster Family as a Team: Setting the Pace and
        Roles for Contact with the Natural Family
    III. Open Discussion
    Appendix
        Sample Chart of Foster Care Activities

Session Seven: Coordination with Case Workers:
Implementing the Process

To the Trainer (themes, skills, goals)
Session Activities
    I.   Preparing for Contact
    II.  Meeting with the Biological Family
    III. Solving Problems Cooperatively
    IV. Open Discussion

Session Eight: Going Home

To the Trainer (themes, skills, goals)
Session Activities
    I.   The "Going Home" Transition: Different Perspectives
    II.  The "Going Home" Transition: Planning Together
    III. Leaving the Training

# CHAPTER SIX

# Substance Abuse
# and Pregnancy

## A FAMILY-ORIENTED
## PERINATAL PROGRAM

This chapter focuses on the treatment of women who are poor, pregnant, and chemically dependent. Certainly, the problem of addiction affects a much wider segment of the population, crossing the boundaries of social class, ethnicity, age, and gender, but there's a special urgency to the plight of this group. They are the bearers of the next generation. Whether their infants are born with positive toxicity or not, the management of the mother's addiction has long-term implications for the women, their children, and society. For this reason, we will describe the formation and evolution of a family-oriented perinatal program in some detail.

There's a second reason for detailing the events, which may be equally important. The history of this program illustrates the kinds of issues that arise whenever a new approach is introduced into an established system, whether it be a clinic, a hospital, a school, or a corporation. The specific crises, compromises, and solutions we describe pertain to this particular setting, but the experience has implications for many other situations.

The perinatal program was set into a well-established therapeutic community for substance abusers, which, in turn, was housed within a department of a large urban hospital. As consultants and trainers from the inception of the program, our designated role was to develop the family component and to help the staff integrate this into their treatment procedures. As the collaboration evolved, the nature of the intervention changed in scope and content. Our contacts expanded beyond perinatal staff to include members of the broader therapeutic community, the women in the perinatal unit, their families, and, eventually, the clients and staff of the ob/gyn department of the hospital. The task of training and consulting increased in complexity. We needed to shift perspectives, relate to subsystem conflicts, and periodically pause to reevaluate our role and priorities.

The intervention brought gender to the foreground. The perinatal program, comprised of women and children, was incorporated into a therapeutic community populated predominantly by males. Gender issues arose, not as a political matter but as a reflection of different realities, and our family oriented approach was at the core of both the tensions and the solutions.

The intervention also raised a question fundamental to any training program: What does it take for a new approach to graft? How does it become part of an institution so that the ongoing procedures reflect the change, the staff trains new people in this way of working, and continuation of the program no longer depends on the people who initiated the approach? We saw a new model grow, peak, and then falter in one setting of the hospital, while expanding and taking hold in another. Why did that happen? What lasted and what did not? Which elements fostered longevity?

In the following sections, we will discuss the setting, the nature of our interventions, the evolution of the program, and the expansion of the model to a setting that was, in the end, better suited to perpetuating the approach.

## THE PERINATAL PROGRAM

The perinatal program was a special project, inaugurated by the director of the hospital's addictions department and supported by outside funding. It was created as a treatment service for pregnant and postpartum women who were crack or cocaine dependent, and was viewed essentially as a new addition to the existing day-treatment recovery clinic. The new client population was to be integrated into the therapeutic community of the clinic, adding only a program coordinator and one counselor. The community's combination of medical care, psychosocial services, and emphasis on self-help was considered particularly suitable for dealing with the multiple problems afflicting the new population. In addition, the day treatment structure seemed likely to attract female addicts, who might regard long-term inpatient programs as threatening to their outside ties.

The staff of our training center, Family Studies, Inc., was invited to help with what had been conceptualized as the "family component" of drug addiction: the impact of chemical dependency on family structure and the impact of family structure on the individual. In actuality, the task was more complex, reflecting both the realities of the situation and our own view of the change process. From the beginning, we had to address the organizational dynamics generated by the entry of a new population into the existing community. Although we had expected some resistance to family-oriented procedures, we hadn't expected to find ourselves in the middle of a conflict between "old" and "new" personnel over treatment and case management policies. Troubleshooting and adaptations began immediately, as an accompaniment to the introduction of a family focus.

In retracing the process of consultation and training, we can identify three phases: the inclusion of the perinatal program in the therapeutic community, the gradual differentiation of this program from its host, and the expansion of the program to another hospital setting. In general terms, inclusion, differentiation, and expansion would be a typical sequence for any program successfully integrated into a larger structure.

## THE PERINATAL PROGRAM JOINS THE THERAPEUTIC COMMUNITY

### The Process Begins

When the project got underway, the first task for the trainer/consultants was to learn something about the setting. We spent time observing, talking with staff, and attending meetings at which administrative and policy issues were reviewed. There were weekly staff meetings, which now included the staff of the new perinatal program, and monthly meetings, chaired by the director of the addictions department. The latter were attended by the perinatal staff, as well as the coordinator and supervisors of the therapeutic clinic.

Because the therapeutic community (TC) was the host culture, and our work was shaped by its structure and orientation, we will begin by describing its population, philosophy, and routine.

## The Host Culture

### The Population and the Model

The therapeutic community was a day treatment center for chemically dependent individuals ranging in age from the mid-20s to the early 50s. Housed within a large medical facility, the clinic combined a self-help strategy characteristic of the therapeutic community model with an array of medical, psychotherapeutic, educational, and social work services. The staff played the dual role of professional helpers and community monitors. Nurses, for instance, handled medical problems as needed, but they also ensured a drug-free community through the routine collection of urine samples. Counselors and social workers helped clients set and pursue therapeutic goals, also keeping track of the emotional tenor of the community as a whole. In addition to internal activities, the clinic maintained contact with staff from other services of the hospital, as well as with outside agencies.

At any given time, the clinic served a population of 30 to 40 clients, most of them male, African-American or Latino, and poor. Many were homeless at the time of admission, and some were HIV positive. Most had long histories of addiction to crack, cocaine, or other substances, and were veterans of other drug treatment programs. To qualify for the TC program, candidates had to be actively involved with drugs, willing to maintain abstinence, and committed to completing 18 months of treatment. During initial interviews, client motivation was assessed, the program was explained, and a treatment plan was agreed upon that included personal goals.

As it was expected that clients would be passive at first, the initial emphasis was on securing their involvement with the community. The first stage, expected to last for at least 9 months, required attendance 5 days a week. The daily routine began with a ½-hour meeting of staff and clients and proceeded through a variety of activities: orientation to the TC model, psychoeducational classes, introductory 12-step seminars for beginners, Narcotics Anonymous (NA) open and closed meetings, self-disclosure meetings, support groups, stress and relaxation workshops, and community meetings at the end of the day. On Fridays and Mondays, before and after the weekend recess, there were "relapse prevention" and "weekend process" meetings. In addition, each client met by individual arrangement with a personal counselor and a sponsor.

Clients were closely monitored for compliance with community rules. A client who violated the rules would be confronted by other clients as well as the staff. Twice a week the main activity of the day was the "encounter," attended by the entire community and facilitated by staff members. In this emotionally charged experience, clients took turns on the "hot seat," where they were challenged concerning progress, denials, community achievements, and manipulative behavior. The encounter served to reinforce compliance with the rules, penetrate the defenses of whoever occupied the hot seat, and encourage emotional expression by other members of the group. In general, the frequent meetings were seen as a vehicle for helping members of the community become open and supportive of each other.

During this stage, it was expected that the client would become increasingly acculturated into the community. Involvement in the program and sustained sobriety were seen as dependent on a combination of personal motivation, community support, and enforcement of the community's values. Seniority was recognized by the assignment of community responsibilities, ranging from sweeping the floor and organizing parties to planning and chairing special meetings, and by moving into a "big brother" role with new members. It was assumed that these marks of progress would create a sense of belonging while developing responsibility and self-esteem.

After approximately 9 months of drug abstinence and satisfactory participation in the program, the client entered a new phase, requiring attendance only 2 or 3 days a week. Known as the reentry phase, the focus was now on helping the client adjust to life in the outside world—including financial matters, housing, work, legal issues, family, and other important relationships. By the time the client graduated from the program, it was expected that he or she would be employed, in school, or in job training; would have resolved problems that might jeopardize sobriety and continuing recovery; and would maintain some relationship with the clinic—such as a sponsor role with new clients.

The process was not always as smooth as the plan. Desertions were frequent. Some clients never made it past the orientation phase, others engaged in a pattern of irregular attendance until they eventually dropped out, and still others regularly attended but remained emotionally detached. Slips and relapses occurred, slowing the advance through stages and extending the length of treatment. A few were asked to leave the program, typically for violations of the "no drugs" rule. On the other hand, some clients overadjusted to the community, resisting movement into the reentry phase and toward graduation. Despite all of its inevitable problems, this was a generally successful example of the therapeutic community model.

## The Community's Attitude toward Families

Since we were particularly interested in a family approach, our first observations at the weekly staff meetings focused on references to the families. What was known? What was discussed? What were the attitudes? Perhaps it's no surprise that family matters were hardly a factor. Clients were discussed in terms of individual success and failure, their relationships to other community members, and their interactions with staff. Little or nothing was said about the relationship to family or how this might influence recovery. In fact, the staff knew little about family background, realities, or relationships.

As we observed the discussions, we came to understand that the community functioned on the basis of two primary tenets: the belief that addicted clients need to focus on themselves and deal with their addiction before doing anything else, and the conviction that the community is the healing context. Everything that transpired in the clinic setting was related to the struggle for a drug-free life, and the relationships among community members were fostered as the crucial force for personal mastery. Neither principle drew staff attention to the family as a relevant unit of intervention.

*The Community in Action*

The reality of community relationships was, of course, complex. Friendships developed over the course of the daily activities and extended beyond program hours, when members were expected to provide the mutual support that would prevent relapses. Some relationships, such as the sponsorship of junior participants by senior members, were explicitly sanctioned by the program. Others, such as sexual relationships, were viewed as akin to incest and expressly forbidden. For the most part, contacts among community members reflected the spontaneous dynamics of alliances, enmities, leadership, and the need to give and receive attention. Professional boundaries and objectivity often became blurred as clients competed for the attention of staff members and complained about favoritism, while staff members protected clients from each other. In its intensity and dynamics, the community had many of the characteristics of a family, and indeed was often referred to as the "real" family for some of the clients.

The guiding schema was powerful for the staff. Because of the focus on addiction as the problem and the therapeutic community as the solution, the rest of the client's life was treated as secondary. We learned at staff meetings, for instance, that one client was confronted for arriving late at the clinic because she stopped at her church on the way from her shelter, and that another, who could work nights because he was a baker, was pressed to remain unemployed so that he would not be too tired to participate in the daytime activities of the community. If we asked about families, we were told they were nonexistent ("Joe doesn't have a family"), rejected ("Dave doesn't want his family involved"), rejecting ("Paul's family doesn't want to be bothered"), or toxic ("Brenda's mother is a bad influence and may cause her to relapse").

The thought of involving families emerged only in the reentry phase, in accordance with the belief that clients need to commit to the community and deal with their addiction before they are emotionally ready to negotiate family issues. Even then, families were not included in treatment; rather, they were invited to come in for special occasions, such as parties. The family and the outside world were viewed primarily as a posttreatment resource, to be called upon when a client had reached the point of discharge planning and was preparing to leave the community.

As we came to understand the model of the host culture, we needed to consider our role as family consultants to the perinatal program.

## Introducing a Family Focus for the Perinatal Program

The first clients admitted to the perinatal program were greeted with the standard approach of the therapeutic community. They were expected to develop a close therapeutic alliance with their counselors and to become committed community members for at least 18 months. Family issues were not paramount. If a pregnant, chemically dependent woman had children in foster care, it was taken for granted that her relationship with them would be suspended until she made progress in the program—as demonstrated by her willingness to focus on her addiction and adhere to the 12-step philosophy.

We saw the situation differently. We thought that the perinatal staff would have to become more sensitive to the importance of families as a resource, that they would need to learn how to protect and enhance the clients' connections with children, spouses, siblings, and parents. In effect, we brought an alternative model into the situation, and needed to face the reality that our work would necessarily bring the two models into conflict.

Figure 6.1 illustrates the contrast between the model represented by the therapeutic community and the model represented by a family systems approach. The models place a different emphasis on drug abstinence vis-à-vis family connectedness, embody different conceptions of the family's role, place different requirements on clients entering the treatment community, and advocate a different relational structure to encompass client, community, and family.

Recognizing the power of the traditional treatment philosophy, we were careful to avoid a direct confrontation. We postponed any challenge to specific procedures, did not question the priority placed on recovery, and did not insist on the need to involve the family. Instead, we started with an educational approach focused on introducing the family as a factor. Our strategy had two aims: to raise the interest of the staff in family life so that they could appreciate the potential importance of the family for the recovery process, and to bring forth more constructive beliefs and attitudes

| | THERAPEUTIC COMMUNITY | FAMILY SYSTEMS |
|---|---|---|
| PRIMARY VALUE | Drug abstinence | Connectedness |
| ROLE OF FAMILY | Secondary | Primary |
| | Occasional guest | Full participant |
| | Resource toward end of program | Resource from the beginning |
| | Complicates treatment | Is complicated by treatment |
| | Part of the problem | Crucial to the solution |
| RESPONSE TO NEW CLIENT POPULATION | Must adjust to community culture | Require specific subculture |
| RELATIONAL STRUCTURE | | |

FIGURE 6.1. Alternative approaches to the perinatal program: Therapeutic community versus family systems models.

toward families as an eventual foundation for family-focused interventions. To this end, we offered didactic presentations about family structure, ethnicity, conflicts, and strengths; held weekly case consultations; and conducted demonstration family interviews. Our mission was to train the perinatal staff, but this staff was part of the larger unit and their clients would be interacting with the range of personnel. Therefore, we scheduled our activities so that the extended staff of the clinic could also attend.

Progress came slowly, through detailed discussion of concrete material in which we reframed automatic negatives and expanded the horizons of staff thinking. In one case, for instance, we questioned the staff's perception that a client had been rejected by her family. While the official story was that the family had unanimously ostracized the woman when she became pregnant, we were able to elicit information from various staff members that pointed to a more differentiated picture. The woman's counselor knew of an aunt who was more supportive than other family members; another worker had heard that the client's mother was expressing interest in the baby, if not in her own daughter. When the aunt and a sister accepted an invitation to come in to help us understand the situation better, we conducted a demonstration interview. Working together to create a family map, we were able to generate a fuller picture of the family than the one spontaneously conveyed by the client or contained in the case record. Building on this and other case consultations, we introduced the notion of mapping the family as a way of collecting information regarding who's important in the client's life, who likes her or is disappointed in her, who's taking care of her children, and so on.

The staff responded with interest, and soon noticed that even those who said they didn't want anything to do with their families kept bringing up unfinished business: the feeling of not being liked by one's parents, of having been treated unfairly by a mother who preferred a sibling, of betrayal by a close relative who was "stealing the children from me," and of having disappointed other members of the family. As interest grew, we were asked to provide family counseling for specific clients: Inez had three children placed in different homes and was engaged in a complicated triangle with her mother and her lover. Julie's boyfriend was apparently supportive of her recovery but the staff suspected him of being abusive. Shirley was preoccupied with the prospect of her children being given in custody to her mother, with whom she had an antagonistic rela-tionship. Beth lived in a complex network, and the staff had requested a meeting with all her children, their foster parents, and workers from other agencies.

We used these interviews to model an approach centered on promoting family connections rather than on treating dysfunctional aspects that had been primary for the staff. When Shirley com-plained that her mother sabotaged her plans to go to school and learn to read, we explored something broader, searching for the positives: "Do your children read?"; "Do they know that you can't read?"; "Can you help with their homework even if you can't read?"; "Does your mother read?" What emerged was a richer picture of the family's reality. Shirley's mother not only read but wrote poetry, and the antagonistic relationship between Shirley and her mother was mixed, not surprisingly, with admiration and yearning. From that kind of shared exploration, it became possible to help Shirley build more constructive family connections.

Our input as teachers to the staff and consultants to families was focused on particular cases, limited to a few hours per week. We knew that was insufficient: the structure would also need to change, and we looked for ways of affecting broader policies and procedures.

## Attempting to Change Intake Procedures

If a different approach is ever to take hold, the institution must modify procedures so they will embody the thrust of the model and support newly developing skills. That's a general principle. However, each setting requires a specific assessment in which timing and appropriate mechanisms are considered within context. In the case of the perinatal program, the high rate of client turnover during the first months of the program provided the opportunity for suggesting a change in intake procedures.

As the program got underway, it became obvious that many clients were dropping out after a short period. The perinatal staff accepted defections as the natural effect of the client's lack of motivation, and her inability to adjust to the rules of the community. However, the low census posed a threat to the continuity of the program. Decreasing enrollment called for corrective action and opened the way to more radical ideas. We suggested that the situation might improve if key members of the client's network were involved in the intake procedures as partners in the effort at rehabilitation. Intake might include husbands or boyfriends, parents, siblings, children, workers from protective or foster care agencies—or anybody else in a position to encourage regular attendance at the program. We concretized our recommendation by offering guidelines on how to conduct a family intake.

The first attempt to modify procedures was unsuccessful, at least in terms of procedures we were suggesting. The cast of characters invited to intake meetings remained the same. In retrospect, we realized that a family intake was at odds with the need to build up the program in a hurry. It was still easier, faster, and probably more comfortable to admit clients through an individual interview. On the other hand, intake interviews changed in quality. The staff became more sensitive to the client's network. They began to use part of the individual interview to map families and ask questions about family composition, its quality of relationships, and the attitudes of various family members toward the client's addiction and potential recovery.

In addition, treatment plans developed during the intake interview were now couched in different language and specified broader goals. Whereas previous plans vaguely referred to the remote goal of regaining custody of children currently in foster care, they now made specific reference to maintaining and improving contact with the children, even while they remained in placement. This was an important step forward. In the context of community relations with the hospital, in fact, it was a turning point. The grapevine in this neighborhood had always conveyed a clear message: If you were pregnant and chemically dependent, the hospital would take your infant away at birth. The existence of a program that regarded mother and child as a unit, and that worked toward reestablishing family connections, began to reverse the reputation of the hospital. The number of pregnant, chemically dependent women who voluntarily came to the hospital and into the program increased significantly.

## THE PERINATAL PROGRAM DIFFERENTIATES

The second stage of training and consultation began when the perinatal program developed veterans, that is, when some of the women had participated in the program long enough to form a core. At this point, they presented the therapeutic community—and especially the staff—with a challenge to established procedures. The challenge engendered conflict, but also provided an opportunity for review and revision, and we were able to bring a family perspective more directly into the program.

### Staff Problems

As the perinatal population grew, the problem of turnover was compounded by the ambivalence and tenuous commitment of the women, their inconsistent attendance, and their frequent noncompliance with the rules. Perinatal clients often arrived late, left early, missed days, and participated only perfunctorily in community meetings.

In response, a split over treatment and disciplinary policies developed among the staff. The core staff of the therapeutic community expected the newcomers to abide fully by the standard rules of the program, fearing that anything less would sabotage recovery and undermine client morale. The perinatal staff argued that the special life circumstances of their clients required a more flexible stance. They allowed the women to attend less than 5 days a week or spend fewer hours there, and in general took a more lenient attitude toward rule violations.

In disagreement with this special treatment, the core staff began to impose the customary sanctions on perinatal clients who violated rules. Transgressions increased and disagreements among the staff escalated, with recurrent arguments about whether, how, and who to punish. Partly as a result of intrastaff tension, coordinators of the perinatal program found the job stressful. When the second person to hold that post resigned, we were consulted about a replacement, and a coordinator was hired with a strong interest in family dynamics.*

Staffing is a major factor, and an imponderable, in consulting work with agencies. Changes cannot be dictated, but when an opportunity arises, it's a welcome bonus if the consultants can have input into the assessment of new candidates.

The change of coordinators did not bring an end to staff conflict; in fact, the activities of the new coordinator brought the clash of opinions to a head. He mounted a vigorous and successful client recruitment campaign, based on an active liaison with the hospital's ob/gyn department and with women's shelters in the area. The resulting influx of new clients, at a faster pace than before, accentuated the challenge to existing rules and the disagreements over policy.

## Supporting Gender Differentiation

The split within the staff allowed the consultants to bring different viewpoints into open discussion. We encouraged an airing of the conflict in the monthly meetings chaired by the director of the addictions department, offering analysis and recommendations in a

---

*David Greenan, currently at the Minuchin Center for the Family, became the unit coordinator, and later was responsible for expanding the program to other services.

setting that guaranteed maximum impact on the program's operation. Specifically, we took advantage of this forum, and of the presence of the new family-oriented coordinator, to suggest that the perinatal clients needed to be recognized as a special population, and that they required a program that addressed their needs.

We took the position that gender issues, including the stark reality of pregnancy, largely accounted for the difficulty that members of this group had in accommodating to community rules. The women were arriving at the clinic by a different route than traditional clients. Unlike their male counterparts, they had not worked through a decision about joining the therapeutic community. Most had been abruptly faced with the choice of entering the program or having their babies placed at birth. In comparison with the male clients, many of whom resided at a hospital-based shelter, the women were more connected to an outside network: male friends, children, parents, siblings. Their caseworkers from child welfare agencies, often invested in keeping the family together, tended to encourage those interests. When Paula left the program early to see her daughter, when Tina missed 2 days because her boyfriend brought his children home, and when Christa missed 3 days while dealing with immigration and public assistance, they were encouraged to do so by their caseworkers from child welfare and foster care agencies.

We emphasized the new realities inherent in the introduction of a female, multirelated population into a primarily male and largely self-enclosed community. We understood that the primary job of the staff was to focus on the activities and progress of their clients within the program, but we also urged them to make provision for realities of the outside world important to the women. For the larger staff of the community, that meant more tolerance for ways in which the women participated in the program and followed rules. For the perinatal staff, with whom we worked most closely and who were most directly involved with the women, it meant the development of new program activities in the form of groups that met to discuss family-oriented matters: a parent support group and a family issues group.

## The Parent Support Group

It seemed clear to us that the women in the perinatal program should be focused, at least part of the time, on relationships with their children, not just the ones about to be born but their older children as well. We suggested that this activity be undertaken by child development specialists from the child life department of the hospital, which appeared to be a radical idea. The staff had contact with some of the medical services, using them as needed, but were unaccustomed to incorporating the resources of the larger hospital into their program. We were offering an example of communication and combined service across traditional and rather carefully maintained boundaries.

In accordance with this recommendation, the schedule of the program was modified to accommodate a weekly meeting focused on children and the parenting role. The meeting was held in the child life nursery, creating a warm and child-oriented atmosphere— complete with toys and pictures of children on the walls. The meeting offered the women an opportunity to discuss parent–child relationships, share their experiences and concerns, and learn something about the developmental abilities of their children and how to stimulate their growth.

The introduction of an activity led by the child life staff had a ripple effect, enhancing the family focus within the program. The clients were now devoting part of the program to parenting rather than drug issues, and were brought into contact with other child-focused services offered by the child life department, such as the developmental evaluation of their infants and toddlers and a therapeutic nursery program. After the initial period, the group included fathers and other significant adults in the natural network. In an important development, the group also came to include male members of the therapeutic community who had asked to participate, thus impacting the clinic community. The comment of one male client encapsulates the effect of bringing a family focus into a drug rehabilitation program: "This is the group that I like the most, because here I'm not treated like an addict, I'm treated like a parent."

## The Family Issues Group

The second addition was a twice weekly family issues group, conducted by the coordinator of the program and including a consultant from Family Studies. This group played a major role in differentiating the program from a more traditional approach. It introduced "family" as the central topic for discussion, and sensitized the women to the connections between their interactions within the program and their relationships with their families. Initially used as a sounding board for dealing with difficult family members, these meetings helped the participants move from conflictual to more collaborative connections with their relatives. They began to invite family members in for consultation interviews, framing the invitation in terms of rapprochement and the exploration of difficult issues.

Katherine, for example, described how she had left her two very young children with her aunt 6 years earlier because she felt unable to care for them. Both women expected that Katherine would come for them within 2 years, and the aunt had promised that she would give them back. As more than 5 years passed before Katherine asked for the children, her aunt felt she would need some time to make arrangements. Katherine agreed that this made sense, but she and her aunt were both uncomfortable after this conversation. Talking together was no longer easy, and the aunt made it difficult for Katherine to visit the children.

When Katherine told her story, one of the group members suggested that she take her aunt to court. That was a common reaction in the group to conflicts about child visitation and custody. The family consultant instead suggested that Katherine invite her aunt in for a discussion. Although she felt nervous about the idea, she agreed, and called her aunt to set up a meeting. The meeting had important consequences for both Katherine and the group. The consultant was able to help the aunt move from questioning Katherine's parenting skills to talking about her own reaction to giving up the children, who, after 6 years, felt like her own. Katherine, despite feeling upset, could accept this, and it became possible to work out ways to increase her visits with the children. A blaming, adversarial relationship began to change into one of collaboration.

For the group, Katherine's decision to call her aunt served as a catalyst. Over the next few weeks, two other women in similar situations set up family meetings. The automatic impulse to resolve these issues through the courts was weakening, replaced by the idea that you can invite family members in for a session and work toward the resolution of problems.

For both clients and staff, such procedures represented a major change in thinking and process: satisfying, sometimes exciting, and productive of hope. We thought it possible, although we had no proof, that reconnecting with family members might help these women not only repair relationships but make progress in recovering from addiction. The sense of solidarity and support in the group worked in the same direction, offering a paradigm and supplement—but not a substitute—for family connections. In general, the groups formed specifically for this program offered some of the same kinds of support as the various groups and activities of the larger therapeutic community. Different, however, was the predominantly female content of issues dealt with, and the strong connection to relationships and realities in the outside world.

## The Impact of the Babies

The special needs of the perinatal clients became more apparent as the first women admitted during their pregnancy approached the time of delivery. New policy issues arose, and new realities brought about changes both in the physical setting and the focus of treatment.

### Policy Issues

Changes in thinking are not automatically accompanied by the ability to generalize. When new issues arise the tendency is to fall back on traditional assumptions and procedures rather than work with less familiar models. Thus, the birth of the babies became a fresh source of conflict within the staff. The leadership of the community expected the city's child welfare agency to provide a homemaker who would care for the infant at the client's home or shelter so that the mother would be free to attend the program. Some child welfare workers agreed, but others pressed for the mother to focus on her baby, even at the price of limiting her participation in the program. The community staff reacted with an intensification of distrust: "What's the hook, if they're so free to decide between the baby and the program?" "Wouldn't it be irresponsible to help these babies stay with these mothers?" Caught in the middle of the argument, the perinatal staff vacillated between the two positions.

Again, the conflict over policy allowed the consultants to

suggest a procedure emphasizing the special characteristics of the perinatal program. We took the position that the *family* should enter the program. We insisted on two points: that the protection and nurturance of the mother–child bond was an essential component of the perinatal program, indeed, its main justification, and that the presence of the babies should be considered an enhancer of the recovery process rather than an impediment. On these grounds, we challenged the homemaker solution. Rather than separating the babies from the mothers, the program needed to find ways to keep them together for as much time as possible while the mother was a participant. That position triggered a reexamination of policies, involving several levels of authority within the hierarchy of the hospital. Eventually, it led to decisive changes within the structure of the perinatal program.

## Changes in the Physical Setting

The first question was whether the hospital would accept the presence of the babies. The issue involved both those babies who were not technically patients and those who were born with positive toxicity. There had been some anxiety among the nursing staff that babies born HIV positive might present a risk of infection for clients of the clinic. At the request of the director of the addictions department, the chief epidemiologist of the hospital reviewed the situation and delivered a ruling that emphasized two points: inclusion of these infants in the program was acceptable, and certain guidelines must be followed for the health and safety of all the babies. Clients who might spread contagious diseases to the infants were to abstain temporarily from attending the program, an adequately furnished area should be provided for diaper changing, hands should be washed before infants were handled by anybody other than the mother, and so on.

These guidelines, and the heightened concern for the safety and well-being of the babies, led to changes in the physical environment. A large room was set aside for the exclusive use of the perinatal group. Furniture was rearranged, cribs were installed so that the babies could nap, colorful pictures were hung on the walls, and equipment was provided to refrigerate and warm formula. Later, as the babies grew, mattresses, mats to crawl on, and toys were provided. The perinatal portion of the clinic adopted a distinctive family look, and the nursery became a "home room" where the women could congregate to talk and relax.

## Changes in the Focus of Treatment

Inevitably, there were changes that went beyond the physical. With the babies very much present and in the care of their mothers, there was an increase in the time devoted to the client as a parent, as opposed to focusing on chemical dependency. The parent support group now consisted of real dyads, and the child life staff was able to work directly on the capacity of mother and child to send and receive cues, on feeding and caregiving styles, and on the mother's understanding of her child's development. The role of the child life department also expanded as a result of logistical complications. The community staff was concerned that the encounter groups might be too emotionally intense for the babies, or, conversely, that their presence might curtail the emotional intensity that was an essential ingredient of the situation. The child life department took up the slack and, as behooved professionals, went beyond routine babysitting activities. They organized a "developmental stimulation" program for the infants, conducted twice a week while the mothers were involved in encounter groups. The encounter sessions were modified by the staff of the therapeutic community in order to be more respectful of women, and to reflect the fact that many had suffered abuse in the past.

The babies also affected the topics under discussion in the family issues group. Now conducted amidst children, cribs, and play mattresses, the group focused increasingly on the practical implications of motherhood, and its interconnection with other aspects of family life. What became important were themes about the support that mothers were receiving or not receiving, requesting or not requesting, from fathers, boyfriends, extended family, neighborhood networks, and social services. For most of the women, the new focus also meant a heightened interest in regaining custody of children currently in placement.

## Changes in Group Identity

Finally, the presence of the babies played a decisive role in consolidating the identity of this group as a distinctively female community. Sharing the day-to-day challenges of motherhood, the women gradually developed a strong sense of solidarity, organized around their predicament as mothers facing difficult odds rather than around their status as recovering addicts.

When the first participants reached the reentry phase of treatment and needed to attend job interviews, the women formed an informal baby sitting co-op to care for each other's children. When they learned that a prospective but hesitant new client was going to be inspected by the city's child welfare agency, they spontaneously rallied to stock the woman's refrigerator with food, then used their leverage to convince her to join the program. And when another new client revealed that she was facing a hostile environment in her shelter, one of the veterans said: "They treat you like that because they think you're all by yourself. It's important that they know you're not a lonely person, that you do have a family. And if you don't, we'll be your family." The group then agreed to show up at the shelter, "not to intimidate anybody, but so that they know that you're not alone, that we care for you."

## Helping Families Rebuild

One effect of the family emphasis was that many women resolved to reclaim older children who were in placement. As this issue became paramount, part of the weekly consultation was devoted to the development of skills for negotiating with the system. The staff was taught how to encourage mothers to take initiative in approaching caseworkers and foster parents, and how to coach them through the process. In time, mothers began to run these meetings, taking charge in what was certainly a reversal of the usual hierarchy.

In some situations, the perinatal program became a meeting ground where mothers, children, workers, and foster parents could deal with the dilemmas of foster care. When participants succeeded in regaining custody of their children, consultants helped the staff assist their clients during the challenging process of reunification.

For example, when Sonia entered the program, she was pregnant and subsequently gave birth to a little girl, Tisha. Sonia's rehabilitation was successful, and by the time she graduated from the program she had regained custody of another daughter, 8-year-old Tania. One more daughter, Latoya, was about to be reunited with her mother after 2 years in a residential treatment center. The other children, two boys, lived together in a group home and were expected to remain there for the present. Sonia retained her connection to the perinatal program after graduation. She specifically requested help with Tania who, she felt, was rejecting her, clamming up, and resisting her authority.

We see here the symptoms of a difficult reunification. Having developed in isolation from each other for many years, Sonia and Tania needed to learn, rather abruptly, how to relate as mother and daughter, even while Sonia was struggling with the anxieties of a transition from the sheltered position of client to the travails of autonomous parenting. Given this reading of the situation, the consultant declined an invitation to become yet another expert in charge of Tania. Instead, he offered a context in which Sonia could exercise and develop her own expertise as a mother. Family meetings with Sonia and all her children were scheduled for every other week, and arrangements for assembling workers and the children were left up to Sonia.

The sessions were largely unstructured. During these meetings, Sonia had many things on her mind, discussing jobs and housing as well as matters involving the children. The consultant accommodated to Sonia's realities and her style rather than forcing a family session. He responded when Sonia's concerns veered toward the children, was disengaged when she attended to other business, and became active again when appropriate. He often joined her bantering style, using light humor to inject a family theme, set up a family enactment, or highlight the fact that the children were more responsive to Sonia than to the residential workers.

The central theme in this family was the uncertainty of reunification. Sonia began every session with a barrage of complaints about one or more of the children, about how their behavior stressed her, how all this was jeopardizing her continued recovery, and how she was having second thoughts about reunification. Perhaps she should postpone the return of the children who were still away, perhaps the daughter who had just returned should be placed again, perhaps. . . . The consultant listened, sympathized with her predicament, and concentrated on creating bonding scenarios in which Sonia and the children could experience the connectedness, nurturance, and playful interaction they had missed over many years of separation:

SONIA: Tania has been getting on my nerves. She doesn't do anything for herself. I have to do everything.

CONSULTANT: Like what?

SONIA: Like, when she first came she was so independent. She would comb and wash herself. Now I have to comb and wash her. I shouldn't be doing that. She's not a baby anymore.

CONSULTANT: She asks you to comb her?

SONIA: No, she doesn't ask. She just doesn't do it, so I have to do it.

CONSULTANT: And she lets you?

SONIA: Yeah. She does it on purpose, I guess.

CONSULTANT: I guess she doesn't reject you anymore, eh?

SONIA: Yeah. But now she wants me to baby her.

CONSULTANT: Do you?

SONIA: Sometimes I do. She sort of manipulates me into babying her.

CONSULTANT: Would you show me how you baby her?

SONIA: OK. (*to Tania, in a commanding voice*) Come over here. (*Tania rushes to Sonia and climbs on her lap. Sonia starts caressing Tania; her voice softens.*) I caress her and talk in her ear, like this. (*Demonstrates talking into Tania's ear. Latoya and the boys, who had been playing, approach them.*)

CONSULTANT (*to the children*): Do you want to be there, too? (*The children surround Sonia and Tania and form a big hugging group.*)

SONIA (*laughing*): Cut it off! Leave me alone! (*But she keeps her arms around the children, and the children continue to laugh and hug her.*)

There are no miracles in these situations, nor is there any guarantee that Sonia and her children can maintain a successful reunification, particularly if she isn't helped through the transitional period. Under any circumstances, it's vital that they have a chance to sense and express their connection so that Sonia can feel her importance as a mother, and so that all can have a lifelong sense of "family"—no matter where they live and who else they connect to.

## Consolidating the Family Orientation

About 2½ years after the start of the training, a significant development took place: The coordinator, in partnership with child life staff, initiated a caregivers support group. Participation in the group was voluntary, and open to both clients and other adults involved in the child's life. Meetings were focused on helping participants rebuild or improve their relationships with other adults, particularly those who cared for the children, had custody, or were active in making decisions that affected the lives of the women and their children. The topics ranged broadly over relevant human relationships. One meeting, for instance, addressed conflicts that two couples were experiencing over their roles as men and women, focusing on issues of trust, respect, and being heard.

This development was especially significant because it was conceived and implemented autonomously by the staff. It was a move consistent with a family-oriented viewpoint, but it did not depend on the consultant's input. The staff memo announcing the formation of the caregivers group noted that, because of the basic assumption that sobriety is strengthened by building networks of support, the group would focus on exploring strategies to improve relationships and communication among parents and other adults involved in their children's lives. The tone and content of the memo indicated how far the staff had moved from keeping the family at arm's length to regarding them as indispensable assets in the lives of the clients.

# THE EXPANSION OF THE PROGRAM TO OTHER SERVICES

The original purpose of intervention was to facilitate the establishment of a family-oriented unit, staffed by people who had developed a broad framework and relevant skills, and who could continue the program within the department structure after the consultants left. As time went by, the vision evolved to include an extension of the basic ideas to other settings. The initiative was led by the coordinator of the perinatal program, who had assumed primary responsibility for expanding the family-centered orientation of the program.

The realization that the program must spread to other settings was based on an intimate knowledge of the women and the reality of their lives. They needed a variety of services, and the traditional organization of service delivery forced them to seek care through separate agencies located in different places. Aside from the toll on time and health, they were not easily able to sustain attendance at the perinatal unit. The coordinator began to search for a structure that would integrate some of the crucial services. Medical care, housing, and treatment for chemical dependency were primary. A major requirement for such a network was that all elements must be accepting of families and concerned that the women maintain contact with their children.

The ob/gyn department of the hospital was the principal site of program expansion. This department could provide medical services for the clients of the perinatal unit, obviating the necessity of traveling in order to obtain prenatal care. The department already had a high-risk clinic that provided special medical treatment for chemically dependent women. A liaison with the perinatal unit was, at the very least, a convenient arrangement for drug treatment referrals. Beyond that, members of the high-risk staff were generally convinced that the women should not be faced with separation from their infants. They knew that the women who came to them were reluctant to talk about the problems of homelessness, abuse, and foster care for fear their new infants would be taken away at birth. The staff believed that their clients would profit from a safe and helpful forum for discussing their issues.

To an extent, the groundwork for a cooperative network with a shared viewpoint was already in place. Regular case consultations were part of the perinatal program, and had been organized to draw in people who dealt with the woman and her family. Whenever the client was being treated medically at the high-risk clinic, members of that staff had been participants. With an informal, case-bound liaison already established, the high-risk clinic and the perinatal unit were able to implement a more formal working relationship in which the perinatal program looked to the ob/gyn department for referrals and medical services, and the high-risk clinic looked to the perinatal staff for training, on-site activities, and drug treatment. In that context, the coordinator instituted a weekly multidisciplinary meeting, bringing together staff from ob/gyn, the therapeutic community, and the child life department to discuss individual cases. The varied perspectives produced a richer picture and decreased the tendency to focus on pathology. For instance, when a child life worker commented that Sharon was a competent and sensitive mother, there was a shift in the perception of the drug counselor, who had always considered Sharon weak and flighty.

A third corner of this network concerned housing. Still oriented toward the difficulty of daily life for the population of the program, the coordinator looked into the possibility of keeping services within a manageable geographical area. He contacted a local shelter for homeless women, some of whom were pregnant and chemically dependent. In time, the three units became a viable system, referring clients back and forth and attempting to coordinate services.

It may be useful to note that the skills for promoting this network had little to do with family therapy. Instead, they involved sensitivity to the needs of the clients, a survey of community resources, some creativity in thinking "what if," and the ability to recognize key people in each setting who would be receptive and flexible. Given this combination, the basic ideas of the perinatal program could move into the high-risk section of the ob/gyn section of the hospital.

Training and consultation activities at the ob/gyn clinic took different forms. As already noted, the coordinator conducted a weekly meeting in which the staff of the clinic exchanged information with staff members from other services. In addition, there were training sessions with personnel of the high-risk clinic, focused on the concepts and skills that would be necessary for working with the women and their families.

Direct contact with the clients was an important aspect of the intervention. It began informally: Trainers would come to the clinic on the days the women came in for medical checkups, sit in on informal groups, activate discussions among the women, and help to clarify important issues. Perhaps the most significant development was the establishment of a new structure. Veterans of the perinatal program—women who had successfully participated in the program, delivered their babies, and remained drug free—became senior peer facilitators for women in the high-risk clinic. They worked with groups, drawing on the knowledge and leadership skills developed in the therapeutic community. The consultant became an advisor, offering support to the leader and sharing observations about leadership style and the content of the discussion.

The peer facilitators were particularly effective in encouraging the women to enter the drug program; not only did they come from the same community, they also represented a hopeful and successful outcome. When they brought their own infants to the meetings, they were implicitly underlining the mother–child bond as a force in conquering drug dependency. The presence of the baby was palpable evidence that the child had not been taken away, despite the mother's history of substance abuse. As time went on, these groups expanded, both in membership and focus. They came to include companions, older children, and extended family, and spawned a separate couples' group that met weekly to discuss the issues of relationships and parenting.

## WHAT HELPS A PROGRAM TO SURVIVE?

At present, what is the relationship between the perinatal program, as embedded in the therapeutic community, and the program in the high-risk clinic? The former has tended to dwindle and the latter is thriving. There's something of a mystery here. What elements give a program staying power?

Without question, the perinatal program was a successful experiment within the therapeutic community. For some years it grew, bringing at least minor changes to the therapeutic community, and producing desirable and verifiable effects. In an evaluation of what they term a multisystems, gender-specific model, the staff of the host department at the hospital have described the outcome of the intervention. They compare the first stage of the perinatal program, which addressed gender-specific needs but lacked a family orientation, with the second stage, which involved the intervention that was described earlier in this chapter. Using the hard data of urine toxicology and client retention, they report significant improvement for perinatal clients treated in Stage 2, as compared with those treated in Stage 1, whereas there was no such improvement for a control group of nonperinatal clients (Egelko, Galanter, Dermatis, & DeMaio, 1998). Yet, as time has gone by, the number of perinatal clients in the therapeutic community has decreased drastically, and the program is hardly maintained in that setting.

One explanation is obvious. The perinatal program was funded through a special grant and the money ran out. The coordinator moved to the ob/gyn setting as a consultant, and no staff at the therapeutic community was specifically attached to the program. But why didn't it become part of the ongoing operation of the department, particularly since members of the staff were sufficiently proud and impressed to publish the positive results? Was the original philosophy of the therapeutic community so powerful that it absorbed this smaller program? Was it a matter of personnel? Competing demands and other commitments?

Perhaps these are all the wrong questions; or perhaps the answers can only be suggested by looking at the success of the model in the high-risk clinic of the ob/gyn clinic. Here the approach is an integral part of ongoing procedures and the results continue to be satisfying. In this setting, there has been a notable increase in the delivery of infants who are full term, drug free, and born with a normal weight. As a consequence, many more of the women have retained custody of their babies.

Why did the program in the high-risk clinic take hold? We can only point to the several factors that are probably involved, and the fact that they are multiple may be part of the answer. In combination they become powerful.

One crucial factor is gender, and all that accompanies it. Ob/gyn concerns women; it deals with specifically female realities. That's not in itself a sufficient explanation, of course. Almost any woman is familiar with the gap between her needs and concerns, on the one hand, and the treatment she usually receives from ob/gyn services, on the other. But the staff of this particular service was knowledgeable, committed to the women in their care, and convinced that babies and family were an important part of life— even for chemically dependent women. They did not need to replace an established orientation with a new one; at least in attitude they were essentially there. They could understand and agree that the pregnancy was not an addendum to chemical dependency but the core of the woman's life, with implications for her current relationships and the future life of her baby. They were excellent candidates for training, for enhancing their skills, and for adapting their program in order to empower the women in their care.

It was also undoubtedly important that the coordinator continued to work with the staff of the high-risk clinic. His energy and creativity were essential to the growth of the program, even though the approach became institutional. Like many innovative efforts, the program lost a significant proportion of its original funding, in time, but the clinic continues to follow a family-oriented model.

Finally, the program is part of a broader network, which probably is part of the answer. There's a functional liaison with local shelters, and the family-based model is integrated with necessary medical and personal services. The program comes close, therefore, to the immediacy of life for this population in their own community. That may be one of the most salient explanations for its success. Whether for males or females, perinatal or not, a program for the multicrisis poor may need to be family oriented, integrated into daily life, and supported by the community in order to have staying power. Self-sustaining does not mean isolated; it means sufficiently supported from within its own context so that it can continue to function and grow in place.

# CHAPTER SEVEN

# Institutionalizing Children I

## RESIDENTIAL CENTERS

In this chapter, we will take a more historical and evaluative approach, looking at a variety of residential settings for children, noting changes over time, differences in approach, and the relationship of such institutions to families. We will then describe a short-term consultation with a residential center in which the aim was to change the nature of their service from a focus on children toward a family-friendly approach. Finally, we will present a general set of recommendations for residential centers that work with children.

## FROM PAST TO PRESENT: THE EVOLUTION OF ATTITUDES AND PRACTICES

History tells us that in the Middle Ages cities cordoned off their undesirables: the retarded, the psychotic, the poor. They were herded onto "Ships of Fools" and sent down the river until they reached other cities. The channeling of the odd and different into secluded centers began in 1656 with the founding of the Hôpital Général, when all the strange and psychotic people in Paris were hospitalized for what was considered "their own protection" (Foucault, 1965). It was at this point that the medical establishment claimed ownership of the labels defining mental health and illness and declared itself judge of when internment was necessary.

The power of the establishment to make such decisions has a parallel in today's society, where residential centers for children are often utilized as a solution for behavioral problems. The tendency to separate difficult children from their parents through institutional placement is more pronounced, however, when the families are poor and involved with social services. Under these circumstances, the department of welfare, mental health professionals, and the judicial system often act *in loco parentis*, taking on the job of protecting the children by placing them in special settings.

There are two assumptions behind this procedure: first, that the families not only are helpless to control or heal their children but generally are the source of pathology; and, second, that prevention and healing depend on removal of the children from their pathogenic context to a safe and neutral place. It follows from this perspective that the children should be placed in institutions where treatment can be provided, and that in time they will emerge, stronger, healthier, and ready to return to their families.

In this organization of the process, it's assumed that a child can move freely from home to institution and from institution to home, changing for the better with each crossing. It's also assumed that, when finally released, the child will find a family that has kept an open place for its absent member and will welcome the return with ease and gratitude. But the transition is often difficult. Child and family may not adapt easily to each other when they're reunited, and if we take a systemic perspective we understand why. The boundaries between institution and family have usually been tightly defined during the period of placement, despite the fact that permeable boundaries would have allowed more preparation for the future. And there has usually been little emphasis on family reorganization, although new family patterns often are essential for a successful reunion.

If systemic ideas have not been important in residential centers, what has been emphasized, and how have services been organized? It's useful to look at the evolution of such institutions over the past decades, noting the guiding point of view and the organization of their services—as well as indications of change over time. In the next sections, therefore, we will describe four settings covering a span from the 1950s through the 1980s. They have partly been selected because one author (S. M.) served on the staff of each and knew the institution well, but they also illustrate basic ideas and trends. Like most such institutions, all were supportive of children, aiming to alleviate problems and to prepare their charges for life outside the center, and all four were well staffed, well respected, and considered effective in their time. They varied in their view of the locus of pathology and their approach to treatment, but none of the three earlier institutions carried the emphasis that we highlight in this book: Diagnosis of the individual should be embedded in an understanding of the family, and treatment must include family and context.

We first will describe three institutions that were prominent during the 1950s and 1960s, noting the central ideas around which they were organized, and detailing the process through which the third institution shifted its focus and became involved with families. We then will describe an institution for children that developed a family focus during the 1970s, incorporating this perspective into its organization and treatment procedures.

## The 1950s and 1960s: Three Residential Centers

### Hawthorne Cedar-Knolls

In the 1950s, Hawthorne Cedar-Knolls was an institution for emotionally disturbed children, located on the outskirts of New York City and run by the Jewish Board of Guardians. Initially a sectarian institution, it was already nonsectarian by the 1950s, with a large number of children from other ethnic minorities. Most came originally from urban neighborhoods. The children lived in cottages under the supervision of cottage parents and there was a continuous monitoring of life in the milieu. However, the heart and head of the place was in the treatment center, where the children had individual sessions conducted primarily by social workers trained in psychodynamic psychotherapy.

This, of course, was the practice of most institutions at the time. The focus was on the individual child, and there was little room to consider the families and neighborhoods from which the children had come, or to assess their role in shaping behavior. An incident from this period illustrates the orientation of thinking and treatment at this institution: A young, sexually promiscuous adolescent spent most of the time during therapeutic sessions in obvious attempts to seduce her therapist. In discussions with a supervisor, the therapist was advised to explain transference and countertransference to the girl, and to indicate that a sexual response would not be useful for treatment. It never occurred to the supervisor or therapist that it would be important to explore her social background, or the way in which sexuality was a transactional coin in her community, or the possibility of sexual abuse in her family. While we're more alert to social forces now, it's still not uncommon for institutions to function with this same individual orientation, in which the context of the child is not considered part of the significant data.

At Hawthorne Cedar-Knolls, the immediate context—in the form of group life—was monitored by the staff but was given little consideration as a dynamic force. Yet the child group was powerful and controlled a good deal of behavior. It was guided by its own system of values and justice, as the following incident suggests: The wallet of a therapist was missing one day, not an unusual occurrence in itself, and such matters were usually handled by the staff through the cottage parents. However, in this instance the therapist explained the problem to the child who was known as the leader of the group. That evening, after a "kangaroo court," the wallet was returned and the perpetrators chastised by the children themselves. But this process was unusual; in general the informal organization of group life was not explored or utilized.

## The Residential Centers of Youth Aliyah

These centers, in Israel, had a different orientation. Unlike U.S. institutions that emphasized the individual, these centers focused on the organization and power of the group. First established for adolescent and preadolescent children who had come from Europe to Israel as survivors of the Holocaust, they later expanded to include children from Yemen, Morocco, Tunisia, and other Arab countries, as well as India and Iran.

The first step in absorbing this microcosm of the world's children took place on the kibbutzim. Here the children lived in groups under the guidance of an educational leader. They went to school, worked part of the time, and participated in the ongoing life of the kibbutz. For some of the children, the transition from one culture to another presented a hurdle that was too high to jump. Given the tight social organization of the kibbutz, their emotional distress and aberrant behavior were considered unacceptable, and it was deemed necessary to move them to another setting.

The children were sent to residential institutions run by Youth Aliyah, an agency concerned with absorbing young immigrants into the Israeli culture. In these institutions, the educational ideology and social structure were essentially the same as that of the kibbutzim. The children were organized in small groups around an educational leader. The therapeutic and educational focus was on the milieu and the life of the group. There were individual counselors for children who showed serious disturbances, but personalized therapy was not the rule. In any event, the orientation of such counseling was different from that of U.S. therapists. These counselors had been trained in the European tradition of *heil pedagogues* (educational therapists), and some followed the teachings of the Russian educator Makarenko (1973), who maintained that the consequences of misbehavior by any individual member must fall on the entire group.

Neither Hawthorne Cedar-Knolls nor the Youth Aliyah centers included families in their therapeutic work. Family factors were not part of the dominant ideology and were irrelevant for the treatment. In each setting, it was expected that therapeutic change would occur within the institution, and that it would then transfer to the world outside.

## The Wiltwyck School for Boys

In this respect, the Wiltwyck School for Boys was no different, at least throughout most of its history. It was a residential center for boys labeled as juvenile delinquents and referred by the courts. Most came from black and Spanish Harlem in New York City. The institution was located outside the city, with the evident intention of providing distance from the negative influence of disturbed families and urban culture. The school emphasized behavior control, maintaining a "token economy" to quantify rewards and punishments. In addition, each child had a therapist, usually a social worker, who saw him for individual, psychodynamically oriented sessions. The institution was open to change, however, counting among its board members some influential individuals who were alert to social trends, and who represented creative thinking in the area of mental health.

During the 1960s, President Lyndon Johnson announced that the country was embarked on a "War on Poverty," stimulating an increase in the attention paid to poor families and in the development of services to meet their needs. At that point, Wiltwyck became interested in the families that had begotten the children who populated the school. The staff had no ready ideas for working with the families and no skills for integrating families into therapeutic sessions. However, change was in the air, and the field of mental health was offering new possibilities for exploration. Ideas about family systems and family therapy were developing in California, Washington, DC, and New York, and were spreading across the country. These new ideas were exciting to the team of professionals who had come to Wiltwyck to explore new forms of treatment. The determination of this team to work with families marked a watershed in the history of institutions for children, and the focus on poor families was unique.

Technology was helpful in the effort to break new ground. The Wiltwyck group tore down a wall, built a one-way mirror, installed a video camera system, and declared themselves family therapists—ready to work with families who had been considered unreachable. They invented techniques as they went along, meeting families, growing more comfortable with the process, and learning. In the end, they devised an extended session with three stages: First, two therapists met with the whole family; then one met with the parent(s) while the other met with the siblings; and, in the third stage, the family reassembled to meet with both therapists. The purpose of the three stages was to clarify how different subsystems organized the thinking and behavior of family members.

After each session, the therapists and observers met to discuss the session and learn from the experience. Over time, they developed a set of active techniques for therapeutic interventions, based on these exploratory efforts and on their growing understanding of families.

The work at Wiltwyck has been described in a book called *Families of the Slums* (S. Minuchin, Montalvo, Guerney, & Schumer, 1967). It seems useful to quote from the discussion of the

Wiltwyck families in that book, bringing into focus how, 30 years ago, the stresses of urban poverty were seen as shaping the organization of poor families.

The following excerpt describes the functioning of the families, and captures features that guided the evolution of this new therapeutic approach. It should be noted that, for the first time, child behavior and development were described as part of the interpersonal transactions among family members. The focus was on the family as a system rather than on the child alone.

One essential feature of the family and home environment is its impermanence and unpredictability. These characteristics make it difficult for the growing child to define himself in relation to his world. . . . Objects and events have a transient quality. A bed shared by two or more children can be turned over to a different child or to a semi-permanent visitor while its original occupants are crowded into a section of another bed. The geography of the home and its arrangements impede the development of a sense that "I have my place in the world." Meals have no set time, order, or place. A mother who prepared four individual and different dinners one day, according to the wishes of the children, will prepare nothing another day, so that the children have to look in closets for available food, making their meals out of potato chips and soda.

Interpersonal contacts have these same erratic and impermanent qualities. In these large families, care of the young children is divided among many figures. Mothers, aunts, grandmothers, as well as older siblings, care for the young child. Sometimes they shower him with stimulation, and at other times he is left alone for long periods while he wanders through the house unattended. There can be elements of security in this multiple care, but danger lurks in those periods when the child is lost in the interstices of responsibility. Multiple, erratic nurturing figures can increase the child's sense of an unstable world and hinder his movement from a diffuse to a more focused sense of self.

In the socialization of the child, these families seem to be characterized by two major features: parents' responses to children's behavior are relatively random and therefore deficient in the qualities that convey rules which can be internalized; and the parental emphasis is on the control and inhibition of behavior rather than on guidance.

. . . Patterns of parental reaction operate like traffic signals; they carry the instructions of "don't" at the moment, but they do not carry instructions for behavior in the future. . . . The child cannot determine what part of his behavior is inappropriate. As a result, he learns to define the limits of permissible behavior by reacting mostly to his parents' mood responses. He learns that the "don'ts" of behavior are related to the pain or power of the mother or other powerful figures. "Don't do this because I say so," or "Don't do this because you make me nervous," or "Don't do this or I'll beat you." Lacking norms to regulate behavior, and caught in experiences that hinge on immediate interpersonal control, the children need continuous parental participation to organize their interpersonal transactions. The transactions are inevitably ineffective. They perpetuate a situation in which an overtaxed mother responds erratically to a confused child, who behaves in ways that will assure him of continuous contact with an outside controlling figure." (S. Minuchin et al., 1967, pp. 193–194)

The type of family therapy developed by the Wiltwyck team sprang from these observations of the family as a system. Since family members communicated in ways that seemed chaotic, expressing feelings but no clear message, the staff devised techniques directed at the clarification of meaning. Because control moved suddenly from ignoring deviance to responses that were violent, and because the responses were frequently global, the staff evolved techniques to identify the triggers at an earlier point, and worked with the family on developing responses that were moderate in affect and clearly targeted. As family members were not used to the exploration of inner feelings, tending to act out affect in confused transactions, the team worked on techniques that would facilitate the understanding of relationships and would help the family explore new patterns.

In all, what developed was a therapy geared to perceived family needs, aiming to create a direction and a sense of hope in the family. The idea of the staff was that people would learn to function competently in the social laboratory of their own family, and that they would be able to transfer their new competence to the demanding context of their difficult and poverty-stricken lives. From our current perspective, these efforts seem politically naive, since they excluded the realities of the environment, but they were revolutionary for their day. It was the first time that the family was considered the source of healing rather than only the source of pathology. And it was also the first time that a family-based treatment procedure to combat juvenile delinquency was devised and implemented.

After a while, it became an accepted fact that the family must be involved in a child's treatment, and that many of the procedures in this residential center required modification. Intake was revised, home visits became more frequent, and the staff began to include family members in their reactions to the child's behavior at the institution. Like many stories in the field of mental health, this story unfortunately had an ambiguous ending. The grant that had supported the project ran out and team members moved on to other activities. The institution relocated, found itself in financial difficulties, and eventually was closed down. The legacy of the program, however, extended well beyond the life of Wiltwyck. The structural school of family therapy, with its emphasis on active therapeutic intervention, sprang from this experience, exerting a profound influence on family therapy throughout the 1970s and 1980s.

## The 1970s and 1980s: The Philadelphia Child Guidance Clinic

With family therapy a growing discipline, and the experience of Wiltwyck already part of institutional history, it was possible to plan new settings that incorporated changing ideas about families and institutions. The opportunity to implement such a plan arose in the 1970s, when the Philadelphia Child Guidance Clinic prepared to build its new center. The director (S. M.) and the architect shared the idea of an institution with open boundaries. Children would be able to move from an outpatient facility to a day hospital to inpatient facilities, and vice versa. The inpatient facility would have two apartments for the short-term hospitalization of families. Children's Hospital, with which the clinic was affiliated, would provide medical care for the children, while the staff of the clinic would offer consultation about the psychological problems of the hospital's pediatric patients. The outpatient arm of the clinic was to be expanded, actively reaching out to the local community. The basic idea was to organize the institution so that it could provide a continuum of family-centered care and services.

The inpatient unit is most relevant for our discussion. It was organized as an open facility, working in collaboration with the families of children who were the identified patients. Intake extended over two or more sessions, beginning with a family interview. At that time, a contract was drawn up between family and clinic about the goals of treatment and the obligations of each party toward the achievement of those goals. The contract focused on the changes that the family expected from the child while in the institution, as well as the family changes that would be necessary to support the child's successful return home.

Treatment was a combination of milieu, individual, and family therapy. The family sessions included all members of the staff who worked with the child: teachers, nurses, and child care workers, as well as the family therapist. The parents were asked to visit the school to observe the child's behavior in that setting, and parents and teachers together set the academic goals. Home visits were an essential part of treatment. They were not part of the reward or punishment structure within the institution, and they were never canceled because of the child's disobedient or aggressive behavior.

Plans for termination began at intake. A child was expected to stay on the inpatient unit for only a brief period. Therefore, it was necessary to discuss family changes and plans for discharge during the initial contacts. Once a child returned home, therapy continued at the outpatient facility, with clinicians from the inpatient unit participating in family sessions during the period of transition.

There was a good deal of theory behind this work, and a continuous evolution of new interventive techniques. But, what is important here is the formal structure of the inpatient unit, since it became a model for subsequent consultations with residential centers. The structure expressed our basic view: When a child enters a residential setting, the institution is making a family intervention—knowingly or unknowingly. If the institution focuses on the child alone, ignoring the family patterns in which the child's behavior is embedded, treatment is likely to be ineffective. The institution must be structured with open boundaries, incorporating the family into the life of the child at the institution and including family members in clinical interventions.

## MOVING ON: CREATING CHANGE IN A RESIDENTIAL CENTER

We come now to the 1990s, and to the current challenge of transforming residential centers into settings that are friendly to families. How is it possible to turn systemic concepts into powerful tools, capable of affecting the way an institution is organized and the way it implements procedures?

We present here an example of a consultation that stimulated change through a relatively brief intervention. Many of our training programs with residential institutions have lasted a year or more, but some have been considerably shorter. It seems most useful to describe a short-term consultation, since the concentrated time period highlights the details of specific steps, and also suggests that a brief but intensive intervention is an economic way to begin the process of change.

In presenting our work with the Ridge Center, we will be drawing on a particular consultation, but we also have included details from other centers in order to provide a composite picture of the approach.

## The Ridge Center: A Short-Term Consultation

The Ridge Center was a traditional residential institution located on the outskirts of a large metropolitan area. When the director contacted Family Studies, he requested a consultation that would help them to improve their services. According to his description, the institution had modified its individual orientation over the past 5 years and was now attempting to incorporate a family approach into its procedures. However, they were experiencing some problems. The director was requesting both an evaluation of their procedures and suggestions for change. It was agreed that the consultation would take 4 days and would be held at the institution.

The consultation began in the usual way, with a preliminary meeting between the consultants and the executive leadership of the center. Present were the executive director, the director of clinical services, the head nurse, the director of social services, the staff psychiatrist, and the consultant. The staff described a residential center for 50 to 60 school-age and early adolescent children, most of whom were from African-American or Latino families. The children lived in cottages run by a child care worker and most went to school at the center, although some attended schools in the community. Each child had individual and family therapy with staff social workers.

Two basic concerns emerged at this meeting. The leadership of the center was concerned with the length of stay. Over the history of the Ridge Center, children had remained at the institution an average of 2 years. The center had changed procedures and included families, but the length of stay remained fixed at about 18 months. One area of concern, therefore, focused on this problem: Which organizational procedures were maintaining children in the institution longer than necessary, and what could they do about it? The head of clinical services also was concerned about the parents, who were now included but were essentially passive and tended to become dependent. How could the center foster initiative in the parents instead of dependency?

With these institutional problems as the focus of consultation, a plan developed for utilizing the 4 days, including an assessment of what was happening and recommendations for change. For the first day, the plan called for a visit to the various sites at the center, separate interviews with the group of child counselors and the group of teachers, and a meeting with a group of consumers—parents of children who had been or were still at the center. The second day would focus on the process of intake. The third day would be concerned with treatment interventions, and the fourth would involve feedback, discussion, and a set of recommendations. While this plan emerged from discussion at the preliminary meeting, it's actually generic. The coverage would apply to almost any institution, although the details might vary according to the availability and convenience of participants.

### The First Day: Visit to the Center

The day started with a visit to the children's quarters. They were neat and well kept, but they displayed the usual lack of concern for aesthetics characteristic of most institutions, as well as a comparative dearth of details that seemed personal to each child. In every cottage, and in the school, there were blackboards in prominent places listing the rules of behavior. The left-hand column listed the wrong behaviors and the points a child would lose as a result of misbehaving in the dining room or disrupting the classroom. The right-hand column described and quantified good behavior.

This was a clear indication of the token economy, tied to behavior, that is so common in residential centers. For the consultant, this procedure was questionable and not geared to the principles of child development. Children need periods of invisibility while they experiment and fumble. A sense of being watched and held accountable for every move curtails spontaneity. However, the consultant made no comment, since the immediate milieu was not of primary importance in this situation. A consultant needs to set the priorities and pass over certain matters. That principle applies to any intervention, whether with families or larger systems. In fact it would apply if an institution conducted an internal assessment of their organizational procedures in order to plan for change.

The meeting with the child care workers was something of a novelty for this group. Although accustomed to meetings that tapped specific information about the children, they were seldom asked for broader opinions. They expressed the kind of complaints that often arise if this group is contacted, and which have some validity. They didn't feel respected by the clinicians and thought their information was not valued. Although they knew more about the children, in some respects, than did the social workers, they had no way of communicating directly with the families. Child care workers reported to clinicians about the behavior of the child in the cottage, and this information was communicated to the family. The workers neither observed nor participated in family sessions, so their understanding of the family and how the child fit in was always through the eyes of the therapist. Child care workers experienced the barrier between themselves and the families as impermeable, and they regarded this as an indication of their low standing in the hierarchy of the institution.

The discussion with the child care workers triggered two ideas for the consultant. One was that the situation required a general institutional review. Decisions about the role of child care workers in relation to client families belonged in-house. It was important, however, that the perspective of the workers be understood, and that their functions be modified to fit more closely with the ultimate aims of the center. A productive review would require the participation of the workers, the executive staff, and the clinicians.

The second idea concerned the implications of this "barrier" for the families. The distance between the child care workers and the family sent a message to the parents concerning the child's daily life at the institution: "Don't touch; don't ask; don't enter. This isn't your concern." Again, that aspect was probably out of staff awareness and worth bringing up for discussion.

The meeting with the teachers was discouraging, especially at an institution seeking to maintain a family orientation. Without exception, the teachers had only negative comments about the parents. They were invested in the children and described themselves as exerting considerable effort to counter the destructive effects of past experience, but had little sympathy for the welfare population. They focused on their lack of responsibility and damaging relationships with their children, and generalized these criticisms to the families of the children in their care. Given such strong reactions, it was startling to learn that the teachers did not know the families at all. Families were never invited to visit the school, observe classes, or meet with the teachers. The teachers could not answer specific questions about the background of any child, although they were generally critical of the families and the home environments.

The combination of minimal information with negative attitudes is one we have run into often, when the various people concerned with the same children must create images of each other from stereotypes. The foster care situation comes immediately to mind. Initially, foster parents may have negative opinions about the parents of their foster children, but their images are usually modified when they actually meet, begin to share information, and plan together for the child. An increase in teacher–parent contact at the Ridge Center would most likely change teacher attitudes. It might also promote the more active role for parents that the clinical director was seeking.

On the afternoon of the first day, the consultant met with the consumers. The center had invited two sets of parents whose children had been in the institution and were now at home, as well as two single mothers whose children had been at the center for over a year, and the parents of a child who had recently entered. All in all, a good sample.

The parents were intelligent observers of the situation, felt friendly toward the staff, and thought that the center had been helpful to their children. They talked about the need for increased communication between staff and parents, but these comments were vague and not very critical. They may have felt more unsure about the purpose of the meeting than did the child care workers or the teachers, but if their responses were guided by loyalty, that was a tribute to the institution. These parents were basically satisfied.

The meeting with the parents produced little new information. The consultant thought it useful, nonetheless. Such a meeting conveys a concrete message to the staff about the importance of dialogue with the families, particularly if the parents are encouraged to comment on the staff's behavior and suggest ways that families might become more involved. Conducted periodically, meetings between staff and parents might evolve into a productive forum.

## The Second Day: Intake

The second day was focused on intake procedures. The day began with an intake interview, observed through closed-circuit TV by both the consultant and staff. The family was Latino, with two parents in their 30s, an aggressive 10-year-old identified patient, and two younger siblings. The session was conducted by the intake social worker, with the staff psychiatrist participating as an observer. As usual, the family was preceded by a file from the referring hospital in which issues of child abuse and neglect were indicated as possibilities.

The interview was conducted by the intake social worker in a friendly, relaxed manner, and was relatively short—lasting about 45 minutes. For most of the session, the parents answered questions and described their son's difficulties, particularly during his hospitalization on the children's psychiatric unit from which he had come. After the session finished, the psychiatrist left with the child for an individual interview. The family was taken on a tour of the institution and the parents were asked to fill out forms for medical consent. The family was then reunited and went together to the child's cottage, which was empty, by design, of other children. Here they were formally introduced to the child care worker. They went then to the school, equally empty of children, where the same formality was repeated with the teacher. With that, the parents and the siblings left and the child remained at the center.

In debriefing the intake procedure, the consultant brought up one of the primary questions from the first meeting: "What can be done to decrease parent dependency and encourage parent initiative?" He suggested that the origins of the problem had been evident in the intake interview. Clearly, a family-oriented ideology coexisted with procedures that promoted a separation between family and institution.

The pro-family philosophy articulated by the executives dictated an intake process and treatment procedures that included the family. However, a concentration on the child, along with a peripheral role for the family, was still the most prominent aspect of the approach. The procedures indicated to parents that pathology was located in the child, and that the institution was equipped to handle the problem without any help. Parents were told, "We like you (pro-family), but you're not competent to deal with the child" (child-protective). Hidden behind the articulated ideology were traditional procedures, a holdover from the many years during which residential centers felt the need to protect children from the pathological influence of their families.

In the afternoon, the consultant conducted an intake with another family. The session lasted 1½ hours, suggesting by its length that time spent with the family was considered an important part of coming to know the child. The consultant focused on family functioning, and on the role of the family in maintaining the child's symptom. He emphasized areas of strength in family and child, encouraging family members to explore alternative ways of functioning that would increase the parents' competence, mobilize sibling supports, and change the child's symptoms. Finally, he questioned the need for residential treatment. He commented to the family that he had seen evidence that they had alternative ways of being that could be helpful, but that, of course, he didn't know the family or the child very well and he might be wrong. Since that was so, he asked the parents to convince him that residential treatment was necessary. The session ended with everyone agreeing that a stay in the institution could be useful, but the consultant said he was doubtful that the center could succeed without the help of the parents.

Subsequent discussion with the staff focused on differences between the two types of intake, including the distinct messages the parents had received about their participation in the child's treatment. The first intake was exploratory and respectful, with the parents as informants about the child's problems, but the real diagnostic session was conducted by the psychiatrist, who met with the child in an individual session. After the family session, contact with the parents took on the semblance of a sales pitch, reminiscent of some schools in which parents and children see manicured lawns and the staff describes the excellence of the program. The parents were not allowed to see a classroom or any other children, since the rules of confidentiality protected residents from the scrutiny of new consumers, and nobody invited the parents to talk to child care workers or teachers about their child's habits, favorite foods, preferred games, or attitudes about learning. The staff paid little attention to the families of new recruits, essentially tuning them out as they got on with their busy schedules, while the parents left with a sense of relief that the center would do its best for their son. If there was a sense of emptiness on their return home, they were unlikely to attribute it to the barriers that the institution had erected between them and their child.

The second intake focused on understanding the family as a whole and the child as a subsystem. The diagnosis centered on the family: how it functioned; what repetitive patterns appeared; what the sibling group was like; how the child fit into that group and into the family as a whole; what could be seen of rigidities, flexibility, and possibilities. The consultant encouraged dialogue among family members, taking a position as an observer of their conversations. He joined the family, supporting positive skills and possibilities in family members, and asked questions demonstrating his ignorance and his need to be educated in the ways of the family. In expressing his doubt of the center's capacity to help, and in accepting the parents' push for residential treatment, the consultant was communicating an important message: "Without you, I'm sure we will fail." His expression of concern and of qualified competence was an urgent invitation to the family to come to the center and to work together with the staff.

## The Third Day: Treatment

The focus of the next day was on treatment procedures. The staff interviewed a family in the morning and the consultant saw a different family in the afternoon. The first family included Melissa, a Puerto Rican single mother who was 35 years old; 12-year-old Pedro, who had been at the center for more than a year; and Mirta, his 14-year-old sister. This family had a history of impermanence. They had moved from a number of houses in rapid succession, and had been living in a homeless shelter for 6 months before Pedro came to the center. According to the records, he had been stealing since he was 3, first from his mother and later from neighbors and local stores.

The session, conducted by the family therapist on the staff, began with a friendly exchange of greetings. The therapist had a good relationship with the mother, although she never contacted the adolescent daughter, who was clearly bored and remained uninvolved throughout the session. Pedro was visibly pleased to see his mother. He told her at length about an incident at school in which other children had been rough with him. Melissa reacted sympathetically, advising him to talk with the teacher. She went on to bring him up-to-date on the family news, including the recent arrival of a relative from Puerto Rico. The therapist then began to talk with Pedro about how he was getting along, and the rest of the session was centered on the child. Afterward, the family went to the dining room, had lunch, said good-bye to Pedro, and returned to the city. The session had the aura of a pleasant visit for the family, interspersed with some individual therapy for Pedro.

In debriefing the session, the consultant commented that the therapist had a nice and friendly attitude toward the family, but that the session had been bland, without much leverage for change. He attributed that to the timing of the session, which was injected tangentially into the child's ongoing life at the center and had no urgency or emotional force. Because Pedro was now basically related to staff and children at the center, family members were paradoxically experienced as visitors. The family, in turn, had created new grooves that did not include Pedro, so he had become as peripheral to their ongoing life as they were to his.

The consultant suggested that, to make family therapy a useful tool, it generally should be conducted after a home visit, when the family brings the child back after a weekend together. While the child is at home, old patterns are reactivated as the family explores the possibilities of living together. When they bring the child back and all the participants are between two worlds, the therapist has the opportunity to probe family conflict, sample the sources of irritation that are still fresh, and explore novel possibilities.

This suggestion gave home visits a new meaning and a new importance. In light of that change, a staff member asked what would happen if a child misbehaved and the home visit needed to be canceled. Her question brought back the issue of the locus of treatment. If pathology is located within the child and therapy is aimed at individual dynamics, it may be necessary to focus on infractions of the rules. However, if the goal is successful reunification of the child with his or her family, home visits are an essential part of treatment and should not be canceled.

In the afternoon, the consultant interviewed a family composed of a grandmother, aunt, and 12½-year-old Joanna, who had been at the center for a little over half a year. The girl's mother had died of AIDS when Joanna was an infant, and she had been reared by Tessa, her grandmother, and Lilian, her aunt. Two years earlier, Lilian had moved to her own apartment, where she was now living with her boyfriend. Joanna had been shuttling between grandmother and aunt, who reportedly had different views about where she should live and how she should behave. She had been referred to the center because she was inattentive in school and had become increasingly depressed.

The consultant invited Joanna's individual therapist and child care worker to attend the session, as well as the family therapist. He started the session by saying that, since the child care worker would only be present at the beginning of the session, the family first might want to ask him about the child's life in the cottage. The grandmother asked whether Joanna was respectful and well behaved in the cottage, and Lilian wanted to know if Joanna had any friends, as she didn't seem to talk about that much. The child care worker was friendly and, after describing the routines at the cottage, he answered their questions, assuring them that Joanna never caused trouble and that the other girls liked her. However, she was still quite withdrawn and had few friends. When the child care worker left the session, he said he would be available if needed. The individual therapist was silent throughout the session, having indicated that she would simply be an observer in order to maintain the confidentiality of her relationship with Joanna.

After the child care worker left, the consultant became more active, bringing the conflict between grandmother and aunt to the foreground. Lilian wanted the child to come to live with her, but Tessa questioned her competence and her ability to control her niece. Given the nature of the pattern and the positive response of Joanna to Lilian, the consultant thought it important to probe the quality of the relationship between the girl and her aunt, and to explore the possibility that Joanna might go home to live with Lilian. He encouraged a dialogue between them. At the same time, he made a point of not responding when the grandmother interrupted, instead paying attention to the plan that Lilian and Joanna were exploring together. The session ended with a recommendation of increased home visits for Joanna at Lilian's apartment, and a suggestion that all three family members work out a way for Joanna to see her grandmother as well.

The discussion following the session focused on three areas: the inclusion of the child care worker in the session, the meaning of separating individual and family therapy, and the way in which the consultant had moved the session along. The consultant stressed the strategic importance of the child care worker's participation in the session as an indication of the family's right to know about the life of the child at the center. He then asked the group to explore the rationale for dividing individual and family therapy between two practitioners, each of whom was equally trained in both forms of treatment. Staff members suggested that one therapist would be in a better position to use information creatively if she assumed both individual- and family-oriented roles. There was also some discussion about using a second person as an occasional cotherapist or peer supervisor, rather than splitting functions and maintaining a careful and perhaps unnecessary confidentiality.

The staff was particularly interested in the therapeutic stance of the consultant, who had actively fomented disagreements and supported one member of the family over another. But they were also confused. What about neutrality and fairness? In the discussion that followed, the consultant made three points, two of which are generic for family therapy and one with particular relevance for this situation: First, bringing family conflict into the session is an essential part of the process of healing, and, without open exploration of their disagreements, a family is apt to remain deadlocked. Second, "unbalancing" the system creates leverage, the kind missing from the morning session, and can mobilize the family to participate more actively—although a skillful therapist may later shift his or her weight to support a different member if that seems useful. Finally, because there was some indication that Joanna was more comfortable and lively with her aunt than with her grandmother, and because Lilian was more attuned to the issues of a young adolescent, the consultant chose to support this combination. His choice was partly arbitrary, however, as his primary goal was to break the repetitive pattern that was depressing the child.

Some of these points are complex, and staff may not understand the rationale immediately, or be able to implement the bolder procedures when they do. The important part of the demonstration, however, was at a relatively simple level. As in the demonstration intake, this session suggested the importance of including a broad cast of characters, exploring family patterns, and mobilizing the family as active participants in the work of the institution.

## ANALYSIS AND RECOMMENDATIONS

The fourth day at the Ridge Center was used for feedback and discussion: a review of the points that had arisen on previous days and a presentation of recommendations for change. Rather than describing the activities of the last day at that particular institution, we will instead present a generic commentary that highlights issues and recommendations applicable to almost any residential setting for children. Some comments may be irrelevant for a particular setting, and some may seem impossible to implement under prevailing conditions. But according to our experiences, the issues are applicable to most institutions, and we have made the recommendations as generalizable as possible.

### Analysis

The issues fall into three categories: the institution as a setting, perceptions and attitudes, and staff training and orientation. Some details are specific to residential centers, but others hark back to general comments that we made in an earlier chapter about the obstacles to a family-friendly approach. They appear wherever services have traditionally been offered to individuals, and the staff must find their way past barriers they are almost unaware of in order to incorporate families into their work.

#### The Institution as a Setting

Because institutions vary in size, decor, atmosphere, and so forth, it's difficult to generalize about the impact of the setting on families. However, many residential centers are located in areas far from the neighborhoods where the children live, creating difficulties for family members, who must travel a distance in order to visit or participate in activities at the center.

The fact that most institutions are a place apart is no accident. Residential centers were created with the express purpose of isolating children from their customary environments. The decision to create distance was sometimes a form of punishment for the children and sometimes considered a protection for the outside population, but it was almost always intended as a way of counteracting the influence of minority ghettos and the pathogenic effects of the families. When institutions for children first sprang up, the length of stay was undefined but expected to be extensive, allowing sufficient time to inoculate the children before they returned home. During that period, it was an implicit policy to keep the families at a distance.

Times have changed, and long-term institutionalization is no longer a pervasive policy. Also in keeping with modern thinking, new residential centers are frequently small, serving ten to twenty children, and located in the catchment areas where their families live. The former type of institution still lingers, however, and children are sometimes placed in centers distant from their homes because of practical matters such as available openings, the particular diagnosis, and so forth. When that happens, the fact that a seemingly logistical matter is actually a psychological barrier between institution and family generally goes unrecognized.

## Perceptions and Attitudes

This second factor concerns how the family and the institution see each other. There are two primary but distinctive attitudes among families whose children are institutionalized. The first group opposes internment as a decision imposed by regulatory forces such as child welfare, social service agencies, or family court. The entire procedure is resented and the center becomes part of the enemy— the powerful other. The family must necessarily submit to control but will not feel like a partner. With these families, the center has a difficult but essential task. The staff must create bridges to reach the family and must surreptitiously address their anger from the very first contact.

The viewpoint of the second group is almost the complete opposite. They welcome institutional placement as a solution to their problems with the child, and may experience the institution as a boarding school or a better alternative to the neighborhood. Often they feel so incapable of handling the child that separation becomes an acceptable solution for resolving conflict. If that is the primary reaction, family members are glad to leave the responsibility for the child to the center. They hope it will do the job of returning a child who has changed and is now manageable. Families with this attitude are comfortable with traditional institutions that are oriented toward long-term treatment. If the aim is to involve the family, however, the staff must challenge their expectations, finding a way to involve them in the treatment of their child.

That task is often difficult. Institutional attitudes frequently militate against family involvement. The mind-set that perceives parents as pathogenic or inadequate is expressed by procedures that make parents invisible, or that hold them off as long as possible. In their most benign form, these procedures are part of the center's efforts to rescue the child. In a more corrosive form, such procedures reflect the attitude that parents will undo the work of the institution. The staff sets a high, sometimes unreasonable, standard for progress, holding the child at the center until they are absolutely certain of a successful termination. The intention is positive, of course, but few of us think we can work through all of our problems before we can live in the world. Furthermore, as time goes by and both child and family adapt to their current circumstances, the likelihood that they will make a smooth transition when the child is sent home is actually less certain rather than more so. Again, there are parallels to other situations, such as foster placement or internment in a drug program. The longer the stay, and the more feeble the contact between client and family during the period of separation, the more difficult the reunification—even if the treatment program for the client has made good progress.

Finally, the institution often sets up a paradox, albeit unwittingly. The staff expects family initiative as a sign that family members are really interested in the child, and they label the lack of parental participation as disinterest or resistance. However, they do not realize that they have conveyed a clear message of self-sufficiency: "We'll take care of it. We'll call you when we need you." Added to the sense of failure and inadequacy that any family feels when they must bring a child to an institution, the implicit message sinks deep. The family understands that they are neither wanted nor necessary.

## Staff Training and Orientation

Many of the attitudes discussed as institutional matters are expressed through the professional staff and don't need detailed repetition. The sense of institutional self-sufficiency, the high standards for termination, and the evaluation of families as pathogenic are all assumed by those in charge of the child's treatment. We indicated much earlier in this book that psychological training generally emphasizes inner dynamics and pathology: anger, anxiety, conflict, and the mismanagement of relationships. Working with the individual child, therapists at an institution often implement this agenda, and, when they expand to work with families, they may develop new methods without changing their basic orientation. They're usually not trained to search for areas of competence, and have little skill or experience in moving beyond repetitive patterns in order to explore alternatives in the family repertoire. It's a skewed orientation toward human nature, weighing against a productive and empowering collaboration with families.

## Recommendations

Recommendations follow, of course, from an analysis of the issues, and some specifics have already been suggested. Previous discussion has touched on matters such as planning for the location of residential centers, as well as issues of staff training and orientation. The latter would need to be addressed through seminars, case discussion, and supervision, in order to bring family-oriented attitudes to the foreground and enhance the confidence and skill of staff members as they work with families.

The primary focus of our recommendations, however, concerns the organization of procedures at the institutional level. What follow are recommendations for intake, for contact with the family during the period of the child's residence at the center, and for termination.

### Intake

An institution must develop procedures to make parent participation *necessary*. It's not sufficient to welcome families and give them options, or to encourage them to come to the center. It's not even enough to schedule family therapy sessions. The institution must convey the message that the family is expected to participate in the child's life at the center, and that the center cannot succeed without them.

Start at intake. Convey the idea of partnership from the beginning. Schedule a full day for intake so that the family can meet all relevant staff, including child care workers, teachers, and therapists. Invite parents to observe the ongoing life at the center: a class, an activity or recreational period. Parents should get some feel for what a day at the center is like for their children, and they should be accompanied by a staff member who can explain what they're seeing and can illustrate the philosophy of the institution.

Question the need for admission. The intake procedure should carry a strategic stance of uncertainty. Parents need to take the responsibility for requesting that their child stay at the center. If the center accepts their request, it becomes the ally of the family, responsive to its needs. Of course the discussion will proceed differently if the family is resentful than if it is all too willing, but in either case the family must experience an active role in arriving at a decision.

A discussion of this nature focuses the intake on the reasons for residential treatment, and on the goals for the child, the family, and the institution. In most cases, it's useful to create an actual document stating the goals, to be signed by both the family and the staff. That commits both parties to a collaborative effort, and establishes intake as a healing ritual.

A focus on goals also highlights the conditions for discharge. It incorporates the question of termination into the process of admission. Unless we think that residential treatment is a life sentence, that emphasis is highly appropriate. It reminds the staff that they must focus on strengths and possibilities, and it introduces a note of hope for the family. There's light at the end of the tunnel.

The primary purpose of intake is the forging of a partnership, the joining of two systems on a healing trek. Everything else is secondary, including the often lengthy process of filling out official forms. That process is likely to create a bureaucratic feeling, and it dilutes the sense of mutual responsibility. Whenever possible, details of that kind should be left for a second interview.

Since they know their child so well, the parents should be asked to describe details of the child's development during the first contact, and the worker should interview them about the child's interests, preferred food, favorite games, and special friends. They should also be encouraged to bring objects from home that the child can keep at the center, and that will form a symbolic link to a previous and future life.

While it's important for the parents to leave feeling well-informed, they should not go home believing that everything has been resolved. Leave room for some concern. They must grasp the uncertainty of the staff undertaking to help a child who has been separated from familiar people and circumstances. The family must feel, in a sense, that they have been admitted to this institution along with their child.

## The Period of Residence

Once the child has been admitted, other procedures are important. Basically, the institution must maintain and increase family participation in the life of the child.

It's in the nature of residential placement that the sense of separation between child and family increases with time. Emotional distancing is a natural phenomenon that should not be labeled as family resistance. The center must nurture the connection through concrete procedures. It's insufficient to reiterate that the family is necessary to treatment, or even to conduct therapy skillfully. The family must be part of unfolding events, much as they would be if their child were living at home. A worker might contact the family to say, for instance, "Something has happened to Joe's work in school and we're puzzled about the cause. Can you help us?" The request can come in the form of a telephone conversation, a letter, or a suggestion that the family make an extra trip to visit the school and discuss the situation.

Nor does the communication have to concern problems, even though that is the time-honored reason why most institutions—including almost all schools—contact parents. It can be about progress, achievements, milestones: "Joe's been doing very well in school but his accomplishments still aren't apparent to him. Could you come to celebrate with him? Could you bring some reward?" Sometimes the staff can contact the family just to exchange information: "Mary fell down during soccer practice and she skinned her knee. It's nothing serious and it's OK now, but she was upset and a little frightened. Just thought you should know. " The content doesn't matter. Once that idea is ingrained, the staff will find opportunities constantly surfacing. Anything is valid as long as it indicates that, although the institution is in the caretaking role, the parents are the responsible people.

It's important that this contact with the family be visible to the child. Joe and Mary need to understand that the staff and their families are partners.

During the child's stay at the institution, part of this communication may occur between the child care worker and the family, but the clinical staff has an important role extending beyond the officially scheduled therapy sessions. Sometimes the staff will make contact by phone or letter, and sometimes a clinician may bring a child home on a weekend pass, taking advantage of the opportunity to hold a session in the family's own setting. Receiving staff members on their home turf can strengthen family pride. It's important, however, that the family see a visit or a home-based session as part of the clinical effort on behalf of the child, and not as an inspection of the home or of family members.

Whatever the level of ongoing contact, the staff and family should meet at monthly intervals to reevaluate the treatment program and calibrate the goals.

## Termination

Residential treatment is actually a continuum of care, beginning with intake and moving to termination. Home visits should increase over time, as a way of testing the possibility of discharge from the center. Discharge should be considered possible when the family and child can live together and treatment can continue on an outpatient basis. It's always best to continue contact through the period of transition. If possible, a staff person should attend some sessions at the outpatient facility, and should visit with the family, on occasion, if a meaningful relationship has been established.

With the introduction of such changes, most children should be able to leave an institution within a year, or, in some cases, in less than 6 months. There are provisos, of course, related to such factors as the severity of the child's problems, the family response, and the age of the child. In general, our recommended procedures are best suited for preadolescent and early adolescent children, somewhere between 8 to 13 years of age. Younger children benefit more from other types of treatment and, for the most part, do not belong in institutions at all. Older adolescents require some modifications that bring group approaches to more prominence, and that highlight issues of autonomy and selectivity in their relationships.

Whenever young people must be institutionalized, however, and whatever their ages, we have found it important to be aware of the significant people in their lives, and to work with them. In this chapter, we have presented a model that relates to families as partners in treatment when their children are institutionalized. In our experience, the process is productive for the child, the family, and their future together.

CHAPTER EIGHT

# Institutionalizing Children II

## PSYCHIATRIC WARDS

$\mathbf{A}$mong residential services for children, child psychiatric wards present a particular reality and deserve a separate exploration. That's partly because the staff on a psychiatric ward carries a unique tradition, orientation, and status, but it's also because hospitals serving the children of the urban poor are often embedded in communities with special qualities and needs.

## PSYCHIATRIC SERVICES AND THE FAMILY

In most of the settings we have described, the staff expects to carry out their responsibilities without the help or interference of others. In psychiatric settings, however, where the staff is professional, well trained, and accustomed to both responsibility and respect, their sense of self-sufficiency is apt to be especially strong. A senior psychiatrist at a major hospital, in a tone of bemused self-criticism, described the operation of the children's service as analogous to a garage: "You leave your disabled child parked with us for a while, and when your child is fixed we'll call you to come and pick him up."

Psychiatric services are rooted in the medical model, and thus the staff has always been accustomed to working with the individual patient. That focus seems natural, and in the current climate is combined with an increasing emphasis on the biological basis of thoughts and emotions. The staff concentrates on exploring the inner world of fears, fantasies, anger, and confusion—attending to this distress by rearranging meaning, prescribing medication, or both.

Oddly enough, social disorganization in U.S. ghettos has reinforced this orientation. As homelessness, drug addiction, and violence have increased, social services have been unable to contain the flood of social pathology, and the child-psychiatric staff in troubled neighborhoods finds itself faced with byproducts of social distress. Poorly trained to deal with this situation, the staff tends to focus on their own area of expertise: the internalized organization of experience. When the inner world of the individual is the focus of diagnosis and treatment, the social context to which a patient may be responding remains outside of staff awareness.

For the population with which we're concerned, the nature of the psychiatric staff presents another problem. The staff is generally middle class, introspective, articulate, and psychologically oriented. The families, however, are from lower socioeconomic groups that often are ethnically diverse; their members tend to be more action prone and less emotionally reserved. Arriving at the hospital with their children, the families feel out of their element. Some have language difficulties, making communication with the staff awkward, and because many already had negative experiences with helping systems, their first reactions are tinged with suspicion. Expecting cooperation and respect, the staff may interpret family reticence as resistance to treatment.

Often, the staff is inadequately trained to work with families, a point we have made in almost every context. They are unaccustomed to involving the family in ward activities, highlighting home visits, or dealing with the prolonged estrangement that is the natural consequence of separating family and child. The staff builds an understanding of the family by exploring internalized constructs and interpreting the behavior of the child on the ward. Under these conditions, the staff sees only part of the equation. The responses of family members are invisible, and only the inferred family can be dealt with in therapy.

Even if motivated to work with family and child together, staff members may lack the necessary skills. What we have noticed in their first efforts at such work is that the staff often cannot translate the very skills they have honed so carefully for child therapy. They may be critical of the families, although they seldom are with children, and may find it difficult to be inventive and relaxed in a family session, even if play and friendly contact form a large part of their work with the young.

In reality, the first steps toward working effectively with families are conceptual rather than technical. The staff must accept the idea that the child is embedded in a larger social context, and that when a child is admitted to the hospital, the family has been admitted as well. Every move the hospital makes, and every change in the child, will reverberate in future family interactions—whether attended to or not. With that mind-set, it would become clear that assessment and healing require skills that can mobilize the forces in a child's life, and that the goals for change must go beyond the dynamics and biology of the young patient.

That, of course, is not the prevalent mind-set on most psychiatric wards. Spurred by the current emphasis on short-term hospitalization, treatment is increasingly defined as a search for the right medication, and it has become typical for poor children to move from one institution to another. The hospital stay may be short, but the child may subsequently remain in foster care or a residential center for a lengthy period of time.

The following description of a consultation illustrates alternative ways of working. In the staff presentation of the case, one sees the acceptance of internment as an inevitable environment for the child, the staff's overriding preoccupation with medication, and the peripheral role of the family. The intervention of the consultant disrupts this organization, mobilizes the family as participants, and opens the traditional approach to review and discussion.

## Questioning the Self-Evident:
## A Case Consultation

In the 1990s, the mental health department of a northeastern state asked one of the authors (S. M.) to conduct a consultation at a children's ward in a state hospital. The main purpose was to provide an example of a family-oriented approach that could be used for teaching and discussion purposes throughout the statewide system. The department was also concerned with an issue discussed in Chapter 7: Children were staying in the hospitals too long. The problem disturbed administrators for obvious financial reasons, but professionals were more concerned with the effects of lengthy internment on the children's development.

During preliminary discussions, the consultant suggested that the staff of the hospital select the case of a child who had been in their care for more than a year. They chose Mark, a 10-year-old boy, who had spent a year on another psychiatric ward before coming to this unit.

The consultation took place in 1 day and the process had four parts. Given the different circumstances, the steps are not identical to the four-part process at the Ridge Center. However, both procedures reflect the same systemic orientation in which information, intervention, and feedback involve a broad cast of relevant people in family and professional staff. In this case, the consultant first met with the staff who had daily contact with Mark and then interviewed Mark and his family. After the session, he met again with the staff, who had been observing the session from behind the one-way mirror, and discussed his recommendations. The fourth part opened up to a wider audience. The consultation had been videotaped and was the basis of a closed-circuit conference for child psychiatric workers around the state.

Excerpts of the consultation are presented below. They illustrate the fundamental conceptual differences between the traditional treatment that had been guiding the work with the child and a treatment that highlights inclusion of the family.

## The Meeting with the Staff

Nine members of the staff had something to do with Mark's control and well-being, and all were present at the meeting: individual therapist, child counselor, psychiatrist, family therapist, teacher, art therapist, nurse, social work intern, and psychologist—who was also the unit director. This part of the consultation lasted 1½ hours. Since it was evident that the psychiatric presentation of Mark represented the dominant ideological discourse in the ward, we transcribe that section of the meeting in full.

CONSULTANT: Is Mark on medication?

PSYCHIATRIST: Yes. The ADD [attention deficit disorder] was what first came to our attention. He was on Ritalin when he came to us. They ended up there with a combination of 40 milligrams of Ritalin, 60 milligrams of Mellaril, and 3 milligrams a day of Klonopin, with the aggression and the attentional problem as the target symptoms. The separation-anxiety issues were not particularly a focus of the medication efforts.

Here we tried him on Klonopin for a time then took him off, and the difference between on and off is enormous. He is effectively unworkable in class or cottage without medication.

We then tried him on tricyclics; he's presently on triycyclic antidepressants. He's at the upper end of the range of therapeutic doses for adults.

He's better on triycyclics than he was on Klonopin but, as you gather, his self-control can still break down easily. He has some frustration tolerance. He can move from seconds of frustration tolerance to an entire psychotherapeutic session where he can maintain continuity. So, in a relaxed, comfortable environment, there is some capacity for participation in a verbal psychotherapy.

Recently we began a copharmacy of lithium with the antidepressants. He's presently getting 600 milligrams a day. We haven't observed a noticeable change in the aggression at the present dose and we will be trying further dosages. I would say our expectation is that either we'll see further significant change in the level of impulsivity that still makes him a hospital patient, from the medication trials, or a continuation of the slow gradual improvement in self-control.

We're a long way from expecting self-control in the home situation. That can still destabilize independent of Mark, and it can destabilize Mark when it does.

While many child psychiatrists might question this particular diagnosis and treatment of Mark, it does seem that the prevailing ideology of the psychiatric establishment is embedded in the report.

What does it say about children? Mark, the child, is deconstructed into a series of emotional and ideological segments that determine the target of specific medication. "The aggression and attentional problems" are "the target symptoms," "separation anxiety issues" are "not particularly a focus of medication efforts," and so forth.

How does this approach affect the form of treatment? Given the reliance on a match between a symptom and a particular medication, treatment resides in trials and approximations until the ideal correlation is found. Procedures either consist of increasing the dosage or of "copharmacy," in which the current dose is combined with other medication. If there's no improvement, it simply means the proper match hasn't been found and a trial with another medication or combination needs to be conducted. The language carries pseudoscientific certainty, but the procedures are actually a blind series of trials.

And what is the aim? The evidence that Mark benefits from copharmacy is assessed in terms of behavior control. If Mark doesn't change, it's evident that the dosage needs to be increased or modified. The psychiatrist's summary of Mark is so compelling that, when the child's counselor makes a comment related to mastery after the psychiatrist's speech, it draws no attention. She says, "The more skills Mark achieves the better he behaves. He didn't know how to ride a bike and now he does, and he gets a lot of pleasure from it." To this group, her comment sounds simply descriptive and of little significance. The same thing happens when the psychologist makes a relational observation: "Since there is no family, the unit staff takes surrogate roles." This statement of staff involvement in Mark's life remains unexplored as an intervention. Rather, it's taken as a response to a perceived void—a curious construction, actually, since Mark has a large family concerned with his well-being. In the end, only Mark's biology stands as the treatment target.

## The Family Session

After the staff meeting, the consultant interviewed Mark and his family. Present at the beginning of the session were Mark; his mother; his 12-year-old sister, Janice; an aunt; and an 8-year-old cousin, Jody, who was the son of another aunt. The session lasted 2 hours.

The consultant started the session by asking Mark to describe his large extended family, indicating their ages and relationships. As Mark does this, the consultant evaluates his cognitive skill and his ability to communicate. Mark describes a family that is close and supportive of its members.

After this, the consultant moves on to work with the family. The following excerpt highlights only the segment that explores the relationship between Mark and his mother, since the interchange with mother and son illustrates clearly what was different in this approach.

CONSULTANT (*addressing the mother*): Why is Mark here? (*then, immediately, to Mark*): Why are you here, Mark?

MARK: Because I have problems.

CONSULTANT: Why are you here and Janice is not here?

MARK: Because she's better than me, right?

CONSULTANT (*to Mark*): You should ask Mother why you're here.

MARK (*to the mother*): Why am I here?

MOTHER: Because you have a lot of problems with me, a lot of problems with school. (*to the consultant*) He just wants to do what he wants. (*to Mark*) You have a lot of problems with me. It really came to a point were I couldn't handle you being home.

CONSULTANT: It seems you're saying that he's here because you couldn't handle him.

MOTHER: That's one of the reasons.

CONSULTANT (*lightly*): Why are *you* not here?

MOTHER (*surprised, and laughing*): Why am *I* not here? I don't know about that.

CONSULTANT: Mark, what do you think of this idea? If Mommy can't handle you, she should be here.

MOTHER (*to Mark*): You think I should be here?

MARK: No.

CONSULTANT: The fact is that Mark will be here for a long time if you can't handle him. So there are two reasons why he's here, and one of them is that you can't handle him. Are you ready to take him home?

MOTHER: He has improved in a lot of ways, but when he comes

home on passes he doesn't want to listen to me. He doesn't show respect. But sometimes . . . he has improved a lot.

CONSULTANT: I will ask you a strange question. You said that he has improved. Have you improved as well? It's a two-way street, isn't it? It deals with how you and Mark get along. As soon as you will be able to take care of him, they will release him. If your relationship changes, he will change. It's a different way of thinking, isn't it?

MOTHER: Yes, it is. . . . But I think you're right to the point, because it does have to do with me and him.

The consultant then asks the mother to talk with Mark.

MOTHER (*to Mark*): I want you at home. When I put you in the hospital I expected you to be 3 months. It's now 2 years. I want you home. You understand that? And I want that we should get along better.

Mark hides his face and doesn't respond. He looks disconnected from his mother and the scene.

CONSULTANT (*to the mother*): Do something that helps Mark to listen to you.

The mother addresses herself directly to Mark, asking him to sit looking at her, and repeats: "I want that you and I get along better together."

MARK: I want to go and play with Jody.

MOTHER: If you wait, the session will finish soon and you will have time to play with Jody.

MARK: OK, I'll wait.

The consultant gets up, shakes the mother's hand and congratulates her for her effective handling of Mark. The session continues in this vein for another hour. The consultant focuses continuously on the mother's competence in handling Mark and highlights the moments of conflict resolution.

The organization of the session calls attention to the way this consultant approaches the core questions: Who is Mark? What is his context? How should treatment proceed?

The consultant used the first 15 minutes of the session to make contact with Mark. He explored the child's knowledge of his extended family, and, while they talked together, the consultant drew some diagnostic conclusions about Mark's level of intelligence, his capacity to concentrate, his way of connecting with strangers, his concept of self, and so on: a 10-year-old with somewhat idiosyncratic language and a short attention span, who withdraws under stress but responds appropriately in a one-to-one conversation; probably of normal intelligence.

Beyond these general conclusions about Mark's capacities, the consultant looked at this child in context. He had spent 20% of his life—2 years—on a psychiatric ward, but he was also part of an extended family to which he was emotionally connected. His long sojourn in the hospital was reframed as a result of his mother's difficulty in responding appropriately to him rather than as a product of his internal pathology. Dysfunctionality was located between Mark and his mother, both had a profound effect on each other's behavior and ways of thinking. The hospital staff never explored this reality, helped mother and son to develop more functional patterns, or mobilized support from other family members.

What were the treatment procedures in this session? Since the consultant looks at Mark as a part of something rather than a discrete entity, he knows that working with the child alone keeps the therapist ignorant of the way in which the family organizes the child's behavior. He focuses his intervention on making the invisible part of Mark's world visible. He highlights the mother's part in keeping the child in the hospital, and encourages her to challenge the hospital and take Mark home.

There are many unexplored issues here, including the sister's position in the family, pressures on the mother, and potential sources of support that might come from Mark's aunts or other members of the extended family. It's the beginning rather than the end of the story, but the primary intention is to launch the staff on a radically different way of thinking and of conducting treatment.

## Meeting Again with the Staff

In the meeting after the session, the consultant's directives were similar to the recommendations discussed in Chapter 7: Increase home visits; conduct family sessions in the hospital after home visits; conduct family sessions in the home; work on increasing the mother's competence with Mark; support positive patterns but explore conflicts, helping the family to increase their repertoire for handling periods of difficulty; include Janice in some sessions; and mobilize members of the extended family as supports for the mother. The consultant suggested that the staff immediately begin to plan for discharge, increasing the length of time for home visits during the preparatory period and arranging for home-based interventions at discharge.

### Closed-Circuit Presentation to Statewide Workers

The last step allowed for questions from the personnel of child psychiatric wards throughout the state, who had followed the consultation on closed-circuit television. Most of the questions expressed the traditional orientation of the workers: their preoccupation with pathology, their primary concern with the negative influence of families on the children, and their sense of mission as rescuers of the young patients in their care. None of the listeners questioned or commented on the psychiatric view of Mark, the problem of extended internment for a child, or the implications of long-term pharmacological treatment. Clearly, the orientation of the hospital staff was familiar to the observers, and, in addition, there was a code of loyalty among members of the establishment that precluded challenging their colleagues.

In this particular setting, the problems became moot. The statewide system was reorganized in response to a growing trend toward short-term psychiatric hospitalization for children, and the unit was closed within a year. While the trend is positive, however, it does not create an essential shift. It does not change underlying attitudes, reduce the dependence on medication, or expand the treatment to include the family or the social context.

In this consultation, issues concerning the community were not particularly relevant, but in some situations those issues are primary. In urban hospitals, where children of the poor are taken for psychological treatment, problems often arise because of limited contact and understanding between the hospital and the surrounding community. We consider this reality in the following section.

## PSYCHIATRIC SERVICES
## AND THE COMMUNITY

Psychiatric settings for children of the urban poor are generally located in city hospitals, and the communities they serve are often beset by a variety of problems. The hospitals have become a way of dealing with the spin-off from social disorganization, and for handling distressed children whose families are homeless, involved with drugs, suffering from AIDS, or torn apart by violence.

The children admitted to the psychiatric wards of these hospitals are usually diagnosed with behavior disorders, and they look different than the psychiatric population of an earlier time. Forty years ago, many of the children who entered Bellevue Hospital in New York City were diagnosed with childhood schizophrenia. They would twirl around and around, grimace, jump into the arms of strangers, withdraw completely, or exhibit other bizarre symptoms that seem to have disappeared in our time—except in relatively rare cases. Certainly, the description doesn't cover the child psychiatric population in today's cities.

What brings an urban child who isn't clearly psychotic into a psychiatric hospital? Among the various explanations, one is certainly rooted in the realities of the immediate context. As an example, consider the events of one evening on the crisis unit of a particular urban hospital. On that evening, the team needed to deal with three children in rapid succession. Two were brought to the hospital with suicidal ideation. After preliminary work, both were sent home to be monitored by their families and treated at the outpatient unit. The third child presented a less serious picture, with less risk of self-destructive actions, but this girl was admitted to the ward. The difference lay in the family situation, which was considered inadequate for maintaining her safety.

In each case, the estimate of risk could not be a function of the child's psychological state alone; rather, it was a judgment of the interaction between the child's state and the safety provided by family and the environment. The judgment may be right or wrong in a particular case, but the assessment is necessary. Given this situation, some hospitals have an unofficial category of patients they call "boarders," who are admitted tentatively without a formal intake process. The category has been created for children who may be inappropriate candidates for psychiatric admission but who have no place else to go. As a social problem, the situation is alarming. As a professional challenge, it requires a drastic review of procedures once the child is admitted.

Clearly, whatever the circumstance, we believe that the staff must seek out and work with the people who form the child's primary social network. If they address themselves exclusively to the child in the ward they will be intervening in the family and the community without a map, essentially navigating blind. In so doing, they may be steering the child—wittingly or not—toward an institutional or foster placement once the short-term hospitalization runs its course. That's a recurrent sequence in the current climate, but it skips over the more economic and humane possibilities that would look to family and community for an understanding of the issues and the resources for healing.

In the following sections, we will present two cases admitted to the same hospital during our period of consultation. Both involved a need to understand and relate to the community. Since one admission occurred at the beginning of the consultation and the other 6 months later, the descriptions illustrate the changes that can occur when a family focus has been introduced and is implemented by the psychiatric staff.

## The First Case: Relating to the Latino Community

The first case involved a crisis situation. A city hospital with a child psychiatric ward found itself in trouble with the surrounding community, which felt that the staff was biased against Latino families. The case that created the crisis involved a 10-year-old who drove his parents' car for four or five blocks in city traffic before being stopped by the police. He was taken to the hospital, confused and frightened, and when the parents, a Puerto Rican couple, came to pick him up they were told that he must remain in the hospital for observation. When they returned the next day, the psychiatrist told them that their child was hyperactive, required medication, and must remain in the hospital for a week until his response to the medication could be evaluated.

The parents refused to give consent and the hospital took the case to court. The judge ruled that the parents were neglectful, and agreed with the hospital that an involuntary commitment was necessary. The parents took the case to the Spanish media and the case became a political "hot potato," polarizing the Latino community and the city hospital.

How is it that a hospital created to provide services to a community becomes its enemy? The explanation resides partly in perceptions and labeling, and partly in the tendency to use power rather than to explore the different perspectives. For the child's parents, the boy was reckless, had endangered his life and the lives of others, and had disobeyed parental rules. They were frightened and angry, but also somewhat impressed by the child's unexpected skill in maneuvering the car through city traffic. For the hospital staff, the child had shown a lack of judgment that reflected internal problems. His impulsivity and lack of control required investigation. They were also critical of the parents, whom they felt had endangered the child's life by their neglect. The hospital took over the care of the child, *in loco parentis*, and the court supported the medical profession.

Surely there were other possibilities, long before the community and the social institutions squared off to do battle. In a middle-class suburb, this would have been considered a child's prank, albeit a dangerous one. Hospital staff and family would most likely have met swiftly, discussed the situation sympathetically, and the child would have been released into the care of his parents. If judged the prank of a precocious child, explanations and discipline would have been left to the parents; if judged a function of child impulsivity and unclear parental control, outpatient therapy would have been suggested.

This Latino family deserved the same consideration. The issue was not simply a matter of avoiding organized community rage but of serving clients and community effectively. The hospital needed to adopt the same collaborative stance that would be typical in another neighborhood, exploring the problem and its solution with a family that was concerned and competent, although ethnically different from the staff.

## The Second Case: Cultural Sensitivity to the Experience of Immigrants

The second case has been referred to briefly in an earlier chapter. Sixteen-year-old Liliana, one of three children in the family, was brought to the psychiatric ward by her frightened parents after telling them she had taken a large dose of pills and wanted to die. The psychiatrist and psychologist who conducted the initial interview were skillful and empathetic. They explored Liliana's depression and her story of social isolation. She felt imprisoned at home by her parents, who imposed rigid rules that cut her off from peer contacts, and the staff understood her suicide attempt as an expression of impotent rage against her family.

The second interview was conducted with Liliana and her mother. Since the mother appeared to speak only Spanish, a bilingual social worker acted as her translator. The mother described the family's difficulty in adjusting to this country after arriving from South America 5 years earlier. Liliana avoided looking at her mother during this discussion, seeming depressed and withdrawn. The psychiatrist then suggested that, since Liliana spoke fluent English, she could translate her mother's comments, and he asked her permission to dismiss the translator. This simple intervention allowed the participants to explore the very close relationship between mother and daughter. The mother was also depressed, and it was clear that Liliana felt protective of her.

The third session included Liliana, her father and mother, her 21-year-old brother, and her 23-year-old sister. All the children spoke fluent English, and the father was also able to express himself in English—although with difficulty. To everybody's surprise, the mother began to speak a bit of English during the session, and her use of the language was almost as proficient as her husband's. When some difficulty arose in clarifying the meaning of a family member, the son spontaneously took on the task of translating from one language to the other.

During the discussion it became evident that the adaptation of this family had been difficult, and that their economic and social condition had spiraled downward since leaving their country of origin. The father, who had been a reasonably successful businessman, worked here as a security guard and was presently unemployed. The son had been imprisoned for drug dealing, and Liliana's sister, who once had a bout with crack, was now free of drugs and looking for work. The mother was cleaning offices to keep the family afloat.

As this information emerged, the staff began to look at the situation with a new appreciation of the contributing factors. They understood that despairing and concerned parents were controlling their adolescent daughter in an attempt to save her from the dangers of a frightening neighborhood—and in order to forestall the kind of antisocial behavior they had seen in the older children. The focus of staff intervention expanded, moving from the pathology of an adolescent to the complex issues caused by immigration and the ineffective attempts of the parents to protect their children. The staff clarified the salient issues and encouraged a discussion between Liliana and her parents in which all three worked on viable patterns of control and freedom. Liliana's siblings were asked to coach her on the basis of their experience, and the family was encouraged to find sources of social contact and support in their own community. Liliana improved after some sessions, and shortly after was discharged.

While this case is less dramatic than the previous one, it may be more typical. It reminds us that a psychiatric staff can proceed skillfully on the basis of traditional concepts and methods, arriving at a clear DSM-IV diagnostic assessment. However, broadening their perspective to include factors outside the individual allows for more effective interventions that can help the family as well as the identified patient. In the long run, such interventions may prove the more economic, shortening the patient's stay in the hospital, and perhaps improving the relations between hospitals and communities.

The examples in this section have concerned the Latino community, but of course the question of hospital–community relations is much broader. Despite the cultural mix that has always been America, we continue to be semiliterate in multicultural matters, perhaps especially in relation to meaning and mores among economically deprived sections of the population. When children from immigrant families are admitted to psychiatric wards, the staff is apt to apply established diagnostic categories to their behavior. They may not realize that silent withdrawal is a characteristic mechanism in a particular culture, especially in the face of an authority as daunting and unfamiliar as the hospital staff, or that explosive behavior mirrors community reaction to official intrusions into their lives. Even more to the point, they may not know how to access the family or other members of the community who can be helpful in understanding the circumstances.

Perhaps unwittingly, a psychiatric staff often makes conventional assumptions about family dynamics and structure, relying on forms characteristic of the dominant culture. When a young patient comes from a low-status African-American background, for instance, the staff may not understand the far-flung family map, or be oriented toward exploring its resources. The family may not be nuclear in structure and the parents may not be available. But grandmothers, siblings, godparents, or aunts may be sources of support, and may be able to provide an understanding of the child's behavior more specific to the particular situation than the generalized notions usually applied.

Although it's helpful if the staff includes some bilingual members who share cultural characteristics with the local community, that's not easy to arrange, nor is it a solution in itself. What's most important is the will to slow down the process of admission and treatment, and to work closely with the parents of an impulsive 10-year-old or the family of a suicidal adolescent. A professional staff is generally overworked, and reality demands adaptations to new management systems and the mastery of new information about human behavior. Nonetheless, hospitals are situated within communities that are the usual source of patients. When the community is poor and ethnically varied, the staff must be aware both of its tensions and its resources. Despite cultural confusions and obstacles, the psychiatric staff should be in contact with the network of people important to the child. It may help to remember that whatever is difficult for the staff, crossing cultural barriers, may be equally difficult for the patient, who must cross in the other direction, and that the help of the family is a resource for understanding and treatment.

## COMMENTS AND RECOMMENDATIONS

We can return to the discussion of residential centers as a springboard for commenting on child psychiatric wards. Residential centers for children were influenced by educational sources, and by a tradition that required attention to daily events in the lives of the children. The staff knew that they must organize the child's experience at the center, that theories of teaching and learning, the use of authority, and the exercise of control were all relevant, and that each child had previous experience in all these matters at home.

Therefore, the dialogue between a family-friendly consultant and the staff of a residential center could start with perceptions of the family's influence on the child's life. The staff initially might take a pro-child, anti-family stance, but explorations concerning the family also could serve as a good point of departure.

In psychiatric hospitals for children, on the other hand, the staff pays less attention to the milieu, the social structure of the child group, or how family patterns shaped the child's experience of teaching, learning, and control. The concept of hospital, with its medical connotation, skews attention toward diagnosis, illness, and individual treatment. That focus is reinforced by the succession of diagnostic manuals that dominate psychiatric practice, and by the mandate that every child must carry a diagnostic code to insure third-party payment. The focus is reductionistic in general, but for children from multicrisis poor families, who have no other recourse and no skills for challenging the process, it's particularly damaging. An ideology that narrows the observation of children to discontinuous areas of the nervous system keeps a child like Mark on psychiatric wards from the tender age of 8 until he's 10.

Fortunately, the era of long-term hospitalization for children is coming to an end, which brings us to a crucial question. If children now stay in psychiatric hospitals for only a few weeks, will there be an accompanying positive change in the organization and orientation of the units? Will hospitals develop a practice that includes family and community outreach? It's logical to argue, as we do, that the pressure for quicker movement presents an opportunity to explore and mobilize external resources as a support for the child's functioning, but that may not be the primary effect. In the immediate future, the current orientation toward the organic underpinnings of behavior will probably be the dominant force, along with a continuing emphasis on control through medication. That approach is not inevitable, however, and not the only available model.

It would be useful for psychiatric administrators and practitioners to consider the model that family physicians have developed, with the goal of providing collaborative services for their patients (McDaniel, Campbell, & Seaburn, 1995). In this collaborative health approach, the family physicians have started with the premise, or perhaps the recognition, that the health of any one family member is intimately related to the family context. With a psychosociobiological view as their base, they have moved toward the creation of collaborative health teams comprised of family physicians and specialists in family theory and therapy. The teams work together as a unit, sharing information and expertise. If we substitute the idea of a mental health team for the medical teams of these collaborative units, we have a promising model for child psychiatric wards, in which a group of workers can share perspectives and expertise. Of course, most psychiatric wards are currently organized into multidisciplinary teams. The model we are describing, however, emphasizes the shared nature of the work, rather than a technical mix of different disciplines.

Introducing a collaborative model into a psychiatric ward would probably prove to be a major disruption. Hierarchy and status are well established, and our experience as consultants and trainers has suggested that psychiatrists as a group are not particularly interested in collaboration. When we started training in one setting, most of the staff were present, but as the year progressed the attendance of psychiatrists became erratic. Psychologists, social workers, psychiatric residents, and interns continued as enthusiastic participants, implementing a change in practice on the wards. Unwittingly, we began to rely on these workers as the champions of new procedures, which of course is never a solution as it simply reinforces a separation of professionals within the staff. Effective training and the creation of collaborative teams requires an acknowledgment of the current reality, and a sequential plan for bringing as much of the staff as possible into an active role.

A family-oriented consultant may do well to start with some theoretical lectures for the total staff, presenting the major concepts of systems thinking, as well as concrete ideas about the organization of families, the relevance of such ideas to the presence of children on psychiatric wards, and the spectrum of possibilities for their treatment. Specialized training in family therapy can then be offered to a core group of psychologists, social workers, nurses, and psychiatrists, with sessions open to interested observers or auditors. Given the special status, history, and probable resistance of staff psychiatrists, it would probably be productive to hold some separate meetings with this group, during which they can discuss their reactions to the approach, explore the relationship between family work, individual treatment, and the control of symptoms through medication, and arrive at some clarity about their role in a collaborative structure. Those most interested would become part of the group developing a particular expertise in working with families and community. This group, combining professionals from different disciplines, would push the envelope of the institution outward, increasing the permeability of hospital boundaries. They would form an outreach team, bringing information about extended family, school, churches, and community to team meetings in order to create an integrated systemic approach.

A team approach, organized in this way, would not attempt to change the biological orientation of the psychiatric staff, or denigrate the use of medication. Rather, it would look at the biological orientation as a partial view, to be supplemented by a systemic orientation toward children in context, and open to a case-by-case discussion of the most effective procedures. Like any process requiring the accommodation of different viewpoints, the dialogue is apt to be intense and, at times, argumentative. But in the long run it should result in a more knowledgeable and efficient approach to the treatment of children, both while they are resident on psychiatric wards and after discharge to their homes and communities.

# CHAPTER NINE

# Home-Based Services

Home-based services take a variety of forms, but they share at least one feature: They're organized so that the services will be delivered primarily in the homes of the clients. That single fact offers a unique opportunity to become family centered. When a worker enters the home of a client, everything in the structure suggests that the context is part of the intervention. The living quarters and the neighborhood are the client's turf, and the setting maximizes the possibility that family and other important members of the network can be brought together. In addition, the act of coming to the client's home suggests that the service establishment is reaching out. The aura of authority that characterizes an official setting is muted and the reality of the family's life environment is acknowledged.

In this chapter, we will discuss the factors that create a match between possibility and practice, as well as the kind of training that helps a home-based staff maximize the effectiveness of their interventions. We will begin with the history of home-based services, noting the varieties of approach that have characterized different programs, as well as the issues that arise from the perspective of a systemic, family-centered point of view. With that as background, we will then describe a supervisory training program for agencies funded by their state department of mental health to deliver home-based family-centered services to their clients.

# EARLY ROOTS AND LATER DEVELOPMENTS

Home-based services have a long history. It's not our purpose to review the field at length, but it's useful to survey both the nature of such services over time and the major characteristics of selected programs during the last decades.*

The beginnings go back to the turn of the century, when volunteers went out into the community to help the needy, and social workers conducted most of their work in the homes of poor families (Berry, 1994; Tavantzis, Tavantzis, Brown, & Rohrbaugh, 1985). As professional training and organized services grew, and as the scope of the problems increased, service delivery was increasingly located in clinics, agencies, foster homes, and institutions.

In the 1970s, the pendulum swung back. Policymakers and practitioners had become concerned with the way in which the delivery of services tended to dismantle families, especially families of the poor. In challenging the established procedures, they were supported by the social–political climate of the time, and by accumulating data concerning the effects of prevailing services. For instance, it was evident that an increasing number of children were being placed in foster care, shuttled from place to place, and never returned home. The process was costly, and it was destructive for the children and their families. Advocates were suggesting that a concentrated focus on building family strength would offer a humane and less expensive alternative to prevailing practices.

The Adoption Assistance and Child Welfare Act of 1980 (Public Law 96-272) expressed the need for reform. It underscored the value of family preservation, and created significant financial incentives for programs that would maintain children in their homes or reunite the family after placement. Federal efforts continued into the early 1990s. The Family Preservation and Family Support Initiative was passed in 1993, providing substantial funding for the states that was specifically earmarked for family-oriented services. Because of its stated philosophy and the provision of funding, this federal initiative bolstered the point of view that the

---

*The reader interested in more detail is referred to Berry (1994), Bryce and Lloyd (1980), Maybanks and Bryce (1979), and Nelson, Landsman, and Deutelbaum (1990), among others.

family was a legitimate unit of service in its own right, and that family-oriented interventions need not be cloaked in individual language. Shortly thereafter, a shift in the national mood reduced federal support for such programs, but "home-based services" is still recognized and funded as a category, particularly at the state level.

Home-based programs have been described as sharing certain characteristics, or at least goals. Providing services primarily in the home is one obvious aspect, but other less easily implemented features have also been central. They include a focus on the family as the unit of service, rather than just the child; an expectation that parents will participate and remain in charge; and utilization of the family system, natural habitat, and community resources in the mobilization of services (Bryce & Lloyd, 1980).

As the programs developed, they also shared other more concrete features. They tended to be intensive and short-term, providing multiple visits and "on-call" care over a period of weeks or a few months. Workers carried a very small caseload at any one time, often not exceeding two families, so that they could be available as needed. The intervention was usually crisis oriented, meaning that the families were at risk of having a child placed in care, and the goal was to help the family resolve their difficulties sufficiently to avoid placement.

Avoiding placement has been the usual criterion of success. Research evaluating a variety of programs suggested a success rate between 70% and 90% at the end of most programs, and sometimes up to a year later. However, reviewers caution that the studies are often not well designed and the meaning of the figures, therefore, is unclear (Berry, 1994; Tavantzis et al., 1985).

Home-based programs have been sponsored and funded through different sources, such as state, county, and city departments concerned with social services, welfare, mental health, mental retardation, children and youth services, and juvenile delinquency. To an extent, the different sources have shaped the definition of the central problem and the kind of services offered. Home-based programs sponsored by the social service and welfare departments of an area, for instance, have generally addressed the family's basic needs, focusing on practical help for the family's economic, household, and life management problems (Berry, 1994). However, the programs have also differed in the underlying theories that shape the interaction of workers with their clients and the kind of services they offer, and these have not necessarily been tied to particular departments or presenting problems.

Because the various approaches are differentially related to a family-centered point of view, we will review selected programs below, noting briefly the characteristics of programs based on social learning theory, a solution-focused model, and an ecological or family system perspective.

# DIFFERENT APPROACHES
# TO HOME-BASED SERVICES

## Social Learning and the Improvement of Skills

Social learning theory, which developed within the field of psychology, has generated specific techniques for helping individuals modify their behavior and interactions with others. The *Mendota Model*, first implemented as a home- and community-based program in 1969, was an early example of a program incorporating these techniques (Fahl & Morrissey, 1979). Since the program evolved within an institution for disturbed preadolescent boys, the new model indicated a radical change in thinking and venue. Instead of treating children at the institution, staff now went out to the homes and schools, maintaining the children in their natural environment and keeping the families intact. Although the change in structure was radical, the procedures were not. Workers continued to focus on the individual child, using social reinforcement principles to encourage behavioral change in such areas as learning, following directions, and accepting limits. Parents were seen as needing to acquire more effective parenting skills, and were expected to learn from observing staff techniques for child management.

*Homebuilders*, the first home-based family preservation program to command national attention, also falls primarily under this rubric. Started in 1974 in Tacoma, Washington, the program trained its workers in social learning techniques that would increase parent effectiveness and interactional skills, although workers also provided practical help in the homes, and employed a variety of humanistic/experiential techniques that highlighted values clarification and self-esteem (Haapala & Kinney, 1979; Kinney, 1991). Homebuilders spread rapidly through the country during the 1980s, perhaps stretching too thin and generating unrealistic expectations. When follow-up data failed to demonstrate significant differences between Homebuilders and other, more flexibly implemented approaches, the program lost its prominent position.

Although Homebuilders was not basically oriented toward working with family organization as an interacting system in the way we deem necessary, the program nonetheless served an important function in relation to intensive, short-term, home-based services. The work and publications of this group brought high visibility to the concept, so that funding became more readily available for subsequent programs. Their experience also provided a useful example of issues to be considered in designing flexible and family-centered home-based services.

## The Solution-Focused Model

The solution-focused approach, developed as a specific model by Berg, de Shazer, and their associates, has become one of the most widely used approaches to home-based services on the contemporary scene (Berg, 1994). The core of the model is its emphasis on solutions rather than problems. Proponents assume that all families have experimented with solutions to conflicts, but that their experience remains invisible to them because they tend to concentrate on problems instead. On the basis of this reasoning, the intervention focuses on recalling positive moments in the past, exploring conceptions of a satisfying outcome, and encouraging the repetition and extension of such solutions. The worker functions as a coach or guide, conveying an optimistic view of the family's capacities.

The model emphasizes respect for the family, a feature that is clearly important in working with families who are poor, faced with multiple crises, and likely to feel powerless in relation to social institutions. However, questions arise concerning the implementation and philosophy of the model. In practice, workers are seen to confuse respect and empowerment with a prohibition against challenging the family's initiative. For fear of seeming disrespectful, they're often unable to coach the family or redirect attention to areas that the family may be unaware of or avoiding. Most important, the model expressly avoids the open exploration of conflict. As we have noted in earlier chapters, families often founder over their inability to face and deal with disagreements. From our perspective, they cannot be helped to function more effectively unless the worker helps them explore their patterns, recognize what is dysfunctional, and experiment with new ways of resolving their differences.

## Ecological and Family System Approaches

In a sense, any home-based program that connects the family to community resources has an ecological orientation. There have been many programs of this nature, providing a variety of environmental services to families, and aiming to strengthen the ability of impoverished and troubled clients to use available resources (see Berry, 1994). Some programs hold particular interest for us because they address multiple levels of the family's needs, problems, and connections, and because they're concerned with patterns rather than individual behavior or skills.

An early and interesting example was the program developed by the *Iowa Children's and Family Services* for treating high-risk, multiproblem families in their homes (Stephens, 1979). The model combined an ecological orientation toward the family's place in the community with a systems view of family functioning, and an approach to treatment that used family therapy techniques. As noted by Stephens,

> Intervention is directed toward changing the problem-solving efforts of troubled families which have heretofore been ineffective. These efforts have a patterned structure that needs to be altered at the point where it is maintained, whether within the family system or at the interface of the family and the helping systems. (p. 288)

What is noteworthy about this statement is the implication that intervention should be flexibly designed, changing levels as needed, and that an understanding of the issues depends on assessing repetitive patterns both within the family and between family and service providers. The statement also makes clear that, from this point of view, it is the *current* organization of such patterns, and not individual or family history, that sustains the problem, and that these patterns must be addressed if interventions are to be productive.

A more current example is provided by *Families Work*, a program developed for families with a delinquent or unmanageable adolescent at risk of placement (Tavantzis et al., 1985). This program combined the principles of home-based services with those of structural and systemic family therapy, working intensively in 6-week renewable cycles and focusing particularly on periods of crisis.

Tavantzis and his colleagues noted that most interventions were based on individually oriented theories of problem formation, proceeding on the assumption that families will change once individual members come to understand their feelings or improve their behavior. Their own program focused on family organization. Interventions emphasized current patterns that disturb family life, concentrating on how such problems are maintained instead of on their origins.

Since the population consisted of families whose adolescents were out of control or delinquent, the group identified the aspects of family theory most relevant for this situation. They focused on likely areas of dysfunction, such as the boundaries between generations, hierarchy within the family, and clarity of authority, approaching the families with a working hypothesis concerning difficulties to be addressed. This approach has interesting implications for other situations in which the client families share common features, such as a three-generational structure, children in a particular age group, or drug-dependent adolescents. Certain assumptions about family organization and issues can be made in any of these situations, however, it's important to note that theoretical generalizations are simply a point of departure. In any situation, the most important information concerns the organization of the particular family, and the relation of their repetitive patterns to difficulties and potential resources.

This program's techniques for working with families would be familiar to any professional worker who has implemented structural interventions, emphasizing the importance of initially "joining" the family before introducing change, making change feasible by reframing behavior and setting manageable goals, and enacting change in family sessions as a first step toward exploring and integrating new patterns. However, some suggestions imply the involvement of larger systems. Program designers note that, by agreement, participants suspended their contacts with other services for the duration of the intervention. In addition, the proponents suggest that first efforts should go into organizing helpers before restructuring the families, and that the home-based worker should function as the case manager. These are useful suggestions, although difficult to implement.

## THE CURRENT SITUATION

The brief review of programs in the previous section is certainly not comprehensive, but it does reflect the range of forces that have shaped home-based services since the 1970s, and the variety of programs that developed as a result. The move toward providing services in the home stemmed from social concern for the poor, the realization that service delivery was often ineffective or destructive, and the political will to support change. Although the programs were all meant to improve the quality of service, they reflected a variety of theories concerning problem formation and the procedures that would best serve their clients.

Currently, home-based services are a widespread modality for working with poor families. They're funded with the express understanding that services will be brought to the family at home, but the mandate may not go beyond that concrete fact, neither spelling out standards or requiring certain procedures. It's generally assumed that the provider understands that the basic aim of this service is to help the family with its problems and avoid placement, that workers are equipped to use their skills for these purposes, and that the agency will mobilize community resources to provide the necessary "wraparound" services. Since most providers are responsible and experienced, these are reasonable assumptions, but only to a point. From a systemic, family-centered perspective, the fundamental question raised at the beginning of this chapter remains relevant: Given the potential of the home-based structure, what is the correspondence between intent and possibility, on the one hand, and actual practice, on the other hand?

An assessment of current programs would need to consider several areas of concern. We can review and summarize the generally shared goals and the pitfalls that prevent their effective achievement as follows:

| Goal | Pitfalls |
|------|----------|
| The enhancement of enduring problem-solving skills for the family. | Crisis containment as the goal, and success defined by the prevention of placement. |

It may seem strange that placement prevention is described as a pitfall. The avowed purpose of most home-based interventions is to contain an immediate crisis and forestall the need to remove a child from home. A calming of the waters sufficient to keep the family together is usually the criterion of a successful intervention.

Yet, that is only a short-term goal. As evaluators of home-based services have reminded proponents, "Effectiveness should also be explored using criteria other than prevention of placement, such as the quality of the family functioning and the impact on the child's growth and development" (Fein, Maluccio, & Kluger, 1990, p. 10). If a family is not to reappear as soon as the next crisis arises, the current intervention should be an opportunity for growth, enabling family members to take control of their own lives and to stem the process of disintegration.

| Goal | Pitfalls |
|------|----------|
| An understanding that the locus of any problem lies within, or is shared by, the family, so that the family must be the unit of service. | A continuing view that a particular individual is the target of service, even if it is rendered in the home. |

A contract for home-based services almost always carries the directive that the family must be the unit of service, but it seldom specifies that psychological services are part of that requirement. Home-based workers, in turn, are often skillful in carrying out the social and economic aspects of the mandate, mobilizing services and community help in such areas as housing, welfare, transportation, medical necessities, and household assistance, but they do not extend the family orientation to therapeutic interventions. The view that the individual child is the target of psychological services is sustained by theoretical assumptions, the organization of referrals, evaluations of progress, and insurance requirements.

| Goal | Pitfalls |
|------|----------|
| Interventions involve extended family and are directed at the forms of connection, empowerment, and conflict resolution that will strengthen the family's ability to function. | Workers are unskilled in dealing with interactive patterns or helping the extended family to change the patterns that are maintaining their problems. |

Most home-based workers are unprepared to deal with family patterns, even if they see and understand them. They're usually able to support individuals, but often lack the skills for mobilizing an extended family, or for facilitating systemic changes that can create and sustain improvement in the functioning of family members.

| Goal | Pitfalls |
|------|----------|
| Coordination of services, allowing for the reduction of duplication, fragmentation, and intervention by multiple helpers. | Continued fragmentation and duplication caused by poor communication, and by implicit jurisdictional problems concerning hierarchy, decision making, and integration. |

For home-based workers, recurrent questions concern the chain of command, and the appropriate pathways for changing procedures when clinical judgment suggests that such action is advisable. Who should make the decisions about modifying services, extending them beyond the designated period, or terminating a case? And how flexible is the home-based mandate? Can some sessions be held elsewhere than at the home if there is a constructive reason for doing so? The questions arise in connection with specific cases, but the problem is general, underlining the urgent need to organize the system so that the work is coordinated and collaborative.

In the remainder of the chapter, we will describe a training and consultation project, sponsored at the state level, that involved agencies under contract to deliver home-based services. The presentation is not intended to assess the program, but to provide an example of how close attention to the details of intervention can clarify the process and bring the intervention closer to the goals of the service. As in other chapters, we have modified some details, partly to protect privacy and partly to highlight generic principles.

# A TRAINING AND CONSULTATION PROJECT

It's important to note at the start that this project was organized by the mental health section of the state apparatus. Although a variety of departments contract for home-based services, the caseload and requirements of the mental health service have some specific features. The cases usually carry a diagnosis for an identified patient, and home-based services are often seen as an alternative to hospitalization or a special out-of-home placement. Families referred through this department do not always require economic and life management supports, but they do require therapy. The staff must have skills for assessing family patterns, while remaining aware of the officially identified problem, and must be able to help the family explore more adaptive ways of functioning. Therefore, in this chapter, case examples are focused primarily on the details of family contact and family therapy, although issues involving larger systems inevitably arise as well and are crucial to the discussion.

## The Origins of the Project

The project arose out of the concerns of the mental health administration about the nature and quality of home-based services. The situation was typical of many other settings, where categorical funding had become available for such services and contracts had been awarded. Responsible agencies had submitted respectable proposals and become state providers, but nobody knew exactly how services were being implemented. There was no unified conception of what home-based services meant, beyond the idea that they were to be delivered in the homes of children at risk of placement, or who had been discharged from mental health institutions.

The contact between the department and the trainers began

with a series of visits to various agencies, a period of demonstrations and discussions at these sites, and conversations with staff and administrators about goals and needs. It became evident that the attitude toward further training in family therapy was mixed: enthusiastic on the part of some and wary, at best, on the part of others. The latter attitude stemmed partly from political concerns, since advocacy groups for families of mentally ill patients are alert to any approach that seems likely to blame families. Resistance also came from people who were primarily focused on the child, and who saw the trainers as part of a movement toward family preservation that might endanger children.

Nonetheless, the department and the trainers were able to work out a conjoint plan for a pilot project that seemed economically feasible and that had two related purposes. The project would provide training in family assessment and therapy for workers on the front line. At the same time, the process would provide the department with a clearer understanding of how agencies were implementing their services, and would allow for the development of standards and guidelines.

## The Structure of the Project

### The Settings, the Participants, and the Rotation of Training

At the start, the department selected two regions to participate in the project. Each region was composed of five participating agencies. In each agency, two workers were selected for training. If possible, one participant also held an administrative position within the agency. Both were usually expected to become supervisors at the termination of the project.

A training group consisted of 10 members, two participants from each agency within the region. Each group met twice a month. The trainers met every other week with each group, for a total of 10 full-day sessions in each region. The meetings rotated among agencies and the core group of 10 members attended all of the sessions. As each agency became the host of the week, their total staff could observe the training through a one-way mirror. Mental health staff from the central office of the region also attended some meetings and participated in the discussions.

## The Training Day: The Setup and the Experience

The structure of the training day at each setting was the same. In the morning, one member of the agency team presented the history of a family in treatment, and the family was then seen for a live session. In the afternoon, the second worker presented a videotape of a session conducted in a family's home. Discussion and teaching were interwoven throughout these procedures.

In presenting the morning cases during the first weeks, the workers followed their customary format: They provided a description of the problems presented by the identified patient, how the worker saw his or her needs, and how the family members responded to this child or adolescent. The trainers, however, had a different internal checklist for understanding a situation. In addition to listening to the history of the identified patient, they noted other details: the participation of different providers, the family organization and dynamics, the family's participation in maintaining the symptoms, and the emotional involvement of different family members. They also listened for indicators of family strengths, the position of the worker in the therapeutic system, the worker's understanding of his or her own therapeutic style, and so on. Perhaps it's not surprising that the workers would have overlooked such complexity. It would be a major goal of the training to expand staff understanding concerning family organization and the complexities of the therapeutic system.

After the case presentation, the worker met with the family. The session was observed by the group, and the trainers conducted a running commentary beyond the one-way mirror concerning the therapeutic process. As the staff began to interview families, it became clear that most workers had a particular pattern of intervention. They tended to be supportive, but also very central and directive. They provided a mixture that moved between respectful support for the family and formulas for problem solving. Therefore, another major aspect of the training would be directed at identifying and elaborating on skills that help families change.

Midway during a live session, one of the trainers joined the worker in a cotherapeutic consultative position, opening up new avenues for exploration. The other trainer remained with the group, commenting on procedures they were observing. The morning concluded with a debriefing of the experience.

The intention of the trainers was to teach inductively from the clinical material, using available opportunities at every step of the process. It would have been preferable to begin the training with a theoretical review of family therapy, but, in the limited time available, the decision was made to concentrate on actual practice. For the participants, this intensive focus on the details of their work was both gratifying and threatening. During the first two or three meetings, the supervision created confusion and resentment, but the mood changed rather quickly to an acceptance of the process. The support of the group probably was important, as well as the division of labor between the two trainers, which allowed one to support the worker while the other challenged or redirected the therapeutic process. Whatever the reasons, the groups were learning. Although their knowledge of family theory and therapeutic techniques remained quite limited, the understanding of their clients and the style of presenting the families became thoughtful and more comprehensive.

During the first 1½ hours of the afternoon, the group watched a videotaped session conducted by the second worker of the host agency in a family's home. Stopping and starting the videotape allowed for an interruption of the process, and a concentration on details. The discussion centered on the thought processes of the worker during the session, and a consideration of the match between these ideas and the nature of the intervention. During these discussions, participants became increasingly active. Although at first hesitant, they became commentators and critics of each other's styles of intervention.

The last 1½ hours of the day were devoted to an open discussion of generic issues. As the project continued, group members used the time to provide follow-up information on families that had been seen before, and to consider how to proceed further.

The fact that the 10 members of the core group rotated through the agencies created unforeseen dynamics. Initially, the trainers were mainly concerned with stopping the process and calling attention to the automatic responses of the workers so that they could explore new ways of thinking about their clients. But the presenting workers had another audience that was invisible to the group and trainers. In most cases, it was the first time that staff members were presenting their work so openly to their colleagues in the agency, and they were concerned that the reception would be critical. The situation was particularly difficult for presenters who were also in an administrative position, and they were understandably afraid of losing face. Feelings of having been exposed and not protected constituted a large part of the tension during the first sessions. As noted, however, the aura of confusion and resentment tapered off once the core group members got to know each other and could act as buffers between presenters and the agency staff. It would probably have been advisable to begin the training without observers so that the sense of safety and familiarity in the group could develop without strain.

In most respects, the rotation of the training among agencies, and the participation of extended staff as each agency hosted the training day, were positive features. Team members found themselves visiting agencies treating similar clients but with a different organization and treatment procedures. Some agencies focused particularly on collaboration with other providers, others were family focused, and still others primarily addressed children. Some had day-respite or residential facilities so that children could move from outpatient to home-based to residential services and back again as needed, without changing therapists. By visiting different agencies and spending the day in detailed discussion of how services were implemented in each setting, participants were able to observe their own agencies from a variety of different perspectives.

Another unexpected but positive feature was the festive aspect of the training day. Every agency prepared elaborate lunches for the participants and the staff, so that the day became special and the staff of the agency felt involved. In some way, the family therapy training day became a positive, theoretically stimulating force for each of the host agencies.

The fact that there were two trainers allowed for an interesting teaching process in which the trainers could focus on different areas and take complementary roles. In general, one trainer paid attention to the worker's style of intervention and the match between thinking and practice, while the other focused on family dynamics and relevant therapy techniques. Of course, they sometimes commented on the same issues. However, their perspectives were frequently different, conveying not only their particular observations but an implicit message that multiple realities can exist within a consistent framework. It seems likely that the tolerance of their own differences, on the part of the trainers, facilitated acceptance of the training and encouraged participants to dare new things and expand their styles.

## The Emergent Issues

A number of issues emerged as the consultations proceeded. They were similar, of course, to the generic issues described earlier in the chapter for most home-based programs. Given the mental health focus of the agencies and the particular mandate of this training project, however, the areas of concern were located primarily in the contact between agency workers and their client families. The emerging issues fell into four categories: the handling of child-focused situations within the family context, working with the extended family, understanding the relationship between family empowerment and family therapy, and the effective management of multiple providers in relation to any one family.

In the following sections, we will present brief summaries of clinical cases as examples of family systems thinking and of the therapeutic techniques that follow from this perspective. They are organized under the above-mentioned four categories in order to illustrate each issue with specific situations. It should be obvious, however, that the division is artificial: In almost all cases, most of the issues would appear if we were to describe the situation and the necessary interventions in enough depth.

### Child-Focused Situations within the Family

Regardless of family characteristics, and even when the relationship between family dynamics and the child's symptoms was evident, workers tended to focus on the child's specific problem. It's not that the families were completely ignored. In fact, it was always evident to the workers that parents were involved in some way, either as protectors, sufferers, or contributors to the symptom, and they were usually invited to attend the sessions. What the trainers needed to challenge was the assumption that family members lived in separate psychological spheres, and that the family was background while the child was center stage. Even though the locus of treatment had changed in home-based services, the family was not the focus of the intervention.

It's not very surprising that this mind-set shifts slowly, if at all. As we've noted repeatedly, traditional training prepares most staff members to focus on individuals, and bureaucratic procedures make it difficult to change. The identified patient must carry a DSM-approved diagnosis, and the agency is contracted to provide services directed at this condition until the patient improves. Yet in most agencies there is certainly a sense that workers are there to help the family. Quite often, what the trainers saw was a confused set of interventions, mixing an individual focus with family sessions, and proceeding without a clear idea of how these different aspects were related.

In each of the following two cases the problem of the identified patient has been specified and targeted for treatment. The staff understands that these children live, or have lived, in a difficult family context, but they have not found ways of recognizing the family patterns, or of working with the fact that the child's symptoms are embedded in the organization of the family.

*Problem: A 9-Year-Old Adopted Boy Who Has Anxiety Attacks.* The household in this case consists of three people: 9-year-old Luther, his adoptive mother, and another woman, a friend, who has been living with them since the boy was adopted at the age of 2. Luther has nightmares, and some days his fears are so strong that he develops palpitations and nausea and is forced to leave school.

When Luther was 2, his father killed his mother and then killed himself. At that point, he was adopted by his present mother. The mother works in the post office, and Luther's "aunt," who is more often at home because she has a part-time job, has been primarily in charge of child care. The family has been in therapy for 5 months, referred for home-based treatment because of Luther's symptoms. The focus has moved back and forth between current stresses in family and school and the traumatic event in the child's early life. Mother and aunt participate in the sessions as concerned adults.

As the therapist meets with the family, the trainers and project participants remain behind the one-way mirror. The trainers comment on the particular shape of this family. One woman is the adoptive mother, but the other woman has been the caretaker. During the session it becomes clear that the two women are competitive about who is the "real" mother. As they begin to argue about Luther's behavior, he becomes agitated and begins to hyper-ventilate. The adoptive mother talks about the possible need for hospitalization and the aunt insists that the child remain at home.

One of the trainers joins the session and focuses on the different styles of the two mothers. He supports the importance and insights of both, also suggesting that Luther cares about each of them and reacts to their disagreements. As this conversation pro-ceeds, the symptomatology of the child subsides.

In the comments of the second trainer and the discussion after the session, certain points are emphasized. One concerns the unusual nature of this family group, in which the presence of two mothers who sometimes disagree has confused the boy and raised fears of abandonment. Since the relationship of the women with each other is neither legal nor sexual, however, the family organi-zation has not been the focus of staff attention or therapy. The staff primarily has been drawn to traumatic events of the past, giving less weight to dynamics in the current household. As this becomes clearer, discussion centers on the way that interactional patterns among family members maintain Luther's symptoms, and on alter-native approaches to the therapeutic sessions.

*Problem: A 13-Year-Old Girl Who Refuses to Go to School.* The school has been concerned about 13-year-old Yolanda. She's a bright girl who repeatedly has been truant. The family has been referred to an agency for home-based treatment. Both of Yolanda's parents are in their 50s. Her father, a factory worker, recently lost his job, and her mother has been left partially paralyzed by a stroke. She is unable to talk or express herself in writing, although she understands what people say and participates in the family meetings with guttural sounds that her husband and daughter have learned to translate.

The worker presents a videotape of a session conducted at home. Without success, she has been trying to deal with the girl's truancy: instituting a system of rewards and punishments, instruct-ing the father to wake up Yolanda in the morning, and suggesting that he accompany his daughter to school most days of the week. As the different strategies fail, the worker designs new possibili-ties. Yolanda, a bright and polite youngster, is friendly with the worker and never openly defiant, but some days she still fails to go to school. The session with father, mother, and Yolanda focuses on the school problem, and on possible reasons for the child's behavior.

What becomes evident to the group as they watch the session is that the therapist is the hardest-working person in the room. She has replaced the mother as the problem solver and is stuck in her role as family protector. The discussion first centers on the style of the therapist, and the fit between her interventions and the needs of this family. The trainers suggest that she experiment with a less central and directive role. She might increase the use of questions during her interventions, and hesitate before deciding on solutions and offering them to the family.

The trainers then ask the group to think about the symptom and about the family. How could they see things differently? What emerges is the idea that the girl's refusal to go to school is related to her expertise in reading and translating her mother's guttural sounds, and is therefore a protective act. Yolanda has become her mother's helper, and doesn't trust her father to protect her mother as well as she does. The group plays with different perceptions of family members, and the worker comes up with the idea that the mother is a Mystery Woman. Her thoughts always need to be interpreted by family members, who can never be sure of her wishes.

The focus of discussion and learning, in relation to this family, had three parts. First, the group considered the meaning of this child-focused situation within the context of the family, noting how the understanding of Yolanda's truancy changed when the staff saw her behavior as a response to family realities and family dynamics. Secondly, the group had the experience of using imagination to develop therapeutic metaphors. The idea of a Mystery Woman, and of Yolanda as a fairy godmother, became intriguing images with which the worker and the family could explore what was essential and what was dysfunctional in their handling of a difficult situation.

Finally, the therapist's style was a major point of discussion. Since a therapist is always limited by his or her idiosyncrasies, training is partly a matter of exploring alternatives for interventions and expanding the worker's repertoire. In this case, the worker was alerted to her directive style and the usefulness of taking a less central position. In a follow-up report, however, she described her dilemma when the father became ill during a session, the mother was helpless, and Yolanda was unable to handle the crisis. She made a rapid decision to take charge, and resolved the situation successfully. For the worker and the group, the experience was a reminder that change is complex. An expansion of one's style involves an alertness to old habits and the development of new techniques, not the abandonment of judgment or the atrophy of old skills.

## Working with the Extended Family

In learning to look beyond the individual client, workers seem to move first toward the patterns established together by parents and children. However, the patterns that sustain a problem often involve extended family. Grandparents, aunts, uncles, and cousins are rarely part of the therapeutic focus, even when they live in the same house or neighborhood and are in frequent contact with each other.

In illustrating this, we will describe two cases where extended family were part of the problem. The first case involves a grandparent. The close involvement of grandparents in the lives of their offspring is a pervasive phenomenon, and the nature of their relationship with the nuclear family should be part of any worker's internal checklist for exploring the family's reality. The second case, which is less typical, involves something of a family "clan." In each case the training focuses on making the staff aware of the importance of these figures, and of the need to include them in the treatment. With help, members of the extended family can become part of the solution rather than part of the problem.

*Problem: A 17-Year-Old Oppositional Son in Conflict with His Mother.* This family is composed of a single woman in her 40s and two sons, ages 17 and 13. The family had been living with the mother's boyfriend, but they moved out of his home when the mother became concerned about his cocaine habit and his strong influence on Josh, the older boy. The family is currently living with the mother's parents. Since the move, there have been continual arguments between the mother and 17-year-old Josh, with the younger boy siding with his mother. The mother and children have been in treatment for 5 months at the home of the grandparents, who have not been included in the sessions. While setting up the session with the trainers, however, the worker invited the grandmother to attend.

The session takes the usual route of an argument between the mother and Josh, which continues for some time. When the trainer enters he asks the grandmother how she can help her daughter. She responds with a forceful indictment of her daughter as incompetent. She says that, because her daughter feels guilty about failing to protect the children from her boyfriend, she treats them as companions and doesn't control them. As the grandmother elaborates on her daughter's shortcomings, she is eloquent and unstoppable, while her daughter shrinks visibly and becomes tearful. At this point, without missing a beat, Josh takes up his grandmother's indictment. He's equally critical, and his attack seems just as powerful. However, mother, who has been crushed and silent in the face of her mother's criticism, responds fiercely to Josh's attack. The pattern of fighting between them repeats itself, including the participation of the younger boy, who sides with his mother.

At this point, the worker intervenes to calm down the intensity of the conflict, but the trainer takes a different route. He addresses Josh, asking if he has noticed how much he resembles his grandmother in his attitudes, and how he has taken on his grandmother's job to judge and improve his mother. By reframing the boy's behavior, the trainer has changed the meaning of the conflict between the mother and son so that it now includes the grandmother.

This kind of intervention has its pitfalls. The trainer knows it's not useful to alienate the grandmother, and he prepares the way by listening respectfully to her version of the story and commenting on the clarity of her insights. Once the new framework is accepted, he introduces a graphic metaphor that can be useful for the therapist and the family during subsequent sessions. He comments that the boy has become a ventriloquist's puppet, and points out how strange it is for him to become his mother's parent. At this point the mother seems to take courage. She confronts the grandmother with her feeling of having been depowered since she moved back with her parents. She feels that she has been treated as a child, and needs to respond to the very rigid rules imposed by the grandmother in her house.

After the session, the group explored how the participation of different family members in therapy clarifies repetitive patterns and changes the meaning of the symptom. The mobilization of extended family also brings more resources into the movement toward change. As a result of this session, the worker invited the grandfather to become a participant in the therapy.

*Problem: A 12-Year-Old Girl with Hallucinations of Seeing Ghosts.*
Twelve-year-old Sofia has been hospitalized because of visual hallucinations. She's now out of the hospital and staying with her
grandparents. Sofia is part of a large family living within a closely
knit Greek community, and family members are in constant contact
with each other. The grandparents and the families of two daughters and a son live in one building. The worker had invited all the
members of this extended family to participate in the session, which
was conducted in the home of the grandparents and videotaped
with the family's consent.

The group observed the beginning of the taped family session,
during which a discussion that began with Sofia and her mother
escalated into a family free-for-all: grandmother and two aunts on
one side, the mother, brother, and grandfather on the other. The
argument was intense, and at some point Sofia bolted out of the
room. The family continued arguing, seemingly unaware that the
girl had left. The therapist, feeling absolutely paralyzed, tried to
move the family back to a consideration of the girl's problems, but
she was unsuccessful and the argument raged on.

The therapist presented this segment of the session as an
illustration of her difficulty in managing the family and making
progress with the problem. The group reacted by first celebrating
the therapist's convening of the whole clan; clearly their presence
was relevant. Then they considered the core of her dilemma.
Having assembled the family, why was she unable to use her
understanding of family dynamics in this session? What was in the
way, and how could she empower an involved, intensely caring
family to handle their conflicts and be helpful to each other?

All of the group, including the therapist, understood that the
issue in this family had to do with coalitions. Family members
tended to form factions and to fight for supremacy no matter what
the topic. Nonetheless, the therapist focused on the girl, trying to
get the family to think and talk about Sofia's problem. Since the
therapist had realized during the session that much of the problem
lay in the family pattern, the question for the group was why she
did not deal with that, and what she could have done at that
moment.

The answer to her paralysis was fairly obvious. The therapist
knew she could not comfortably handle the intensity, and that she
did not know what to do in the face of family conflict. That was a

common problem for members of the group, and indeed for many therapists learning to work with families. The intensity of affect is apt to be higher when families are assembled in the room than when clients become angry in individual sessions. However, the uproar was part of daily life in this family, and was certainly part of Sofia's reality. The high-pitched quarreling of warring factions followed many of Sofia's efforts to question authority, even when the beginnings were mild.

The energy and sense of connection in this family is a resource as well as a trigger. The group discussion focused on how the workers could become more comfortable with open conflicts, and how, in this case, the worker might interrupt the argument, pointing out to the family how Sofia is affected by their battles, and mobilizing their energy and concern in an exploration of change.

## Family Empowerment and Family Therapy

Despite some differences in the organization of the agencies, everyone adhered to the idea of family empowerment, which is a basic concept in the ideology of home-based services and exists as a primary goal. The concept, however, can become a trap. If "family empowerment" moves from a therapeutic goal to a politically correct mantra, it hobbles the usefulness of the worker's intervention. In some agencies, the workers' concern for respecting the family curtailed their capacity to look objectively at family patterns, explore areas of difficulty, and help the family move toward new modes of interaction. Therapy, in these cases, was respectful but unproductive.

Therapists often find it difficult, as well, to act on some implications of systems theory. For instance, one of the basic tenets of the theory posits that the behavior of people in an intimate system is interwoven. It follows that family members inevitably participate in the maintenance of symptoms carried by an identified patient. That concept underlies much of the power and practice of systemic therapy, allowing a therapist to explore patterns of interaction and to intervene at different times with different family members. A skillful therapist can effectively explore the family's responsibility for the behavior of its members while retaining a respectful and empowering stance.

And therein lies the problem: A thin line separates the search for responsibility from an implication of blame. Administrative units that contract for agency services are sensitive to political nuances, and are wary of the risk that workers will "derail" into blaming the family while exploring family involvement. Thus, the mandate for home-based services often emphasizes family support, and workers shy away from more exploratory and multifaceted interventions. However, as the primary purpose of home-based services is to help the family with its problems, it's important for workers to develop an informed understanding of the relationship between family therapy and family empowerment—along with the skills to implement their understanding.

To illustrate this issue, we will describe a case involving a complex family that was resistant to exploring the violence at the core of their problems.

*Problem: A Case of Adolescent Rage in a Stepfamily.* Irma and Jeremy married 3 years ago. It was the first marriage for Irma but the second for Jeremy, who brought his two daughters, ages 14 and 12, into the household. Gail, the older daughter, became physically violent toward her stepmother, so fiercely and with such frequency that her father needed to call the police to restrain her. The family was then referred to a local agency for home-based therapy.

After the violent incident that precipitated the crisis, the father undertook the task of mediating between Irma and Gail, and the overt aggression diminished. The family indicated to the agency workers that they did not want to mention the event again in future meetings, and that they would resolve this kind of problem by themselves.

Behind this obvious problem of violence, however, lay another one. Gail had told her school counselor that her stepgrandfather, Irma's father, drinks a lot, and that in recent visits he has hit her several times. Gail resentfully says that Irma does nothing about it. The family continues to visit the grandparents, and Jeremy appears unwilling or unable to challenge his wife. Clearly, the apparent cease-fire between Gail and Irma is dangerously unstable, and the identification of Gail as a troublesome and troubled adolescent represents an incomplete understanding of the situation.

The therapist receives the family for a session, while the trainers and the group observe from behind the one-way mirror. The therapist first asks the parents what they think should be the

direction and form of today's meeting. This is his customary opening, meant to indicate to the family that they control the intervention, and that the therapist is there to support the family's needs—
as explicitly expressed by family members. It's not wrong, in itself,
especially as a way of opening a session, but apparently it has been
the driving force of the work to date. When the trainer is introduced 20 minutes later as a person who can help the therapist in
his work with the family, Irma objects. She says she feels betrayed,
and that she will protect the family against this intrusion. The
therapist is surprised, having been painstakingly clear about the
reasons for requesting a consultant. However, the trainer leaves the
room, and the therapist spends some time soothing and reassuring
the family before they leave.

The trainers focus the group on two questions: What is the
definition here of empowerment, and what is the goal of therapy?
Interaction with this family has evolved into a protection of Irma—
who has the dominant voice in the family—but has not touched on
the several areas of conflict. Jeremy's opinion and efforts have been
marginalized, and the physical attacks on Gail have been suppressed
as a topic to explore. Because this view of family empowerment is so
limited, serious conflicts have been avoided by the therapist, who
feels that he has been helpful in keeping the peace.

This is admittedly a complex case. There are three families
involved: the newly formed stepfamily, the father and his two
daughters, and the mother and her family of origin. Which family
is to be empowered? To be effective in empowering all concerned,
the interventions would need to take into account the needs of
each unit and the conflicts between and among them.

In discussing this case, the trainers point out that multiple ways
of empowering this complex family exist, and that it's necessary to
intervene in parts of the family system while maintaining a broad
perspective concerning the relation of parts to the whole. They
suggest that the therapist could empower the stepfamily by helping
them create clearer boundaries between themselves and the extended family. They could also use the home setting to facilitate
meetings involving different units and subsystems: individual meetings with Gail, meetings that include only the two sisters, and
sessions with Irma and Jeremy—during which Irma can air her
frustrations in the new stepfamily and Jeremy can be supported in
challenging his wife's protection of her father at Gail's expense.

The specific techniques are not relevant here; of greater importance is the need for staff to see the panorama of issues in this family
and to feel able to introduce major issues into the therapeutic
sessions. Of course they will need to find a balance that supports
and respects family members while dealing with painful matters.
However, if the therapist waits for family members to introduce
difficult problems themselves, he will make little progress, and, in
the end, he will not have been very helpful to the family.

The fact that workers go regularly to the home gives them an
advantage. They can protect the children and mobilize the family
as a healing force for its members without avoiding the need to
explore destructive patterns. Empowerment of a family that respects
their resilience and has long-term staying power requires this
balance, and therapeutic strides cannot usually occur without it.

## Multiple Providers for One Family

A home-based team is responsible for centralizing services in the
home while using the resources of extended family and community
as needed. The key to the effective use of multiple services,
however, is judgment, parsimony, and coordination. Ideally, the
home-based team should function at the center, and should be able
to forestall the fragmentation and duplication in service delivery
that frequently overwhelm a family and slow down progress of the
case.

Balancing need with parsimony is a tall order, and we have
found that home-based workers are apt to err on the side of too
much rather than too little. Their concern for working with the
context of the family sometimes translates into the maintenance of
multiple connections with a host of other service providers. The
home-based program then becomes a holding action for supporting
the family during periods of crisis, while maintaining intact the
previous organization of services. That is an ironic and regrettable
pattern, since the home-based concept sprang largely from a concern about the fragmentation of services. The workers find themselves in an untenable position, responsible for carrying out services
at home, but unable to redirect the ancillary services provided by
other agencies.

In the following three cases, we will see this pattern at work,
and will suggest alternative forms of organization that would prob-

ably prove more productive. The first case is described almost exclusively in terms of problems created by a multiplicity of services. The other two, however, represent more of an amalgamation. They describe clinical issues and interventions—particularly in relation to expanding the individual focus of the staff—but also are set within the context of multiple services. These cases highlight the fact that, if new insights and skills are to be effective, a change in thinking and therapeutic procedures must be accompanied by a reorganization of other parts of the system.

*Problem: Anorexia Nervosa in a 9-Year-Old Girl.* The first case, presented on videotape, centers on a 9-year-old anorexic girl who lives with her grandmother. Janet, the identified patient, is the only figure in a barrage of "spotlights" from all over: hospital, school, nutritionist, psychiatrist, pediatrician, grandmother, and home-based workers.

She was hospitalized for 5 months on a children's ward. Since returning home 6 months ago, she has been attending a school for children with special needs, where the teacher monitors her intake of food, in keeping with the prescription of the nutritionist. Janet is in individual therapy with a child therapist, who has ruled that the home-based workers may not see the child alone because it would interfere with therapy, and who does not return their calls.

The workers keep in touch with the school, and visit the home frequently at dinnertime, monitoring Janet's food intake and supporting the grandmother's effort to put another morsel of food into the child's meager frame.

In reviewing the videotape with the group, the trainers highlight issues raised by the provision of multiple services: the question of who determines the therapeutic focus and procedures in such a case, and the problem that the home-based workers are in a relatively powerless position. The treatment of anorexia nervosa through individual therapy and the tight external control of food intake is not universally accepted as the best approach, but that is not central to the discussion. There are simply too many people hovering over this child, and the work of the team has been curtailed by rules and boundaries set up by others and accepted as inevitable. The team has no contact with the individual therapist, and nobody has been dealing with the tensions resulting from the grandmother's refusal to allow her daughter, Janet's mother, into the house. The conflict of loyalty that the 9-year-old patient may be feeling, caught between her mother and grandmother, has never been explored.

The group discussion raised issues focused on the necessity for organizational changes in hierarchy, coordination, and decision making. To begin with, an effective systemic intervention into the complex field of multiple service delivery would require a greater empowerment of the home-based workers. Backed by the agency, they might first call a meeting of the principal providers to review what had become a cumbersome situation. The goal would be to create a newly empowered home-based staff and a forum for effective systems consultations. As currently organized, the multiple providers were duplicating each other's efforts while increasing the child's dependence and ignoring corrosive tensions in the family. A meeting and review of the situation would aim at a clearer, more integrated plan for helping Janet and her family, considering what must be subtracted and what must be added in a reorganized approach to their problems.

*Problem: Two "Impossible" Children, Ages 8 and 6, and a Mother Who Wants to Place the 8-Year-Old in a Residential Institution.* The family is formed by a divorced woman and her three sons, ages 6, 8, and 14. The parents separated when the younger boy was 2 years old. Father has left the area. The mother is a competent saleswoman, but she declares herself defeated at home by her young sons.

Besides the home-based worker, the oldest son has a therapist, the 8-year-old has a different therapist, and the 6- and 8-year-olds are in the care of a psychiatrist who medicates them for hyperactivity with Ritalin. All therapists were invited to the session and all, except the psychiatrist, attended. As the session began, so did the habitual pattern. The 8-year-old ran around the room, the younger boy followed, the oldest boy chased after them, and the mother yelled instructions. The therapist of the 8-year-old asked him to sit down, and the mother got up and ran to get him. She caught and held him in a restraining manner. The entire episode took place during the first 15 minutes of the session.

Behind the one-way mirror, one of the trainers commented to the group that the mother seemed as hyperactive as the children; she responded to every movement of the boys. Preparing to enter the session, he told them that he would begin by engaging the boys in the kind of interventions he frequently used with young children.

As the trainer entered the session, he said to the 8-year-old that he had seen how good he was at running and wondered if he was really strong. He asked him to hit his hand, as hard as he could. When the boy hit him, the trainer expressed surprise that it didn't hurt. Probably because it was the first blow, he said. Could he do it harder? After four punches, the child was tired and the trainer repeated the operation with the younger boy, commenting again that they were young and not very strong. The children found this game fun, and they laughed when the trainer asked the mother to stand up so he could measure who was the tallest of the three. He then asked her to pick up the older boy and hold him high in the air, after which he encouraged the children to try to pick up their mother in the same way. The trainer then turned to talk with her. The children moved quietly to the corner of the room, where they began to play with the toys.

Behind the one-way mirror, the second trainer commented on the nature of this intervention. It normalized the perception of children who were seen as destructive and powerful, and created a sense of hierarchy with the mother in control. The therapist's message was communicated without direct discussion, as is appropriate with young children, but it also was understood by all the family.

As the session proceeded, the mother described her relationship with the two individual therapists. She found them very helpful, especially since she needed to call them frequently when she became upset and was afraid of hitting the children. As she said that, the children began to fight and the pattern appeared again: the mother yelled, the oldest son tried to calm everybody down, the younger children began to run around, and the mother chased them. The trainer asked the mother to sit down so he could talk with her. He asked her if she could do less, since he had seen her working so hard. She responded by describing family life when her former husband lived with them, about his violence, and how the children would gather around to defend her. She was afraid that the 8-year-old would become violent like his father, and felt she needed to protect him from that terrible outcome by controlling his aggressive behavior.

In discussions with the group and the individual therapists after the session, the trainers pointed out how the 8-year-old and the mother set each other off. If the workers regarded the child simply as hyperactive—concentrating on individual therapy, medication, and perhaps out-of-home placement—without considering the importance of the mother–child interaction, their work would be ineffective. It would not help this family live together, or prevent potential difficulties in the mother's relationship with her younger son.

The therapist of the 8-year-old was asked if he could suspend treatment for the next 2 months, allowing the home-based therapist time and space to work with the family and help the mother be less reactive. It was also suggested that the adolescent boy's therapist continue treatment, but in combination with the home-based worker: trading information, planning together, and evaluating progress over time. The mother's request for residential treatment was put on hold in order to allow time for this more integrated approach.

In addition to these suggestions, discussions with the group focused on three areas: One concerned the techniques for working with young children. Another focused on the difficulty of disengaging from patients. Without realizing it, therapists may come to a point where they "need to be needed" by their patients, and find reasons for not letting go.

The remaining topic of discussion was at a different level, concerning workers' assumptions about the mandate they received from the mental health department. Did they actually have the right to suggest that a therapist from another agency suspend treatment? Based on the assumption that the case manager from the central office deals with the family's right to treatment, and may want individual therapy for members of the family, do home-based workers have the prerogative to challenge this directive? The question was actually part of a larger issue concerning the role of clinical judgment, the locus of decision making in relation to home-based cases, and the coordination of service delivery.

*Problem: A 13-Year-Old Girl with a School Phobia.* It's not very surprising that the roster of cases presented in this chapter or elsewhere in this book would include several examples of children who fail to attend school and are diagnosed as truants or phobic. Problems among children often manifest themselves in this way, and the educational and social systems pick up the phenomenon and refer the child or adolescent for help. There are some common threads in many of these cases, but clearly they have individual features as well, some of which reside in family history and organization. It's useful if the worker can begin with some knowledge of the possible patterns that produce and maintain this symptom, but therapy proceeds in relation to the particular child and family.

In this case, the referral for home-based treatment centered on the 13-year-old daughter of a single mother. Lian had not attended school for a year. She was anxious and fearful, and became agitated when separated from her mother—although her behavior at home was reasonably functional. The mother, Nguyen, was Korean by birth. She had married an American serviceman and returned with him to live in the United States. The couple divorced 10 years later, and Lian's school phobia began 1 year after the divorce.

Lian is being seen by a psychiatrist, who works with her individually and has prescribed medication for her symptoms. Nguyen is depressed, and is also on medication. The team has a good relationship with both mother and daughter. Like the psychiatrist, they see Lian's symptoms as a product of internal conflicts, and their work with the family is intended to provide support until Lian is well. The workers have encouraged Nguyen to take classes in English, and to venture out alone to establish contact with other members of the Korean community.

Watching the session from behind the one-way mirror, the trainers comment on the interdependence of the mother and Lian. They sit very close to one another, respond to each other's gestures, and seem wired together. As one of the trainers enters the session, he asks if they're very close. They both laugh and say yes. He asks the girl to sit on the other side of the room and teasingly asks them if they can endure that degree of separation. Nguyen, entering into the game, sits on a chair with wheels and "walks" the chair closer to her daughter. The trainer labels them Siamese twins and asks if they can read each others' thoughts. They claim that the mother is better at mind reading than her daughter, but the trainer disagrees, pointing out how frequently Lian doesn't go to school because she feels that she must alleviate her mother's loneliness. The symptom is now located in the interaction between mother and daughter.

The group explores how to look at the identified symptom as

a response to a number of relevant forces: Nguyen's immigration to a new culture and her prolonged sense of dislocation, the depression and confusion following a divorce experienced as an abandonment, and the strong bond between mother and daughter. They see Lian's symptoms as a response to her mother's distress and her own discomfort, serving to maintain the proximity they both need. The symptoms provide the rationale for her remaining at home.

In planning for further work with this small family, the group suggests that the therapist explore how Nguyen and her daughter maintain each other's symptomatology; an important goal is to increase the autonomy of each. Some of that effort can be conducted separately—an approach that the worker has already taken by encouraging Nguyen to reach out to the community—but much must be carried out with Lian and Nguyen together, exploring their needs and fears, as well as resentments that will surface as each becomes more independent.

The discussion has been related to systemic understanding and clinical techniques but, as in other cases, the plan faces potential difficulties. The emphasis on medication for each family member, and on monitoring dosage and effects, perpetuates an individual orientation toward the problem and the solutions, both in the minds of the clients and within the mental health system. The work of the home-based staff is embedded in a complex organizational structure, however, and they have no ready pathways for suggesting a change of treatment. They have had little or no contact with the case manager responsible for the family, and no relationship with the psychiatrist who is prescribing and monitoring the medication. It is a situation, like many others, that calls for a different kind of communication among service providers, in which planning and change can be the result of collaborative decisions. It seems unlikely that the work can go forward on the basis of new understanding unless home-based workers can communicate and implement their clinical judgments.

## IMPLICATIONS OF THE PROJECT

The training project is a work in progress. Nonetheless, we know by now that certain matters need serious consideration if home-based services are to be optimally effective, and we have also learned something about the shape of a training program that can stimulate and support workers while they explore new pathways and learn new skills. The most important areas of concern center on the orientation and skills of the staff, the interpretation of the home-based mandate, and the functioning of the larger system.

## The Orientation and Skills of the Staff

Clearly, training in family dynamics and family therapy is essential if home-based service is to become an effective modality for serving families instead of a mere category of service. From the first contact with the family, the home-based staff should be oriented toward assessing family organization, and should have the skills for understanding the dynamics of their relationships. Each case file may move through the system with the name of an identified child client, but a well-trained worker is responsible for including information about patterns that maintain the symptom and the family's potential as a resource for healing. Intake forms and procedures should facilitate that approach.

During family sessions, the worker should be equipped with a pouchful of skills and the ability to mix them judiciously. The desire to respond to client needs and to empower families should not mean that the worker only provides those services requested by the family. Empowering families should be understood as a complex process, involving support for their needs, a challenge to the repetitive patterns maintaining their pathology and their dependence on outside providers, and a respect for the family's resilience and capacity for change.

## The Home-Based Mandate

The provision of home-based services should be flexible, determined primarily by informed clinical judgment. In particular, the locus of therapy should not be dictated by the nature of the funding, often interpreted to mean that services must be delivered exclusively rather than primarily in the home. At the beginning of contact, the family's home may be a particularly useful setting for services, but workers should have the freedom and incentive to move back and forth, conducting sessions elsewhere when they think it important for encouraging increased responsibility and autonomy among family members.

## The Role of Larger Systems

Sponsoring units that award home-based contracts have usually been vague about their standards. Certainly, they should have requirements concerning the credentials of home-based staff and the ongoing procedures for supervision and in-house training, with particular attention to staff preparation for working with families. Central office workers should also evaluate the degree to which their surveillance facilitates or handicaps the development of competence in the client family, working with agency staff to calibrate the balance between control and autonomy.

In this area, as in all others, service providers from the larger system must face issues of duplication, fragmentation, and the protection of turf. We know by now, along with many other observers, that families are the primary victims of unresolved confusions, and that the best efforts of home-based workers are likely to be ineffective if they have no power to change procedures. When the family is in therapy, the home-based worker should be seen as the case manager, with authority to call for different services, require a cessation of services from other providers if deemed necessary, and determine when a case should be extended or terminated.

## The Training Structure

Finally, we return to the idea that home-based workers should be trained in family therapy. We have come to realize that our project had a particularly effective structure. What began simply as an attempt to reach a broad group of agencies proved to be a felicitous structure for creating a positive atmosphere and for enhancing the possibility that new thinking and skills would take hold and spread. This program was elaborate. It's not suggested that the structure can be easily replicated, but some principles can be extrapolated and applied to simpler situations.

For one thing, the open nature of the supervision was a new and highly productive experience in all the agencies. Supervision had been conducted primarily through the verbal presentation of cases, and very few workers had observed their colleagues doing therapy with clients. Open supervision brings some discomfort at first, but is apt to diminish rapidly. The enduring result is a sense of collegial stimulation on the part of the staff, an increase in discussion and mutual support, and a diffusion of new ideas and skills through the agency.

The mix of agencies in this project added an important dimension, but it's unnecessary to go beyond the bounds of one agency in order to duplicate the general principles of the process. It's advisable for an agency to invest in a camcorder for videotaping in the homes so that supervision and in-service training can focus on live material. Opening a wall to create a one-way mirror is a more formidable project, but wherever feasible it creates a host of learning possibilities.

In this project, as in the training programs described throughout the book, the introduction of new ideas and techniques brought resistance and created some unease but, in our experience, the process evolves. As new ideas are connected to real situations, and as the staff acquires more confidence and skills, the atmosphere lightens, the workers are stimulated, and some procedures change. The major problem becomes how to continue the process when the trainers leave. That requires an integration of changes into the structure of the agency, to be sustained by people who have acquired some skill, continue to explore new pathways, and have some responsibility for training new staff.

If the major challenge is how to carry the new approach forward, the home-based training program described in this chapter has probably been optimal in its conditions. In each agency, more than one team member is available to continue the work, other members of the staff have had exposure to the approach on training days, the process of open supervision and group discussion has been established, and so forth. In less elaborate situations, the sustained effects of training in systemic family-centered therapy will depend on committed leadership, and on the conviction of the staff that, by working with the family, they are helping the children and their families to deal with present problems—and more effectively adapt to whatever the future may bring.

# CHAPTER TEN

# Epilogue

We began the book with the story of Angie, a woman whose odyssey through foster care, early sexual and physical abuse, drug addiction, teenage pregnancy, homelessness, and separation from her children would be familiar to anyone who has observed or worked with poor families in the United States. She represents millions of others whose lives begin badly and who lack the resources to change course. If she finally had a fighting chance, it was only because she came into contact with an intervention program that tried to bring together the scattered elements of her family and the helpers who were dealing piecemeal with their needs.

In our final comments, we have a choice: We can highlight either the professional aspects of what we have offered or the social and political attitudes that shape services for the poor. Actually, we must do both.

The professional aspects of this book can be found in the mixture of broad thinking and small detail. The breadth of thinking has an optimistic component that springs from a persistent belief in the untapped resources of families, and the possibility of mobilizing their strengths. It also lies in the primary emphasis on context, on working with the knowledge that the internal life of individuals—whether low-income or well-to-do—is regulated by the fact that they're embedded in intimate and large-scale systems. This ecological view has allowed for a different way of looking at people who are poor and need help handling their problems. Drawing on the growth of systems thinking over the last half century, we have focused on the family as the system that both shapes its members and has the potential, with judicious support, for helping its own.

In applying this perspective to foster care, drug dependence, residential, psychiatric, and home-based services, we acknowledge that we have been swimming against the current, not only because established attitudes hold back growth, but because professional workers and policymakers are unsure of how to proceed. Good will and the motivation to work with families are insufficient; change is based in the details. The main thrust of the book, therefore, is at this level. We have tried to provide images, examples, case histories, ways of thinking in concrete situations, and illustrations of specific interventions in which a worker is faced with a family in trouble. We hope that material provides a useful guide for practical work.

But the book must conclude on a social and political note. Attitudes toward the poor continue to be pernicious: critical, sometimes subtly racist, and insufficiently attuned to the plight of disadvantaged women who are trying to raise their children against heavy odds. Despite a democratic credo of positive values that includes support for the needy, this population is regarded as responsible for their poverty by virtue of laziness and lack of will. The national mood is impatient. People are critical of disappointing results in the past without presenting a viable plan for the future, or the concrete means to support it. In this atmosphere, procedures that disempower and fragment these families will not change. Our last words, therefore, are inevitably political: It is imperative to reverse the inertia and the punitive attitudes that maintain ineffective and destructive systems of intervention in the lives of poor families, and that complicate the already difficult task of professional workers who are trying to help.

# References

As courts remove children, lawyers for parents stumble. (1996, June 10). *New York Times*, pp. 1, B8.

Berg, I. K. (1994). *Family based services: A solution-focused approach*. New York: Norton.

Berry, M. (1994). *Keeping families together*. New York: Garland.

Bryce, M. E., & Lloyd, J. C. (Eds.). (1980). *Treating families in the home: An alternative to placement*. Springfield, IL: Thomas.

Coontz, S. (1992). *The way we never were: American families and the nostalgia trap*. New York: Basic Books.

Egelko, S., Galanter, M., Dermatis, H., & DeMaio, C. (1998). Evaluation of a multi-systems model for treating perinatal cocaine addiction. *Journal of Substance Abuse Treatment, 15*(3), 251–259.

Fahl, M., & Morrissey, D. (1979). The Mendota Model: Home–community treatment. In S. Maybanks & M. Bryce (Eds.), *Home-based services for children and families*. Springfield, IL: Thomas.

Fein, E., Maluccio, A., & Kluger, M. (1990). *No more partings: An examination of long-term foster family care*. Washington, DC: Child Welfare League of America.

Foster Care Committee of the Mayor's Commission for the Foster Care of Children. (1993). *Moving toward a spectrum of care: Foster care services in the child welfare system*. New York: Mayor's Commission for the Foster Care of Children.

Foucault, M. (1965). *Madness and civilization*. New York: Pantheon Books.

Haapala, D., & Kinney, J. (1979). Homebuilders' approach to the training of in-home therapists. In S. Maybanks & M. Bryce (Eds.), *Home-based services for children and families*. Springfield, IL: Thomas.

Kinney, J. (1991). *Keeping families together: The Homebuilders model*. New York: Aldine de Gruyter.

Makarenko, A. (1973). *The road to life: An epic in education*. New York: Oriole.

Maybanks, S., & Bryce, M. (Eds.). (1979). *Home-based services for children and families*. Springfield, IL: Thomas.

McDaniel, S., Campbell, T., & Seaburn, D. (1995). Principles for collaboration between health and mental health providers in primary care. *Family Systems Medicine, 13*, 283–298.

Minuchin, P. (1995). Foster and natural families: Forming a cooperative network. In L. Combrinck-Graham (Ed.), *Children in families at risk*. New York: Guilford Press.

Minuchin, P., with Brooks, A., Colapinto, J., Genijovich, E., Minuchin, D. & Minuchin, S. (1990). *Training manual for foster parents*. New York: Family Studies, Inc. (Available from National Resource Center for Family Centered Practice, School of Social Work, 112 North Hall, Iowa City, IA 52242-1223)

Minuchin, S. (1984). *Family kaleidoscope*. Cambridge, MA: Harvard University Press.

Minuchin, S., Montalvo, B., Guerney, B., Rosman, B., & Schumer, F. (1967). *Families of the slums: An exploration of their structure and treatment*. New York: Basic Books.

Nelson, K., Landsman, M., & Deutelbaum, W. (1990). Three models of family-centered placement prevention services. *Child Welfare, LXIX*(1), 3–21.

The Prevention Report. (1992, Fall). *New approaches to foster care and permanency planning* (Special Issue). Iowa City, IA: National Resource Center on Family Based Services.

Sharkey, M. (1997). *Family to family: Bridging families, communities and child welfare*. Baltimore: Annie E. Casey Foundation.

Stephens, D. (1979). In-home family support services: An ecological systems approach. In S. Maybanks & M. Bryce (Eds.), *Home-based services for children and families*. Springfield, IL: Thomas.

Tavantzis, T., Tavantzis, M., Brown, L., & Rohrbaugh, M. (1985). Home-based structural family therapy for delinquents at risk of placement. In M. P. Mirkin & S. L. Koman (Eds.), *Handbook of adolescents and family therapy*. New York: Gardner Press.

# Index